Convivial Cultures in Multicultural Cities

The large-scale migration brought about by the expansion of the EU over a decade ago led to migration from less ethnically diverse countries to multicultural and super-diverse societies. This book examines the complex encounters between Polish migrant women and local populations in Manchester and Barcelona, with attention to the ways in which difference is negotiated and managed through everyday practices of conviviality, which help to overcome hierarchies and create elements of sameness. Illustrating how cultural differences may become important resources for interaction that facilitates positive relationships, *Convivial Cultures in Multicultural Cities* draws on the narratives of Polish migrant women to shed new light on everyday social relations between migrant women and local populations, including settled ethnic minorities and other migrants. In doing so, it contributes to our understanding of the positional nature of racial identification and complicates our ideas of whiteness and privilege.

Alina Rzepnikowska is Lecturer in Sociology, the School of Social Sciences at the University of Manchester, UK.

Studies in Migration and Diaspora
Series Editor: Anne J. Kershen
Queen Mary University of London, UK

Studies in Migration and Diaspora is a series designed to showcase the inter-disciplinary and multidisciplinary nature of research in this important field. Volumes in the series cover local, national and global issues and engage with both historical and contemporary events. The books will appeal to scholars, students and all those engaged in the study of migration and diaspora. Amongst the topics covered are minority ethnic relations, transnational movements and the cultural, social and political implications of moving from 'over there', to 'over here'.

Wellbeing of Transnational Muslim Families
Marriage, Law and Gender
Edited by Marja Tiilikainen, Mulki Al-Sharmani and Sanna Mustasaari

Tracing Asylum Journeys
Transnational Mobility of non-European Refugees to Canada via Turkey
Ugur Yildiz

Convivial Cultures in Multicultural Cities
Polish Migrant Women in Manchester and Barcelona
Alina Rzepnikowska

Democracy, Diaspora, Territory
Europe and Cross-Border Politics
Olga Oleinikova and Jumana Bayeh

Migration, Education and Translation
Cross-Disciplinary Perspectives on Human Mobility and Cultural Encounters in Education Settings
Edited by Vivienne Anderson and Henry Johnson

For more information about this series, please visit: https://www.routledge.com/sociology/series/ASHSER1049

Convivial Cultures in Multicultural Cities

Polish Migrant Women in Manchester and Barcelona

Alina Rzepnikowska

Routledge
Taylor & Francis Group

LONDON AND NEW YORK

First published 2020
by Routledge
2 Park Square, Milton Park, Abingdon, Oxon OX14 4RN

and by Routledge
52 Vanderbilt Avenue, New York, NY 10017

Routledge is an imprint of the Taylor & Francis Group, an informa business

British Library Cataloguing-in-Publication Data
A catalogue record for this book is available from the British Library

Library of Congress Cataloging-in-Publication Data
A catalog record for this book has been requested

ISBN: 978-0-8153-7792-4 (hbk)
ISBN: 978-1-351-23355-2 (ebk)

Typeset in Times New Roman
by Apex CoVantage, LLC

To all those who took part in my research

Contents

Figures

Series editor's preface

In 2004, ten new countries acceded to the European Union; with the exception of the islands of Cyprus and Malta, all were from Eastern and Central Europe. Whilst the majority of countries in the EU delayed free access to the newcomers, the United Kingdom, Ireland and Sweden permitted immediate freedom of entry.[1] One of the main reasons for the British Government's decision was an assumption that only between five and thirteen thousand immigrants would arrive annually from the Accession (A8) countries. In reality the forecast proved totally inaccurate: at the time of the 2011 Decennial Census, 579,121 Polish nationals were recorded as living in England and Wales, an increase of 521,014 on the 2001 figure. It has been argued that the presence of such a large one-nation immigrant population and its (perceived) impact on Britain's job market and national identity was a powerful influence behind the Brexit outcome of the 2016 referendum; and it is within this heightened anti-immigrant context that Alina Rzepnikowska explores the everyday interactive experiences of female Polish migrants in Manchester.

However, the author does not leave her examination of quotidian female migrant conviviality as a single spatial/national survey. She expands her work further and deeper by presenting a binary study, selecting Barcelona as a comparison. While the arrival of Polish migrants has not been of the same volume as in the UK, their number is growing and the author's investigation highlights another feature of migrant conviviality: the existence of diverse national cultures in one city. In Barcelona, which has been at the heart of the fight for Catalonian independence, one aspect of this diversity is the need for the migrant women to learn both Catalan and Spanish and acquaint themselves with the two cultures in order to interact at a local level with their Spanish counterparts. Having been provided with a dual locational study, the reader is able to compare and contrast the female migrant experience in two major cities and assess the ways in which politics, culture, economic activity, parenthood and racism influence successful conviviality at the grass roots.

This volume is the result of research which the author has undertaken with depth and compassion. It is enhanced by Rzepnikowska's positionality which, as someone of Polish nationality and tongue, has enabled her to interview her protagonists both in the public space and in the privacy of their own homes.

Though rich in methodology and theory – providing detailed background to the concept of medieval *convivencia* – it is the empirical chapters which bring us face to face with the women who find themselves amongst strange cultures and societies. As the author emphasises, whilst some research has been carried out on migrants in the workplace, there has been a paucity of material which analyses the different aspects of female migrant and indigene interaction in a work environment. There is not one overall image. Whilst in some instances there is humour, collegiality and the creation of friendships that extend beyond work, the author also provides examples of exploitation, discrimination and racism. These negative patterns of behaviour call on the migrant to devise strategies in order to overcome the disagreeable nature of the work experience.

Not all the female migrants featured in this volume are single young women; some are mothers and Rzepnikowska provides a fascinating insight into the ways in which motherhood enables the overcoming of cultural and linguistic barriers between indigenes and women of other immigrant backgrounds. In both Manchester and Barcelona migrant mothers provide support mechanisms for each other in both the nursery and the school. Parenthood is shown to enable interaction between British and Spanish families and their Polish counterparts. However, as in the workplace, not all is ideal; in the schools there are examples of racist attitudes shown by some parents towards others and their children – negative patterns of behaviour from which the Polish migrant parents cannot be absolved.

The original research for this book was carried out by the author in 2012 and 2013 but it is important to note that, particularly in the broader context of contemporary[2] British political developments, post the Brexit referendum the author re-interviewed some of the Polish women she originally met with. These recent interviews highlight the ways in which continuing conviviality between the Polish female immigrants and the indigenous population is 'local and specific'. There is no 'one fits all' post-referendum aftereffect, a factor which is true nationwide. For though some Polish immigrants have said that they are not prepared to remain in a country which recorded such a negative response to their presence, others have found their work colleagues and neighbours sympathetic and concerned to maintain relationships that have been worked at and endure. They do not want to go back to Poland. Rzepnikowska's recent interviews also illustrate how suppressed racism has raised its face in certain workplaces where Poles and indigenes are employed, while elsewhere neighbours and workmates have been increasingly supportive of the Eastern European presence.

The in-depth comparative study of female immigrant conviviality which the author originally carried out, and which is documented in this volume, would have been a valuable addition to our understanding of the migrant experience itself. Her further research into what has been a seismic event in European politics not only brings her work up-to-date but additionally enables readers to appreciate the importance and diversity of grass-roots female conviviality within two major cities with multinational populations. It is a book which should appear on the shelves of not only those engaged in the study of migration but of all those concerned with broadening their comprehension of gender, place, space, class, ethnicity, racism and politics and each of those in interaction with the others.

Anne J. Kershen
Queen Mary University of London
Spring 2019

Acknowledgements

This project would have not been possible without my research participants in both Manchester and Barcelona who shared their stories with me. I would like to thank them for their generosity with their time. Some of them became my good friends. Special thanks to Tom Griffiths, Krzysztof Wiszniewski, Dariusz Wilk and Meri Ilić who were key during the fieldwork and welcomed me to their associations and groups. Even though some of you might not know each other, you have a lot in common, particularly your passion for supporting migrants and bringing them together with the local population.

I am very grateful to Bridget Byrne and Chris Perriam for their thoughtful guidance, patience and encouragement, critical and constructive comments, and support over many years. I thank Encarnación Gutiérrez Rodríguez who was very influential and supportive at the early stages of this research project. I am also grateful to Nina Glick Schiller, Ewa Ochman, Hilary Pilkington, Claire Alexander, Maddy Abbas, Wendy Bottero, Eva Duda-Mikulin and Marius Gudonis, as well as Adrian and Gurjeet, for insightful readings of my work and helpful feedback.

I would like to thank the Routledge team for editorial and administrative support and guidance. Some of the chapters in this book are reworked versions of published articles, including: 'Racism and xenophobia experienced by Polish migrants in the UK before and after Brexit vote', *Journal of Ethnic and Migration Studies*, (2018b) 45(1); 'Polish Migrant Women's Narratives about Language, Raced and Gendered Difference in Barcelona', *Gender, Place and Culture* (Special issue: Gendered, Spatial and Temporal Approaches to Polish intra-EU Migration), (2018a) 25(6); 'Conviviality in the Workplace: The Case of Polish Migrant Women in Manchester and Barcelona', *Central and Eastern European Migration Review*, (2017) 6(2); and 'Imagining and Encountering the Other in Manchester and Barcelona: The Narratives of Polish Migrant Women', *Journal of the Institute of Ethnology and Anthropology* (Special Issue: Postsocialist Mobilities), (2016) 15. I would like to thank all the reviewers for their insightful comments.

I thank the Arts and Humanities Research Council (AHRC) for the funding for the research conducted in 2012/13 which made it possible.

I wish to thank my husband, Peter, for his constant support, encouragement and love which have kept me going through the years. I also thank my family, especially my mother Regina, and friends who have been supportive.

Notes

1 The UK imposed a restriction on welfare benefit which had to be applied for.
2 At the time of writing this Preface there is still uncertainty as to the way in which Brexit – if it takes place – will operate and affect the lives of those living in the United Kingdom – both British and non-British citizens.

1 Introduction

Setting the context

In recent years European politicians and academics have engaged in debates on how to come to terms with the growing diversity of migrants and ethnic minorities. This has raised questions of how migrant populations and host societies can cope successfully with the challenges involved in living together. However, this re-emerging idea of having to deal with the issue of living together often falls into the discourse of immigration and diversity causing a problem often discussed in terms of segregation, competition for housing and welfare, as well as conflict between different groups. Immigration is often perceived as "a symbol of a world falling apart and a society that does not hold together" (Back and Sinha, 2016: 517). Migrants themselves are frequently framed as objects of concern and a threat. In contrast, this book offers a counter-narrative to the dominant discourses on migrants by exploring everyday interaction in the multicultural cities of Manchester and Barcelona from the perspective of Polish migrant women. It does so though the lens of conviviality understood as a dynamic process of living together at the local level. It explores the narratives about everyday encounters in both cities not only in terms of ethnicity, but also other categories which often intersect, including gender, class, religion, age and spatio-temporal dynamics. While the book explores various forms of encounter, interaction and engagement with difference, it recognises the importance of conflict, tensions, racism and xenophobia (Back and Sinha, 2016; Gilroy, 2004; Neal et al., 2018). This book aims to address the following questions: how does conviviality emerge in encounters between Polish migrant women and the local populations in both Manchester and Barcelona? What facilitates and what limits convivial encounters? Can conviviality endure despite exclusionary anti-immigration rhetoric, particularly in the context of Brexit?

There has been a growing number of scholars and researchers focusing on conviviality by exploring the ways of living together in urban spaces (Back and Sinha, 2016; Heil, 2014; Karner and Parker, 2011; Neal et al., 2013, 2018; Padilla et al., 2015; Wessendorf, 2014a, 2014b; Wise and Velayutham, 2014). Nowicka and Vertovec (2014: 1) argue that this "convivial turn" (Neal et al., 2013: 320) reflects a deeper concern about "human modes of togetherness". This book differs from the existing literature on conviviality for several reasons. Firstly, it acknowledges the shortcomings of previous studies that mostly focus on a single country case. By adopting a comparative lens, it allows the exploration of the ways in which conviviality is experienced in two cities with attention to multiple settings, including social, political, cultural, national and local contexts. Secondly, while there is a growing body of research on gender and migration (Amrith and Sahraoui, 2018; Duda-Mikulin, 2018b; Erel, 2009; Gutiérrez Rodríguez, 2010; Kindler and Napierała, 2010; Mahler and Pessar, 2006; Phizacklea, 1983; Ryan and Webster, 2008), this book stresses the importance of under-researched migrant women's experiences of conviviality, and it offers a critical perspective aiming to shed light on their daily encounters in multi-ethnic societies. Thirdly, whereas the existing literature tends to focus on relations between host society and postcolonial/non-European/non-white ethnic minorities, this book explores encounters between post–2004 Polish migrants not only with the native population but also with settled ethnic minorities and other migrants. What is particularly interesting about these migrants is their unstable racialised positioning as privileged white Europeans and migrant Others (Rzepnikowska, 2019). This positioning introduces the discourses of whiteness and racialisation to discussions on conviviality. Finally, this book contributes to the field of geographies of encounters by focusing on multiple locations which are often interlinked. It highlights the importance of investigating workplace relations between migrant women and their co-workers from different ethnic backgrounds. Furthermore, while research on conviviality mainly focuses on encounters with difference in public and semi-public spaces, private spaces as sites of convivial interaction have been largely overlooked. Since my interviewees often referred to encounters in private spaces of the homes, whether in the context of domestic work or socialising with neighbours, this book contributes to the understanding of conviviality in a domestic environment.

The book focuses on the experiences of migrant women coming from Poland, one of eight countries (Accession 8 [A8] countries: Lithuania, Latvia, Estonia, Poland, Czech Republic, Slovakia, Slovenia and Hungary) which joined the European Union (EU) in May 2004 – a significant event in the history of European migration. The UK, Ireland and Sweden were the only member states which granted free access of the A8 nationals to the labour market immediately after the EU enlargement. Public and political discourses on migration shifted to controversial discussions about new 'Eastern European' migrants, the length of their stay and their impact on the economy and public services. The profound influence of EU expansion on migration patterns within Europe has triggered an immense interest in research on migratory movements from Central and Eastern Europe, particularly from Poland to the UK. Nevertheless, there is a gap in research on everyday relations between Polish migrants and the local population, particularly in Spain which attracts fewer Poles, although there is a steadily increasing body of research on Polish post–2004 migration (Kruszelnicki, 2008; Main, 2013; Nalewajko, 2012; Władyka and Morén-Alegret, 2013). In Britain, there has been a growing interest in studying Polish migrants' responses to other ethnic groups (D'Angelo and Ryan, 2011; Eade et al., 2006; Gawlewicz, 2016; Nowicka, 2018; Parutis, 2011; Ryan, 2010; Temple, 2011; Cook et al.,

2011b). While the existing research often explores attitudes towards difference, there is still little focus on the actual experiences of conviviality which often differ from attitudes and opinions about different ethnic groups.

The term 'multicultural' used in this book is distinguished from the contested notion of multiculturalism. It describes societies or settings where people of different ethnic, cultural and religious backgrounds live together. This book examines the experiences of Polish migrant women in multicultural Manchester and Barcelona, which have seen rapid population shifts as a result of the arrival and settlement of various groups of migrants. It can be argued that both cities are characterised by super-diversity which highlights complexity in terms of "a dynamic interplay of variables among an increased number of new, small and scattered, multiple-origin, transnationally connected, socio-economically differentiated and legally stratified immigrants" (Vertovec, 2007a: 1024). In recent years, the concept of super-diversity has been widely used by scholars from various disciplines and in public policy, and it has been read in many different ways (Vertovec, 2014). However, the concept has been subject to some criticism. During the IRiS (Institute for Research into Superdiversity) Conference *Superdiversity: Theory, Method and Practice in the Era of Change* in June 2014 at the University of Birmingham, the policy roundtable ('Rethinking policy and practice in/for an era of superdiversity') participants expressed a concern about social inequalities and racism overlooked in discussions on super-diversity. Similarly, Back (2015) and Back and Sinha (2016) offer a critique of Vertovec's conception of super-diversity considered as one-dimensional and neglecting attention to forms of division and racism. Further theoretical and methodological analysis is needed to understand these complexities and the dynamics of super-diversity and social inequalities. Nevertheless, the concept of super-diversity is used in this book as it allows moving beyond a simplistic view of diversity viewed solely through an ethnic lens and the presence of postcolonial ethnic minorities. It also highlights that between and within migrant groups living in close proximity there are individuals characterised by distinct gender, socio-economic statuses, experiences, patterns and motives for migration.

In the following sections I discuss the Polish, British and Spanish/Catalan contexts, including Polish migration in Britain and Spain, and finally, I offer the overview of this book.

Coming from an ethnically and religiously homogenous country?

As Valentine (2008: 333) suggests, "encounters never take place in a space free from history, material conditions, and power". Therefore, when discussing Polish migrants' encounters with difference, it is important to highlight the socio-historical and geographic context of Poland. Situated between the East and the West, Poland had been culturally, ethnically and religiously diverse for centuries (Podemski, 2012). From the fourteenth century, the First Polish Republic was a multi-ethnic country in which Poles, Byelorussians, Lithuanians, Ruthenians, Jews, Germans, Armenians and Tatars lived side by side (Kłosowska, 1994).

According to Dziekan (2011: 37–38), the history of Polish Tatars, who have been present in Poland for more than 600 years, is a perfect example of coexistence of two different cultures, influencing one another, borrowing various elements and leaving out the others. Furthermore, by the end of the sixteenth century 80 per cent of the world's Jewish diaspora sought refuge from persecution in Spain, Portugal and Germany. Even though the Polish state lost two-thirds of its territory after the period of partitions (1795–1918), Poland's diverse ethnic minorities remained, consisting of about one-third of the Second Republic's population (Kłosowska, 1994: 200). However, the tragic consequences of the Holocaust during WWII, border changes and the communist regime, which excluded Poland from the rest of the world and repressed difference, have left it as one of the most ethnically, culturally and religiously homogenous countries in the world (Podemski, 2012). While before WWII ethnic minorities constituted about 36 per cent of Poland's population, they made up merely 2–4 per cent of the Polish population immediately after the fall of the Communist regime (Grzymała-Kazłowska and Okólski, 2003: 24–25).

With the end of socialism, Poland began to deal with arrivals of various groups of migrants, mainly from Southern and Eastern European countries, as well as from Asia and Africa who mostly regarded Poland either as a transit or a temporary place where they engaged in informal trade and short-term employment in several major cities (Grzymała-Kazłowska and Okólski, 2003: 24). During the first years of the political transformation there was an atmosphere of excitement and curiosity about diversity. Nevertheless, in the light of the economic recession and high levels of unemployment in the second half of the 1990s, the initial euphoria about difference was replaced with anxiety, stereotyping and prejudice. Despite some claims branding Poland as multicultural (Kempny et al., 1997), encounters between Polish people with non-white people are still rare in many areas of Poland. Średziński (2010) points out that Polish people hardly have a chance to challenge their stereotypical perceptions about black people, highly influenced by Western colonialist discourses, with reality since they constitute a very small number, between two and three thousand (Ząbek, 2009: 170). Only 15 per cent of all Poles come across Africans in their localities, and 7 per cent are in personal touch with them as students of higher education institutions, sportsmen, doctors and bazaar vendors in large cities (Średziński, 2010: 40). Similarly, there is a very small number of Muslims in Poland who are made up of Tatars, converts and Muslim migrants constituting 0.07–0.09 per cent of the total population of the country (Nalborczyk, 2006: 62).[1] The politics of the current conservative government that came to power in 2015 with divisive nationalistic rhetoric fuelling anti-immigrant attitudes and physical attacks on Muslims or foreign-looking people, indicates that there might be even less ethnic diversity in the country (Narkowicz and Pedziwiatr, 2017). Some of my research participants noted that the presence of their non-white partners and mixed-race children often attracted a lot of attention, staring and surprise in public spaces. Racialised narratives have been more common and acceptable than in countries of mass immigration (Nowicka, 2012). While visual difference has become highly marked in Poland, whiteness has remained unnoticed, unrecognised (by the national community) and under-analysed (by the scientific community) (see also Imre, 2005).

The EU accession of the new member states in May 2004 has resulted in a large-scale migration of Poles to the UK, and a smaller one to Spain, where they have encountered people from different social classes, ethnic and religious backgrounds. To some extent, the socialisation in Poland may influence socio-spatial encounters with difference in multicultural societies. Nevertheless, it is also important to consider various trajectories of my research participants. For instance, several had traveled to and lived in different countries where they encountered difference before coming to the UK.

The context of post–2004 Polish migration in Britain

The post-war labour migration in the UK is often discussed in terms of the arrival of postcolonial migrants from Commonwealth countries, most notably from the British Caribbean and South East Asia in the 1950s. Over the past three decades, the nature of immigration and diversity has changed dramatically in Britain, characterised by diversification of countries of origin, migration histories, gender, age, religion, languages, education, legal status and economic background (Vertovec, 2007a). According to the 2011 Census data, 13 per cent (7.5 million) of the resident population of England and Wales were born outside the UK (ONS, 2012: 1). Geographically, the migrant population is not spread out evenly. The 2011 Census shows that over a third (37 per cent) of London residents were born abroad compared to between 5 and 12 per cent in other regions and Wales (ONS, 2012: 12).

There are diverse groups and diverse diasporic identities of Polish migrants in Britain characterised by multiple patterns of mobility as a result of at least three generations of migratory history between Poland and Britain (Eade et al., 2006). The British Isles became home to a Polish post-war diaspora. Furthermore, in the 1980s, thousands of Polish Solidarity protesters migrated to the UK as a result of the Martial Law imposed in 1981 (Garapich, 2008). Polish migration to Britain continued in the 1990s and early twenty-first century. During the 1990s and up to accession to the EU, Polish migrants were commonly associated with illegal employment and visa overstaying (Duvell, 2004). The status and the situation of Polish migrants changed significantly on 1 May 2004 when Poland joined the EU. They acquired the same rights as other EU nationals who have the right to live and work in the UK without restrictions, to remain permanently in the UK, and to be joined by dependents. Polish migrants constituted the largest single national group among the new arrivals in the UK (Burrell, 2009; White, 2011b). Between 2003 and 2010, the Polish-born population of the UK increased from 75,000 to 532,000 (ONS, 2011a). Poland became the most common country of birth for non–UK born mothers between 2010 and 2014, followed by Pakistan and India (ONS, 2015), and Polish migrants continue to be the largest non–UK national group in the UK (916,000), making up 29 per cent of all EU nationals living in the country (ONS, 2016). Furthermore, Polish is the second most spoken language after English in the UK (ONS, 2011b).

The reason behind the immediate labour market access of A8 nationals into the UK was severe labour market shortages, mainly in low-wage and low-skill occupations in construction, hospitality, transport sectors and public services (Anderson et al., 2006). Freedom of movement attracted many Polish people, especially the young, affected by high rates of unemployment, low wages and lack of opportunities in Poland (White, 2010). Low-cost transport lowered the cost of travel, encouraging 'fluid migration' (Grabowska-Lusińska and Okólski, 2009) with no settlement goal and for an undefined period of time.

Polish migrants are distributed very widely across the country. The socio-demographic profile of over half-a-million Polish minority is highly varied. They are mostly young (Grabowska-Lusińska and Okólski, 2008) and their qualifications often do not match their employment, although this may change over time (Ryan, 2015c). Many speak English and have finished secondary school or have obtained a degree (Grabowska-Lusińska and Okólski, 2009), although some researchers highlight that the majority are not university graduates, and many have poor English-language skills (White, 2011b). They work in a variety of sectors including administration, business and management, hospitality and catering, public services, agriculture, manufacturing and food, and fish and meat processing, as well as construction (Drinkwater et al., 2006). In addition, there has been a growing population of Polish university students (HESA, 2015). According to 2001–2006 Labour Force Survey data, there had been a minor gender imbalance amongst A8 migrants since 58 per cent of registered workers were male (Drinkwater et al., 2006: 7). Even though the numbers of both female and male migrants have increased over time, women have constituted the majority of the migrant population in the UK; in 2013, 54 per cent of the foreign-born population were women (Rienzo and Vargas-Silva, 2014: 3).

Polish migrants in Manchester

Manchester has been a city of migrants since the end of the eighteenth century (Werbner, 1999). During the first decades of the nineteenth century, Manchester attracted people from other parts of Britain to work in rapidly expanding industries. It attracted Irish migrants in the mid-nineteenth century and it was a key arrival city for Jewish and Italian migrants in the late nineteenth and early twentieth centuries. In the post-war period, the city witnessed the arrival of Polish refugees, mainly soldiers who were incorporated into the British armed forces and granted the right to stay in the UK, as well as European Volunteer Workers (EVW) recruited after the war, some of whom had been displaced persons. From the 1950s, Manchester became home to migrants from the ex-colonies of the British Empire – Afro-Caribbean, Pakistani and subsequently Bangladeshis. In the last decade, the city has seen the arrival of Polish and Chinese migrants, as well as Somali refugees. According to the 2011 Census data, the largest ethnic minority groups in Manchester are Pakistani, African and Other White (CoDE, 2013). Most ethnic minority groups are evenly spread residentially across Manchester and the Greater Manchester area. Manchester is one of the most culturally and linguistically diverse cities in Europe with up to 200 languages spoken by residents in the Greater Manchester area (Multilingual Manchester, 2013). After English, Urdu is the language most commonly spoken in Manchester followed by Polish (Manchester City Council, 2014a: 32).

In the post–2004 period, Manchester has witnessed the arrival of Polish migrants, amongst other A8 nationals, who have contributed to a greater diversity of the city. Apart from many Polish grocery shops, there is the Polish Catholic Church in Moss Side, Polish Saturday School at the Manchester Academy, Polish Catholic Social Club in Oldham and The Polish Circle in Cheetham Hill. No local authority in Greater Manchester has published up-to-date figures on post–2004 European migration. The official statistics on the numbers and distribution of Polish migrants in Manchester are very limited. According to the 2011 Census data, Polish nationals are incorporated in an imprecise category of 'White Other', which also includes other Europeans, Americans and Australians. According to Manchester City Council (2015: 29) data, Polish migrants constituted 1.2 per cent of Manchester population and 0.8 per cent of Greater Manchester population (based on self-descriptions). Many of my research participants arrived in deprived areas with cheaper rent and poor housing. However, as a result of improved socio-economic situation, some moved to more affluent residential neighbourhoods.

The context of post–2004 Polish migration in Spain

In contrast to Britain, Spain was predominantly an emigration state until the 1980s. Since its acceptance into the European Economic Community in 1986, Spain has become a country of immigration and a multi-ethnic society (Escandell and Ceobanu, 2009). Initially, as in the British context, the immigration flows reflected former colonial ties between Spain and Latin America, the Philippines, Equatorial Guinea and Morocco. In recent years, Spain has been attracting migrants from other European countries, Northern and Sub-Saharan Africa and Asia (Solé and Parella, 2003; Escandell and Ceobanu, 2009). The number of migrants with residence permits was 5,333,805 in 2012. The three main countries of birth of these migrants were Romania, Morocco and Ecuador (Ministerio de Empleo y Seguridad Social, 2012).

Spain had already witnessed the arrival of anti-communist political refugees from Central and Eastern Europe between 1945 and 1989. The arrival of Polish migrants became more significant in the late eighties when some were seeking asylum to flee the oppressive government while others sought a better quality of life (Ramírez Goicoechea, 2003). They constituted the largest group of migrants from Central and Eastern Europe until the late nineties, and therefore the bearers of all traits attributed to these groups (Hellermann and Stanek, 2006). In the first decade of the twenty-first century, Spain attracted a substantially large number of Romanian migrants, as well as Bulgarians and Ukrainians. In 2005, there were approximately 307,000 Romanians, 89,000 Bulgarians and 63,000 Ukrainians, in comparison to 34,000 Poles (Stanek, 2007: 288). Along with six other member states, Spain adopted a restrictive immigration policy which effectively blocked access to their labour markets for at least two years following accession of the A8 member states to the EU. Spain did not open its labour market to the new accession countries until May 2006. The extent of post–2004 Polish migration to Spain is substantially smaller than in Britain. The December 2014 statistics show that there were about 90,835 Polish migrants living in Spain with residence permits (Ministerio de Empleo y Seguridad Social, 2014), compared to 12,817 in 2002 and 23,617 in 2004 (Ministerio de Empleo y Seguridad Social, 2012). However, the actual number of Polish migrants is likely to be much higher. Initially, Polish men worked mostly in construction, while Polish women worked in the domestic sector often not recognised in the statistics (Nalewajko, 2012). While at first Polish migration to Spain was overrepresented by men, by 1996 women constituted nearly half of the Polish collective (Arnal Sarasa, 1998). Since the transition period, Polish migration has been characterised by a new type of Polish migrant: young, educated, coming from bigger cities, entrepreneurial and students (Nalewajko, 2012). The younger age and higher level of education of post–2004 Polish migrants in comparison to those who left Poland in previous years is a shared characteristic in other EU countries resulting in an increase in the brain drain phenomenon (Władyka and Morén-Alegret, 2013; Burrell, 2009; White, 2010). Many of them came to Spain not only for economic reasons, but also to gain work experience, attend exchange programmes, postgraduate studies (Kruszelnicki, 2008) and language learning courses. They also came to discover the culture, search for new experiences and seek adventure. Their employment often matched their qualifications or served to improve them. They mostly migrated to big cities. Initially, many arrived in Madrid as well as Toledo, Segovia and Avila, where earlier political refugees had settled. Those mainly employed in agriculture and tourism moved to Valencia, Murcia and Alicante, while those with higher education and who were highly skilled often arrived in Barcelona (Nalewajko, 2012; Władyka and Morén-Alegret, 2013).

Polish migrants in Barcelona

As in the context of Manchester, Polish migrants arriving in Barcelona have encountered a very diverse population from Spain and other parts of the world. Barcelona is situated in Catalonia, one of the 17 *Comunidades Autónomas* and a stateless nation, where both Catalan and Castilian-Spanish are official languages. Catalonia is characterised by a strong notion of Catalan language and culture, where its native inhabitants exhibit diverse national attachments to the rest of Spain (Rodon and Franco-Guillén, 2014), although Barcelona has its own identity, distinct from that of Catalonia or Spain. The city has a strong network of community associations, many of which support migrants and encourage interaction between people from various backgrounds. Furthermore, during my fieldwork in Barcelona which began in September 2012, Catalonia witnessed pro-independence street demonstrations, especially in the city of Barcelona on 11 September, the national day of Catalonia, *La Diada*. There had been much tension and anticipation in Catalonia with regard to the question of Catalan independence in the light of regional elections in September 2015, and later when Puigdemont declared Catalan independence in 2017, which resulted in Spain triggering Article 155 of the Constitution and instigating direct rule from Madrid. The elections held in December 2017 contributed to further political complexity.

Barcelona's twentieth-century history of immigration dates back to the times after the Spanish Civil War, in the 1940s and 1950s, when a great number of Spaniards arrived from the rest of Spain to seek employment. In the 1960s, Spaniards from mainly Andalusia and Extremadura continued arriving in the city (Zapata-Barrero, 2014). Since the last decade of the twentieth and the beginning of the twenty-first century, Barcelona has experienced major social changes following the arrival of transnational migrants from very diverse backgrounds, including countries from Latin America, Northern and Sub-Saharan Africa, Southeast Asia, China and Europe (Escandell and Ceobanu, 2009). In the late twentieth and early twenty-first century Barcelona saw significant immigration of low-skilled workers from Morocco, the Philippines, Pakistan, Latin America and China (Władyka and Morén-Alegret, 2013). While in January 2000 the number of migrants living in Barcelona represented 3.5 per cent of the total population, at the time of my fieldwork in 2012, this proportion was just over 17 per cent with the highest number of migrants from Pakistan, Italy, China and Ecuador (Barcelona City Council, 2012a). The migrant population in Barcelona decreased to approximately 16 per cent in 2015, with the highest number of migrants from Italy, Pakistan, China and France (Barcelona City Council, 2015a).

The presence of Polish people in Barcelona dates back to the early twentieth century and is marked by the foundation of the Honorary Consulate of the Republic of Poland to Barcelona in 1930. In 1946 approximately 200 Polish children stolen by the Nazis during WWII arrived in Barcelona (Barbería, 2008). In the first decade of the twenty-first century, Barcelona saw an increase of the Polish population as a result of EU expansion. Between 2001 and 2009 the number of Polish migrants increased nearly eightfold (Władyka and Morén-Alegret, 2013: 147). At the time of my fieldwork in 2012, they numbered 2,224, increasing to 2,453 in January 2015 (Barcelona City Council, 2015b). According to the Municipal Population Census, the majority live in Raval, Poble Sec and Sagrada Familia, but many are dispersed in other areas of Barcelona and they do not tend to live in one particular area (Barcelona City Council, 2012b). Polish amenities and events include: Polish masses in the Catholic churches of Sant Jaume and Santa Eulalia, a Catalan-Polish Cultural Association with a Polish library, a Polish school for children, the Polish grocery store Krakowiak, and the Polonia-Barcelona group that organises events and activities popular amongst recent migrants and people from other backgrounds.

Discourses on Polish migration in Britain and Spain

The theme of Polish migration in the UK has been widely covered in the media and political discourse, affecting not only the way Polish migrants are viewed by the British public but also influencing everyday encounters between Poles and Brits. Migrants from Eastern Europe were initially seen as unproblematic as they posed "few questions of cultural and racial difference from their host societies" (Favell and Nebe, 2009: 206). It is argued that by favouring migrants from the EU, the UK has been implicitly favouring white migrants (Favell, 2008: 704). Nevertheless, as a result of British anxieties over uncontrolled European immigration, the political and media rhetoric has changed. The UK Independence Party (UKIP) controversial poster used during the 2014 campaign read: "26 million people in Europe are looking for work, and whose jobs are they after?" In April 2015 during the BBC One leader interview on April 22, 2015, Nigel Farage, the former leader of UKIP, said he would prefer immigrants from India and Australia to East Europeans, even though he previously claimed his party would not want to discriminate against new arrivals by nationality. UKIP's popularity, based on anti-immigration and anti-European policies, is a possible reason for pushing immigration to the top of the political agenda. Speaking on the BBC One 'Andrew Marr Show' on January 5, 2014, the then Prime Minister David Cameron singled out Polish migrants in the discourse about welfare benefits abuse.

EU migration into the UK was a key issue in the EU referendum debates in 2016. The Leave campaign used the anti-immigration discourse claiming that the main cause of all the UK's issues, including housing shortages or the strained National Health Service (NHS), was 'uncontrolled mass immigration' caused by the right to freedom of movement within EU member states. The debates on whether to remain or to leave the EU reproduced the logic of race through the discourse of immigration, mainly through blame attributed to migrants, not new in British politics. The Leave campaign argued that exiting the EU would allow Britain to 'take back control of its borders' – the slogan previously used by UKIP. Virdee and McGeever (2018: 1806) argue that "many of the key leaders of the Leave campaign voiced a narrative of British nationalism that was more insular and Powellite in tone (i.e. Britain for the British)", at the centre of which were concerns about immigration. Similarly, Amber Rudd in her speech at the Conservative Party conference in October 2017 said that foreign workers should not be "taking jobs that British people could do" (*The Guardian*, 12 January 2017), echoing Gordon Brown's "British jobs for British workers" remark in 2007 (*The Telegraph*, June 6, 2007). In November 2018, Theresa May, the former Prime Minister, used a rhetoric of EU migrants 'jumping the queue' in her speech to the CBI business group. She said that a new post-Brexit immigration system would prevent EU migrants from "jumping the queue" ahead of migrants from non-EU countries (BBC News, 19 November 2018). This sounded like a continuation of May's agenda to make Britain a hostile environment for immigrants introduced as home secretary. Even though it appears that the responses of some politicians to EU migration have not been racially motivated but rather economically, they produce racialised effects (Fox et al., 2012). Burnett (2017: 4) points out that an examination of over one hundred cases of racist violence after the EU referendum "shows a link between the language and behaviour of perpetrators and the rhetoric and policy pronouncement of politicians". Furthermore, Haque (2017) argues that the toxic Brexit campaign has normalised hatred towards immigrants, turning communities against each other.

Similarly, there has been some ambivalence in the portrayal of Polish migrants, particularly in the tabloid media. Initially, some media focused on the positive work ethics of Polish migrants by emphasising hard-working-ness, value for money and diligence. They were constructed as a 'desirable' migrant group and seen as 'invisible' due to their whiteness. With the outbreak of the economic crisis in 2008, there was a rhetorical shift. Polish migrants increasingly started to be perceived as an economic threat responsible for society's malaise: job shortages, unemployment and the strain on social services. In the run up to the EU referendum in 2016, the reporting of immigration more than tripled over the course of the EU referendum campaign, and the coverage of the effects of immigration was overwhelmingly negative, particularly in the *Express*, the *Daily Mail* and *The Sun* (Moore and Ramsay, 2017). Migrants were blamed for many of Britain's economic and social problems. Amongst those singled out for particularly negative coverage were Polish migrants. The European Commission against Racism and Intolerance (ECRI) (2016: 18) criticised British tabloid newspapers for "offensive, discriminatory and provocative terminology". Immigration fears have been particularly fuelled by regular exaggeration of the negative socio-economic impact of immigration in some media and political debates, despite the clear evidence of the positive impact of EU migration (Dustmann and Frattini, 2014). In Britain, as in other European countries, xenophobia and liberalism permitted opinion makers and politicians to discuss migrants and minorities in terms of a threat (Amin, 2013), while the actual convivial interaction between Polish and other EU migrants and the local population has been overlooked.

In contrast, there has been no significant opposition towards Polish migrants in Spain who have generally not been considered as a problem. This could be due not only to the small numbers of Polish migrants in Spain but also an assumed cultural historical, political and religious proximity (González Yanci and Aguilera Arilla, 1996; Nalewajko, 2012). Both Poland and Spain are perceived as Catholic countries with past dictatorial regimes. Also, both guard the external borders of the EU. Furthermore, the absence of a negative framing of Polish migrants could be a perception of Poland as the Spanish ally in a socio-political context (*El País*, 16 May 2004). Poles are often referred to as a model of a migrant group well integrated into Spanish society (Hellermann and Stanek, 2006), and they have been used in comparisons with other immigrants, especially in some media and political debates. For instance, in 1991 Jordi Pujol, former President of the Catalan Autonomous Government, said: "In Catalonia, as in any European country, it is easy to integrate the Polish, Italians or Germans, but it is difficult to achieve that with Arab Muslims, even with those who are not fundamentalists" (Cesari and DeWan, 2006: 236). In this light, it is possible that Polish migrants might be used to distance Spain from its Moorish past, especially considering that Polish Catholicism and preserving religious practices might place Polish migrants in a privileged position in the Spanish imagination (Ramírez Goicoechea, 2003). Recently, there has been a substantial increase in populism following the diversion of migratory routes from Africa towards the Spanish coasts of the Mediterranean. Those at the heart of the debate on immigration have been recent arrivals from Africa (*El País*, 6 August 2018). Nevertheless, while in the UK context the Brexit vote in the EU referendum in June 2016 was closely linked with concerns about immigration and the free movement of EU citizens; there has been absence of anti-immigrant or anti-EU sentiment in Catalonia. In fact, Catalans as members of a sub-state nation with a strong independence movement "may try to distinguish themselves from the nation-state by pursuing liberal/multicultural integration policies" (Rodon and Franco-Guillén, 2014: 669). This book shows how crucial these discourses are in understanding conviviality in various national and local contexts.

Book overview

The book is organised into six chapters. The first part of Chapter 2 explores the conceptual framework for studying conviviality in multicultural cities and the methodology. The first part of the chapter expands Gilroy's (2004) idea of conviviality by drawing on the meaning of the Spanish word *convivir*, which allows understanding conviviality as a mode of living together. Furthermore, it draws on the concept of *convivencia* describing the historical mode of coexistence between Jews, Muslims and Christians in medieval Spain and on contemporary uses of the term reflecting the practices of everyday living together in the Spanish and Catalan contexts. It also draws on geographies of encounters by situating the research in the cities as spaces of encounters between people from different backgrounds. It stresses the importance of place and shared spaces. Conviviality is explored as a process of interaction not always free from racism, tensions and divisions. Therefore, the conceptual framework expands to writings on race, racism and xenophobia. While the literature tends to focus on non-white ethnic minorities, Chapter 2 highlights the importance of concentrating on experiences of Polish migrant women coming from a predominantly white society to multicultural cities. Therefore, it draws on whiteness, which contributes to a wider understanding of complex encounters with difference. The second part of Chapter 2 discusses the research process, the reasons why I chose to study the experiences of Polish migrant women in Manchester and Barcelona, the methods of participant observation, narrative interviews and focus groups, as well as the longitudinal dimension. In this part of the chapter I also reflect on my complex positionality as a researcher studying lives of migrant women with whom I share nationality and mother tongue.

The empirical Chapters 3, 4 and 5 explore narratives about everyday encounters between Polish migrant women and the local population in both Manchester and Barcelona. Their experiences illustrate the ambivalences which are at the heart of conviviality. Chapter 3 concentrates on selected accounts which illustrate complex and multiple encounters within various sites in both cities, including the neighbourhoods, schools, colleges, streets, play groups and places of worship, revealing multi-layered social realities and various forms of interaction. However, the narratives demonstrate that not all encounters lead to meaningful interaction, and this is partly influenced by socio-economic inequalities, competition for and anxieties over jobs, housing and welfare, and the influence of the widespread negative media and political discourse about post–2004 migration specific to the British context. Chapter 3 also raises the importance of the spatial, temporal, gender, class and race dynamics, particularly in the context of the street encounters with men of South Asian and/or Arab origin, marked by fear and avoidance.

Chapter 4 concentrates on often overlooked workplace encounters, especially considering that it is where many people spend much of their daily lives often interacting with those from different backgrounds. The selected narratives explored in this chapter show a complex reality of contact with difference at work demonstrating various forms of conviviality, including the interplay of language and humour as a means of facilitating playful interaction between co-workers. It also shows the possibility of more meaningful forms of conviviality by concentrating on workplace friendships that transcend the space of the workplace. This is contrasted with forced conviviality used as a survival strategy. The chapter also illustrates how convivial interaction can be limited by negative discourses about Polish migrants in the UK and ethno-stratification of the labour market in the Spanish/Catalan context.

In 2017/18, I contacted my interviewees living in Manchester about their experiences in the context of Brexit. Hence, Chapter 5 explores selected narratives which illustrate interviewees' awareness of anti-migrant sentiment and a changing nature of encounters following the EU referendum in June 2016. This chapter shows how the fragile and dynamic character of conviviality is contrasted with more sustained forms of interaction holding up to divisive discourses. The longitudinal aspect of my research enabled me to see how some interviewees have taken an active part in shaping conviviality in everyday practices of living together over time. As the chapter illustrates, this is not always without tensions, ambiguities and divisions. This leads to a better understanding of how people live together in turbulent times of Brexit and the possibilities of resistance to divisive anti-immigration rhetoric. Furthermore, it is important to highlight that this book has been written in the period of uncertainty of the Brexit situation, since the outcome has not yet been finalised. This uncertainty is also reflected in the narratives of my research participants, particularly in reference to their future in the UK.

Finally, in Chapter 6, I draw conclusions on encounters with difference experienced by my research participants and discuss different forms of conviviality influenced by various factors, including spatio-temporal dynamics. I finish by considering forthcoming possibilities by referring to my participants' reflections about the future of living together in Manchester and Barcelona.

Note

1 The Eastern influence in Poland dates back to the medieval times and the presence of Polish Tatars for more than 600 years (Dziekan, 2011). The perception of the East

changed radically in Poland during the Enlightenment as a result of the influence of the Western discourse of Orientalism having a strong impact on Polish culture in the eighteenth century (Wawryk, 2012). According to the discourse of invasion of Europe, Poland has been seen "as a fortress of the Western civilisation" against the "barbaric, cruel, militant and chaotic East" and the powerful civilisation of Islam (Grzymała-Kazłowska, 2007: 232). The negative perceptions of Muslims have been influenced by the Western discourses on Muslims reproduced through mass media, politics and public debates constructing them as a 'problem' due to their numbers, assumptions about terrorism, threat to identity and security, and inability to integrate. These views point to the phenomenon of Arabo- and/or Islamophobia, or what Górak-Sosnowska (2011: 17) calls "platonic Islamophobia" – a negative attitude towards Muslims which often involves lack of contact with these groups.

2 Conceptual considerations and the research

Until recently, social researchers tended to identify and describe problems when studying social relations between different ethnic groups, while successful interaction was often overlooked. In response to this, a growing number of scholars shifted their focus to conviviality to discuss ways of living together in urban spaces where diverse groups and individuals coexist in multicultural cities (Gilroy, 2004; Heil, 2014, 2015; Karner and Parker, 2011; Morawska, 2014; Neal et al., 2018; Wessendorf, 2014a, 2014b; Wise and Velayutham, 2014). As Nowicka and Vertovec (2014: 1) point out, "conviviality across a number of disciplines now conveys a deeper concern with the human condition and how we think about human modes of togetherness". Neal et al. (2013: 320) refer to the "convivial turn" in literature on lived experience and suggest that conviviality:

> may offer a frame of analysis, or a means of describing, social relations, interactions, and connections to places that are not hidebound, conditional and troubling as the concept of community. This does not mean it is trouble-free ... but it may yet be the most appropriate and relevant way of describing and thinking about the rapid and ongoing reconfigurations of multiculture and cultural difference.

Thus, conviviality can be considered to explore and describe complex everyday practices of living with difference in multicultural environments. This book demonstrates how my study of conviviality contributes analytically and empirically to the understanding of different forms of encounter in various settings. At the heart of my exploration of conviviality are encounters with difference in terms of social class, gender, religion and other categories which often intersect and cut across ethnic lines.

This chapter is divided into two parts. The first part sets out the theoretical background of my research reflecting on the key concept of conviviality. It firstly refers to Gilroy's idea of conviviality as a frame for studying encounters between my research participants and the local population in Manchester and Barcelona. My conceptualisation of conviviality draws on the meaning of the Spanish word *convivir* which allows us to understand conviviality as a mode of living together. Secondly, it expands the conceptual framework by drawing upon the concept of *convivencia* describing the coexistence of Jews, Muslims and Christians in medieval Spain and contemporary uses of the term referring to the practices of everyday living together. Thirdly, it draws on geographies of encounters, a body of work focusing on encounters with difference in urban spaces, seeking to document how people negotiate difference in their daily lives (Amin, 2002; Matejskova and Leitner, 2011; Valentine, 2008; Wilson, 2013a, 2017). It concentrates on cities as spaces of encounters between people from different backgrounds and highlights the importance of gendered spaces often overlooked in debates on geographies of encounter. Subsequently, it discusses how conviviality is explored as a process of interaction not always free from racism and tensions. I explain the importance of acknowledging the conflicting side of daily encounters, different forms of racism and xenophobia, and how my research participants can be both victims and perpetrators of racist and xenophobic discourses. The literature on conviviality tends to focus on non-white ethnic minorities. The study this book draws on, on the other hand, fills the gap in research by concentrating on convivial experiences of recent migrants coming from a predominantly white society to super-diverse cities. Therefore, this chapter draws on whiteness which may contribute to a wider understanding of encounters with difference experienced by Polish women in Manchester and Barcelona. The second part of this chapter discusses the research process, the reasons why I chose to study everyday encounters in Manchester and Barcelona, the methods of participant observation, and narrative interviews and focus groups, as well as the longitudinal dimension. In this part of the chapter, I also reflect on my complex positionality as a researcher studying lives of migrant women with whom I share nationality and mother tongue.

Defining conviviality and convivial culture

The focus on lived experience disrupts predominant political, media and public debates which regard migration and cultural difference as a problem and instead shifts attention to the emerging patterns of everyday interaction in multicultural cities. These new patterns are a result of conviviality defined by Gilroy (2004: xi) as "the processes of cohabitation and interaction that have made multiculture an ordinary feature of urban life in Britain's urban areas". For Gilroy (2006a: 40):

> Conviviality is a social pattern in which different metropolitan groups dwell in close proximity, but where their racial, linguistic and religious particularities do not – as the logic of ethnic absolutism suggest they must – add up to discontinuities of experience or insuperable problems of communication.

Thus, racial, linguistic and religious differences are considered as not obstructive to conviviality. According to Gilroy, these differences do not disrupt convivial experiences and communication between people who interact and live together. The question of difference is central in this book since it focuses on migrant encounters with difference not only in terms of race and ethnicity, but also gender and class, which are socially constructed categories. For Gilroy (2004: 105), racial and ethnic differences become 'unremarkable', ordinary and mundane in convivial settings and they do not constitute a hindrance to convivial interaction. Gilroy (2008: 58) argues that "things which really divide us are much more profound [than racial and ethnic difference]: taste, lifestyle, leisure preferences, cleaning, gardening and child care". Wessendorf (2014b) conceptualises the normalcy of diversity as commonplace based on her research in Hackney, where, as a result of the long history of diversification, residents experience ethnic, religious and linguistic diversity as a normal part of everyday life. Similarly, Amin (2013) uses the phrase 'indifference to difference' based on everyday negotiations of difference and shared spaces.

In building on Gilroy's idea of convivial culture, this book recognises that culture is no longer understood as a homogenous body of traditions and customs but as a dynamic social process: "The idea of culture as a set of unchanging and coherent values, behaviours or attitudes has given way to the idea of culture as negotiation" (Simon, 1996: 153). Conviviality offers an alternative understanding of culture based on what people do in their daily lives and how they live together with others (see also Back and Sinha, 2016). For Morawska (2014: 364–365), "culture of conviviality" is shaped by habituation through the repeated practices of individual actors. The habitual practices, situated in particular times and spaces, are explored in this book in order to gain a better understanding of emerging convivial cultures in Manchester and Barcelona.

In applying a cross-cultural comparative approach to the research of everyday experiences of my research participants in two cities, I find Gilroy's (2004) idea of conviviality and convivial cultures very useful, although he does not explore them sufficiently theoretically or empirically. Firstly, he does not offer a clear theoretical framework for conviviality. This leaves unclear how it is conceptualised, how it relates to other concepts and how it could be researched. Secondly, Gilroy focuses mainly on the postcolonial context. Convivial encounters can no longer be solely explored in the context of diversity conventionally characterised by the presence of African-Caribbean and South Asian communities from Commonwealth countries or former colonies but through the lens of super-diversity as a result of an increase of migrants with different ethnic origin and diverse migration histories, gender, age, religion, languages, education, legal status and economic background (Vertovec, 2007a). Thirdly, the impact of gender on conviviality remains underexplored, especially when it intersects with other axes of difference including race, ethnicity, class and age (Morawska, 2014). In this light, there is a need to concentrate on the gender and class dynamics lacking in Gilroy's debates on conviviality. Here, it is useful to refer back to Gilroy's quote which highlights leisure preferences, cleaning, gardening and child care, which are, in fact, classed and gendered. Hence, the class and gender gap in discussions on conviviality is particularly important. As Morawska (2014: 368) suggests,

women might be expected to have an emphatic understanding of or even an affinity with being 'other', and yet their traditional socialization as the defenders of the family hearth and the transmitters of its unique traditions would likely make them suspicious of outsiders.

Hence, this book explores complex migrant women's encounters with difference.
  Some scholars disapprove of idealising encounters between different groups and individuals. Valentine (2008) criticises writers for romanticising urban encounters and argues that contact and proximity between different social groups are not sufficient to produce respect. She uses empirical examples showing that contact with others leaves attitudes and values unchanged and, in some instances, hardened, in particular in the areas of relative social and economic deprivation where the narratives of injustice and victimhood are prevalent and where migrants are blamed for 'stealing' jobs, undercutting wages and taking benefits. Valentine is sceptical about conviviality and she argues that "everyday convivial encounters often mark instead a culture of tolerance which leaves the issue of our multiple and intersecting identities ... unaddressed" (Valentine, 2008: 334). Valentine (2008: 325) argues that taken-for-granted civilities towards others in public space do not necessarily mean having respect for difference. Instead, she shifts attention to 'meaningful contact' understood as "contact that changes values and translates beyond the specifics of the individual moment into a more general positive respect for – rather than merely tolerance of – others". In response to this criticism, it is useful to highlight Neal et al.'s (2013: 318) argument that:

> fleeting exchanges and mundane competencies for living cultural difference are preferable to the conditional 'meaningful interactions' demanded by the UK's cohesion policy agenda and are more realistic than the transformative expectations of the encounter approach.

Furthermore, following Lofland (1973), urban researchers have demonstrated that casual informal encounters can turn into ongoing affective relationships that link them to urban spaces (Glick Schiller and Çağlar, 2016; Pink, 2012). Hence, this book stresses the importance of not only exploring more sustained social relations but also momentary and fleeting encounters which might have significant effects (Nowicka, 2012). Instead of engaging in an argument about meaningful versus fleeting interactions, this book explores the complexity of daily interaction with difference involving various degrees and forms of encounter often conditioned by spatio-temporal circumstances, and classed, raced and gendered dynamics.
  While the existing literature about the practices of living together in diverse multicultural cities often interprets conviviality as limited to superficial, fleeting and casual encounters in public spaces (Amin, 2002; Fincher, 2003; Laurier and Philo, 2006; Valentine, 2008) unlikely to generate meaningful engagement with difference, this interpretation often overlooks a possibility of different forms and understandings of conviviality. Exploring the origin of this concept might shed more light on how it is understood in this book. In Latin, convīv(ere) means

to live together (con 'with' + vīvere 'to live'). In their analysis of the word *convivencia*, Giménez Romero and Lorés Sánchez (2007: 78) also refer to the Latin origin of the word and stress the Spanish interpretation of it as *"acción de convivir"* [action of living together] or *"relación entre los que conviven"* [relations between those who live together]. The authors make a clear distinction between *convivencia* and *coexistencia* [coexistence], which is not always very clear in other languages, including English. Giménez Romero and Lorés Sánchez (2007) highlight that while *coexistencia* marks a mere coincidence in time, *convivencia* involves interaction. Furthermore, in Catalan, there is also a difference between *convivència*, with a clear connotation of interrelation between people, and coexistence which refers more to sharing the same space but remaining separate. Therefore, I use the term 'convivial', as informed by the idea of *convivir*, to describe relations of living and interacting together in shared spaces.

The popular English understanding of conviviality as jovial and festive might prevent capturing other important forms of living together, including friendship, care and compassion (Jamieson, 2000), sharing and exchange generative of a "convivial mutuality" (Overing and Passes, 2000: 16). These under-researched forms represent the social and interactive side of everyday relations often encompassing "the affective side of sociality" ("convivial affect") (14). In the next section, I expand my conceptual framework by drawing upon the concept of *convivencia* in medieval and contemporary Spain.

Drawing on *convivencia*: from medieval to contemporary forms of 'living together'

In my analysis of conviviality, I embrace a historical approach to sociological analysis which demonstrates how social phenomena come into being and how they have been shaped over time by multiple and changing circumstances (Morawska, 2014; Abrams, 1982). The term *convivencia* has a rich historical context and can be traced back to a Spanish philologist and historian, Ramón Menéndez Pidal who used it to describe the existence of different forms in the early Romance languages of the Iberian Peninsula. Influenced by Menéndez Pidal, Américo Castro wrote in 1948 *España en su historia: cristianos, moros y judíos* in which he first used *convivencia* as a pattern of interaction between Jews, Christians and Muslims, who lived together in close proximity in medieval Iberia. Castro (1948: 208) referred to *convivencia cristiano-islamico-judía* based on spiritual communication and tolerance, especially during the first 400 years of the Islamic domination. In the 1971 revised English edition of the book, *convivencia* appears in the chronological division of Spanish history as a period of coexistence between people of the three 'castes' from the tenth to the end of the fifteenth century (Castro, 1971: 584). *Convivencia* is translated as "a living-togetherness" possibly to avoid the common translation of the term as coexistence. In order to avoid misrepresentation of the term and to situate it in its socio-historical context, I use the original Spanish term *convivencia* (and Catalan *convivència*).

Castro argued (1971: 55, 60) that under Muslim domination, even though "the Islamic and Oriental mode of life was clearly dominant", *convivencia* was manifested through the intermarriage between the three religious groups, linguistic exchange, tolerance and "the spirit of shared common life which united all three [groups]". Castro (1971: 62) suggested that even though the three groups followed their religions, there was a "belief in a higher religious harmony" reflected in both practical and spiritual life. He also made a reference to the belief in the same God unifying the three groups. He considered these groups as "a fabric woven of three threads, none of which may be cut out" (94). According to the historian, Christians, Muslims and Jews were an intrinsic part of Spain, and Spaniards are the outcome of mixing of the three groups. This view, however, was counteracted by the historiographic approach described by some historians as the "Castilianist" perspective on Spanish history associated with Claudio Sánchez-Albornoz (1962) who saw Castile as "uncontaminated" by the Islamic invasion and by centuries of interaction with the Jews (Soifer, 2009: 20).

Several scholars have criticised Castro's view of intergroup relations as idealised by focusing only on the positive while overlooking the negative ones (Gampel, 1992; Glick, 1992; Kamen, 2014; Soifer, 2009). Glick (1992) has explored the cultural and social dynamics underlying *convivencia* and he has argued that it is difficult to talk about static and unchanging *convivencia* based on either peace or conflict, since socio-cultural relations varied between the three groups in different historical periods and under changing patterns of dominance.[1] The changing nature of *convivencia* highlights the complexities of the social dynamics of interaction and the changing nature of socio-cultural processes over time and according to specific contexts (Glick, 1992). This is particularly important in research on interaction with difference over time. Kamen (2014: 3–4) reflects on the complexity of relations between the three groups under the Muslim and Christian rules in different periods of time and regions of medieval Iberia and he argues that there was always another side of *convivencia*:

> Communities lived side by side and shared many aspects of language, culture, foods and dress, consciously borrowing each other's outlook and ideas.... Within that social sharing ... there were permanent elements of conflict, arising out of the different political, economic and religious status of each faith.

In response to Castro's idea of *convivencia*, lacking consideration of the uneven distribution of power among the three religious groups, Kamen emphasises inequalities between these groups: "The communities of Christians, Jews and Muslims in Spain never lived together on the same terms, and their coexistence was always a relationship between unequals" (Kamen, 2014: 4). Despite familiarity between cultures as a result of close contact for long periods of time, he stresses that minorities suffered social disadvantages, although laws were not always exclusive. Kamen also emphasises the more aggressive reality of conflicts including riots and massacres in the later stages of the wars between

Christians and Muslims. There was a certain paradox in these complex relations: "Muslims and Jews might dance together in the feasts of Christians, but at the same time they took the opportunity to attack each other" (6). Hence, in the study on conviviality, broader relations of power should not be overlooked, as discussed later in this chapter.

Glick (1992) has warned that exploring *convivencia* through the binary of conflict/peaceful coexistence runs a risk of overlooking complex social dynamics. Therefore, *convivencia* should be viewed beyond the traditional binary of conflict and tolerance in the context of relations between different groups, as a changing and dynamic process. Other scholars have rejected the notion that violence and conflict are necessarily contradictory to peaceful coexistence. Salicrú (2008: 34) emphasises that "in the mediaeval Mediterranean, conflict and confrontation versus coexistence and communication have to be seen as two complementary realities, inseparable and in no way exclusive: sides of the same coin". Similarly, when defining *convivencia*, Gampel (1992) has refused to create an image of "total harmony" enjoyed by all faith groups. Instead, he has rather offered an image of a pluralistic society in which different groups often lived in the same neighbourhoods, engaged in businesses with each other and affected each other's ideas, but at the same time, there was mistrust, competition and occasional hatred. In both al-Andalus (ruled by Muslims) and Christian Spain the dominant group aimed to isolate minorities religiously but not economically, creating an unavoidable tension in between different groups (Glick, 1992). It was this tension, according to Glick, that opened up possibilities for cultural exchange at a market place where ethnic differences were not as important as in other spheres of life. Kamen (2014) points out that the military alliances were made regardless of religion, and that the wars between Christians and Muslims happened mainly over land. In addition, Ray (2005) stressed that *convivencia* should be discussed beyond religious and ethnic markers as it was a product of a variety of identities, including not only ethnicity and religion but also often overlooked class and gender. Giménez Romero and Lorés Sánchez (2007) suggest that *convivencia* in today's world is not something opposed to the conflict and it does not mean absence of conflict. The contemporary understanding of conviviality explored in this book, particularly in the discussions on conflict and tensions, is influenced by the historical reality of medieval *convivencia*.

The echoes of medieval *convivencia* are not only visible in Spanish architecture, language and music, but there is a significant revival of the concept in contemporary debates. The term *convivencia* has been embraced by academics, journalists and politicians and it has multiple socio-political uses in contemporary Spain. *Convivencia* is a term commonly used in the local context to refer to social relations between people at different levels, for instance, between family members, neighbours and co-workers in towns, cities and in the country (Suárez-Navaz, 2004). It is one of the most used words today by different individuals, NGOs, civic and religious organisations, in official documents, and it is usually understood in terms of daily relations between people.

Convivencia is a key term of popular discourse also in Catalonia. In recent years, much of political and academic debate has emphasised the importance of *convivencia* with reference to different ethnic groups living together.

At the policy level, the term *convivencia* is used in discourses on immigration and accommodation of cultural difference. The Spanish central government has a common integration programme, *Plan Esratégico de Ciudadanía e Integración 2011–2014* (PECI) which stresses the importance of *convivencia* translated in the document as "living together" (Ministerio de Trabajo e Inmigración, 2014: 189), and explained as a mode of sociability based on interaction, distinguished from mere coexistence and alternative to hostility (200). In PECI, *convivencia* becomes embedded in the immigration policy discourse in the light of challenges of recently intensified cultural, linguistic and religious diversity which 'needs to be managed'. In Catalonia, the discourse of *convivència* seems to be even stronger. In 2009, the Catalan government promoted a political campaign *Som Catalunya. País de convivència* [We are Catalonia. Land of *convivència*] (Generalitat de Catalunya, 2009) aimed at the whole population to raise awareness of migration and cultural diversity as a reality defining Catalonia and the importance of maintaining social cohesion. This campaign took place in the context of introducing *Pacte Nacional per a la Immigració* [the National Agreement on Immigration]. In 2010, the Barcelona City Council (2010) released *Pla Barcelona Interculturalitat* [Interculturality Plan for Barcelona], a political strategy towards diversity, which also raises the importance of *convivencia*. Cultural diversity in the preceding document is considered as both a challenge and opportunity for *convivencia* and social cohesion: "The diversity of origins, languages, customs, values and faiths, and finally, world views raise new complexities for *convivencia* and social cohesion but also new opportunities" (3). In this context, *convivencia* at the policy level constitutes an integral part of an interculturalist approach to managing cultural difference and shaping social relations between the local residents and migrants. As is emphasised in the document, Barcelona's interculturalist strategy is based on three principles: equality, recognition of diversity and positive interaction. The latter defines the interculturalist approach and differentiates it from multiculturalism.

While recognising *convivencia* as a political discourse, some academic researchers have recently focused on *convivencia* as embedded in daily social interaction between different groups and individuals in shared spaces in Spain and Catalonia (Erickson, 2011; Heil, 2014; Suárez-Navaz, 2004). In her study of Muslims in Granada in Andalusia, Suárez-Navaz (2004) explores examples of social interactions in which migrants engage in the active construction of *convivencia*. Erickson (2011) focuses on *convivència* as an interculturalist discourse shaping relations between migrants and the local residents in Catalonia. Heil (2014) explores experiences of Casamançais in two neighbourhoods, in Catalonia and in Casamance, Senegal, and how everyday practices of negotiation, interaction and translation facilitate neighbourliness. Nevertheless, in this literature gendered experiences of encounters with difference are rather marginalised and the emphasis is largely on non-white and non-European migrants.

Although I acknowledge the importance of exploring *convivencia* in a specific geo-historical context, it is useful to draw on it when exploring contemporary forms of living with difference. The conceptualisation of conviviality in this book draws on the understanding of *convivencia* as not fixed but rather a changing process characterised by complex social dynamics of interaction (Glick, 1992), including unequal dynamics of power and conflict. When exploring encounters with difference, it is important to recognise these complexities and the spatio-temporal dynamics involving not only the positive aspects of living together but also conflicts and tensions. According to Hegel, conflict is an integral part of social existence, and thus it is part of social relations. Furthermore, by drawing on the contemporary forms of *convivencia*, this book follows the understanding of *convivencia* not merely as a theoretical and political discourse but a practical process grounded in daily social interaction facilitating negotiation and accommodation of difference. In the next section, I draw on geographies of encounters highlighting the importance of spatial characteristics shaping conviviality.

Thinking geographically about conviviality

In conducting my research and writing this book, I took on the challenge of using the concept of conviviality in an attempt to generate a new and more comprehensive way of understanding of spatialised social relations. I draw on Morawska's (2014: 358) recognition of the time- and place-specific circumstances contributing to the emergence of conviviality as a process of "continuous becoming" and its forms as changeable due to various circumstances and never fully determined rather than fixed in time and space. In her exploration of the practice of everyday bus travel across Birmingham, UK, Wilson (2011: 634) discusses how "intercultural relations are continuously developed, destroyed and remade". Convivial encounters occur in a space recognised by Massey (2005) as the product of never-finished interrelations and the sphere of multiplicity where different trajectories coexist. Conviviality is generated at specific times and places and by different individuals; therefore, it cannot be explored outside of the context in which it occurs. Thus, I find it more appropriate to use the term situated conviviality, which means it is 'local and specific', "not something that can be replicated in a programmatic way" (Wise and Velayutham, 2014: 425), as it is influenced by encounters in particular space and time, as well as race, ethnicity, gender and other categories which often intersect. The intersectional approach, important in discussing city encounters with difference, acknowledges the complex dynamics between them (Crenshaw, 1994). Hence, this book highlights the significance of situatedness and intersectionality in exploring conviviality.

Cities, earlier characterised as sites of crime and conflict, have been recently reimagined as sites of connection (Valentine, 2008) and "throwntogetherness" (Massey, 2005: 11). Cities can be defined as "spatial formations resulting from dense networks of interaction" (Simonsen, 2008: 145). They have become "multicultural and cosmopolitan melting pots where hybrid identities connect the most intimate relations with the most remote places" (146). Koch and Latham (2011: 515) encourage broadening understanding of how "cities might become more inclusive, more convivial and generally better for the people that inhabit them". Nevertheless, it is important not to treat cities as homogenous entities. The differences are situated within the wider geographical, temporal and socio-political contexts: "each part of a city is distinct from each other part, and is different at different times of the day and night ... depending on the wider sociopolitical context" (Watson, 2006: 2).

Research about migration to cities has often treated locality as containers providing space for settlement (Glick Schiller and Çağlar, 2011), without much consideration of how the spatial characteristics of the cities may influence migrants' experiences of encounters with difference (Rzepnikowska, 2018a). The existing literature on geographies of encounters shows how some city spaces are more convivial than other. Amin (2002: 959) emphasised the significance of "prosaic sites of cultural exchange and transformation" where "much of the negotiation of difference occurs at the very local level, through everyday experiences and encounters". He highlighted that 'micropublics', such as the workplace, schools, colleges and youth centres may serve as sites of inclusion and negotiation. This means that people may step out of their daily environments into other spaces which bring them together with those from different backgrounds and allow habitual negotiating of difference. This is explored in more detail in Chapter 3 on encounters in various city spaces. In these spaces, conviviality is characterised by "being in the company of strangers normalised through habits of co-dwelling or shared labour" (Amin, 2013: 4). However, Amin (2002) argues that public spaces in the cities are not necessarily spaces of multicultural engagement as they are often territorialised by particular groups or are spaces of transit with very little contact between people. In an ethnographic study of encounters between local residents and recent migrants in eastern Berlin, Matejskova and Leitner (2011) found that fleeting encounters in public and semi-public spaces often reinforced pre-existing stereotypes, while sustained and close encounters in spaces of community centres in the neighbourhoods often led to positive attitudes towards migrants. My research findings show much more complexity, particularly when considering fleeting encounters and the changing nature of conviviality.

While most studies of conviviality have focused on interpersonal interaction in different sites of encounter, my investigation recognises the connection between places and people (Amin, 2008) and the significance of the urban infrastructure in regulating relations between 'strangers' (Amin, 2010: 1). Fincher (2003) and Peattie (1998) consider how urban planning plays a part in shaping everyday encounters with difference. Fincher (2003: 10) suggests that the task of the planners should include "recognising, identifying and supporting accessible spaces that welcome people and encourage convivial interaction". Peattie (1998: 248) has pointed out that "conviviality can take place with few props: the corner out of the wind where friends drink coffee together, the vacant lot which will become a garden. ... Conviviality cannot be coerced, but it can be encouraged by the right rules, the right props, and the right places and spaces". Rishbeth and Rogaly (2017: 284) suggest that "architectural design is intrinsic to understanding micro-geographies of conviviality and care". These contributions demonstrate that conviviality should be explored as more than the interpersonal, and that material, structural and spatial dimensions play an important part (Wise and Velayutham, 2014).

While the existing literature in the field of geographies of encounters focuses mainly on encounters with difference in public and semi-public spaces, private spaces as sites of interaction with difference have been largely overlooked. My research participants often discussed convivial interaction in private spaces of the homes, whether in the context of domestic work or interaction with flatmates, neighbours or other mothers they met during playgroups. Therefore, this book contributes to the understanding of conviviality in a domestic environment.

Urban encounters are influenced by different historical and geographic contexts and embedded in broader relations of power, as discussed earlier. Therefore, there needs to be some recognition of power relations among different social groups and individuals which influence interactions in urban spaces. As Wise (2009: 42) points out, "power relations are always present in place sharing as are various degrees of intolerance and cross-cultural discomfort". Therefore, there is a need to address the underlying power dynamics in research of encounters with difference not only in terms of race and ethnicity but also class and gender. Johnson (1994: 107) has called for a new geography based on the ways "in which women and men are situated, move through, apprehend and engage with space". Chapter 3 illustrates how certain spaces can be male-dominated and how these gendered and spatial dynamics affect daily encounters with difference.

It is also important not to forget the complex dynamics of urban encounters. As Watson (2006: 2) aptly suggests, "Moments of tranquillity or harmony can easily erupt into moments of antagonism and violence. Love and hate, empathy and antipathy coexist in ambiguous and ambivalent tension". Similarly, Padilla et al. (2015: 621) point out that "Cities simultaneously celebrate and reject diversity. Growing concerns with racism and xenophobia compete with a preoccupation with tolerance, civility and intercultural dialogue". Racialised, religious and ethnic difference in the city has been often constructed as a threat to social order and cohesion (Harries et al., 2018; Glick Schiller and Schmidt, 2016). Furthermore, Amin (2008: 7) reminds us of the erosion of public space, policing and neglect, resulting in the running down of public facilities and emergence of dangerous streets causing fear and avoidance. This raises the issue of 'less convivial' spaces of the city marked by socio-economic deprivation, fear and avoidance. This book explores in depth these complexities of encounters in various city spaces with attention to spatio-temporal and highly contextual dynamics underpinning more and less convivial encounters in two different cities. The next section highlights the importance of focusing on the complexity of social relations which are prone to racist and xenophobic discourses.

The other face of encounters

My earlier discussion of *convivencia* in medieval and in contemporary Spain revealed the complexity of relations between different groups shaped not only by positive forms of interaction but also conflict and tensions. Conviviality in this book is explored as a process of interaction embedded in social practice which is not always free from conflicts, tensions, racism and xenophobia. The book identifies a tension between conviviality and gendered, racialised and stereotyped perceptions of difference. By doing so, it addresses the critique that the research on conviviality masks racism. As Wise and Noble (2016) point out, this critique stems from traditional scholarship on race and ethnicity that has focused on racism as a starting point and the reproduction of relations of social power as the end. In contrast, this book acknowledges the complexity of encounters and social relations.

In developing the concept of conviviality, Gilroy (2006a: 39) discusses it as "unruly" interaction which "has developed alongside the usual tales of crime and racist conflict". He argues that: "Recognising conviviality should not signify the absence of racism" (40). Gilroy (2006b: 6) reflects on different forms of lived experience in his neighbourhoods: "Alongside racism, resources for the undoing of racism had evolved spontaneously, unseen, unlooked for, unwanted.... There were conflicts, but people resolved them. They didn't always get along with their neighbours, but they overcame those difficulties" (see also Karner and Parker, 2011; Neal et al., 2018; Nowicka and Vertovec, 2014; Valluvan, 2016; Wise and Velayutham, 2014). Back and Sinha (2016: 517) argue that "understanding urban multiculture requires equal weight being given to the paradoxical co-existence of both racism and conviviality in city life". Neal et al. (2018: 29) consider conviviality as "a mode of togetherness but one saturated with and defined by ambivalence – tension, conflict, engagement and collaboration". Instead of viewing conviviality and racism in a dichotomous way, the two can be considered as highly dynamic, at times overlapping each other. The empirical examples in this book show how Polish migrant women experience conflicts, tension and hostility, and often engage in convivial interaction. The research also highlights the importance of conviviality as a process marked by power differentials between different groups, for instance, between the hosts, migrants and settled ethnic and recent minorities, or men and women from different ethno-religious backgrounds. The social dynamics between different groups and individuals are often influenced by the hierarchies of race, gender and class.

Amin (2013: 4) refers to 'the other face' of the daily encounter with difference as 'phenotypical racism' defined as the "precognitive coding of surface bodily differences", for instance, skin colour and clothing as racial markers generating aversion. Nevertheless, at the heart of the racist discourse is not just physical difference but other variables, including country of origin, religion, nationality and language. As Anthias and Yuval-Davis (1983: 67) suggest:

> racist discourse posits an essential biological determination to culture but its referent may be any group that has been 'socially' constructed as having a

different 'origin', whether cultural, biological or historical. It can be 'Jewish', 'black', 'foreign', 'migrant', 'minority'. In other words any group that has been located in ethnic terms can be subject to 'racism' as a form of exclusion.

A deep resentment towards migrants across Europe and beyond in the light of the recent economic crisis and Brexit in the British context has led to new forms of racism, xenophobia and anti-immigrant sentiment. As Gilroy (1987: 43) suggests, the new forms of racism have "the capacity to link discourses of patriotism, nationalism, xenophobia, Englishness, Britishness, militarism and gender difference into a complex situation which gives 'race' its contemporary meaning". European migrants in the UK become racialised and imagined through the category of race because they are migrants (Gilroy, 2006a). The widespread negative political and media discourse about Polish migration further contributes to the construction of Polish migrants as responsible for economic and social insecurity affecting the poor in Britain. Institutional racism is still a major and largely overlooked problem. In the context of Brexit, it has been reduced to a personal or individual prejudice of mostly white working class often labelled as racist. This reduced idea of racism overlooks the underlying socio-economic and political structures that produce and reproduce racism (Clua i Fainé, 2012). As argued in this book and elsewhere (Rzepnikowska, 2018b; see also Haque, 2017), both tabloid media and some political discourses have played an important part in constructing the narrative about the apparent impact of EU migrants as economic threat, particularly to the 'left behind' British white working class with few qualifications (Ford and Goodwin, 2018). The Runnymede report (Khan and Shaheen, 2017) discusses how working-class communities have been exploited by dishonest politicians telling them that the newcomers are to be blamed for their problems, encouraging the white working class to resent migrants.

Even though racism and xenophobia are often discussed as distinct phenomena, they often overlap. There is a risk with using solely the term xenophobia when discussing Polish migrants' experiences, as it may imply their presumed whiteness and deny the processes of racialisation. Sivanandan (2009: viii) refers directly to migrant workers from Central and East Europe as victims of 'xeno-racism': "the treatment meted out to (white) East European immigrants [stems] from a compelling economics of discrimination, effectively racism under a different colour, xeno-racism". Race is not an essential characteristic of migrants "but rather the socially constructed contingent outcome of processes and practices of exclusion. Racialisation does not require putative phenotypical or biological difference" (Fox et al., 2012: 681). In fact, "the nominal absence of somatic difference does not get in the way of xenophobic racism; it turns out racialised difference can be invented in situ" (ibid).

Constructions of the racialised Other do not only refer to non-whites, migrants, people from different religions or with another accent. Racialised discourses also encompass class and gender differences (Byrne, 2006). According to Skeggs (1997: 82), the body carries the markers of class, gender, race and other categories. Similarly, Byrne (2006: 105) argues that "perceptual practices of seeing (and hearing) difference are as important in constructing class as they are with 'race'". In the nineteenth century, the British working class was perceived as the Other by the middle classes and was positioned as a distinct racial group with distinct characteristics. Nayak (2009: 28) highlights that the description of the British working class as white is a 'modern phenomenon' as historically "the bodies of the British urban poor were regularly compared with African natives of Empire in terms of physique, stature, posture, facial mannerisms, intelligence, habits, attitudes and disposition". Nowadays, while the interests of the white working class are often pitched by the media and politicians against those of ethnic minorities and migrants in the UK, widespread classism and explicit contempt of poor white people is often considered as socially acceptable (Skeggs, 2009; Bottero, 2009).

Whiteness

While exploring the narratives of Polish migrant women coming from a predominantly white society to super-diverse cities, I find it particularly important to consider how whiteness is produced through encounters with non-whiteness. The literature on encounters with difference often fails to make references to whiteness. Hence, this book introduces the discourses of whiteness and racialisation to discussions on conviviality.

Black feminists suggested the need to examine white experience as racialised and classed rather than normative. According to black critique, whiteness works as a form of racial privilege which has the effect on the bodies of non-whites. Whiteness is produced by assigning race to others. It operates as:

> a taken-for-granted category, something so ordinary it can pass without remark. It is perhaps unsurprising then that in marked contrast to ethnic minorities, those people designated as 'white' tend to be defined and define themselves not by the colour of their skin but by nationality, occupation, age or sex.
>
> (Nayak, 2007: 737–738)

Therefore, the study of whiteness as a racialised position is to contest its dominance (Ahmed, 2004) and its notion as a 'mythical norm' (Lorde, 1984: 116). Frankenberg (1993: 1) stressed the importance to explore "racialness" of white experience and she categorised whiteness as multi-dimensional:

> Whiteness is a location of structural advantage, of race privilege. Second, it is a 'standpoint', a place from which White people look at ourselves, and at others, and at society. Third, 'Whiteness' refers to a set of cultural practices that are usually unmarked and unnamed.

White privilege is, however, mediated by gender, class and ethnicity, which often intersect. Therefore, whiteness can be conceptualised as "a constellation of processes and practices rather than a discrete entity (i.e. skin color alone)" (DiAngelo, 2011: 56). Whiteness is not a singular experience and its constructions should be situated within the geographical and socio-historical context of the home country partly shaping perceptions of difference. Dyer (1997) recognised the distinction between whiteness of the English, Anglo-Saxons or North Europeans from that of Southern or Eastern Europeans due to the specificity of the former in the past two centuries.

While whiteness has been mostly explored in the West, it has been overlooked in the context of post-socialist societies. Poland was constructed by the West through the use of imperial narrative as the 'Other Europe' perceived as poor, backward and underdeveloped (Wilk, 2010; Wolff, 1994). Scholars have used postcolonial studies to explore representations of Eastern Europe as Western Europe's Other (Buchowski, 2006) and as a discursive construct dating back to the Enlightenment (Wolff, 1994). Owczarzak (2009: 4) argues that "Eastern Europe served as the West's intermediary Other, neither fully civilised nor fully savage". Poland's ambiguous position is described as "not quite-Western and not-quite-Eastern" (11). The fall of the Iron Curtain and subsequently the accession of Poland into the EU in 2004 have constituted significant markers of the 'return to Europe' and helped Poland in asserting Europeanness closely linked with whiteness. Nevertheless, while visual difference has become highly marked, whiteness has remained ordinary, unnoticed and unacknowledged (Imre, 2005). Since race has been associated with non-whites, whiteness has been normalised and invisible. Nevertheless, as I discuss in the empirical Chapters 3 and 4, whiteness is at times re-inscribed when racialised Others become visible in Poland and in host countries. As a result of recent large-scale migration of Poles to other European countries, many have become conscious of being white as a result of contact with non-whites, and at times, not-quite-white through contact with the white hosts (Parutis, 2011; van Riemsdijk, 2010).

The debate about the construction of whiteness in the context of migration has concentrated on how various European migrants, including the Irish, Italians and Jews, became white in the late nineteenth and early twentieth century in the United States and in Britain. Barrett and Roediger (1997) have discussed how Polish, Italian and other European artisans and peasants who arrived in the USA between the end of the nineteenth century and the early 1920s became involved in the process of becoming white and how they acquired 'in between' racial status. In the British context, after WWII, displaced persons benefited from immigration policies with racialised preferences for white workers (Fox, 2013; McDowell, 2009). While Irish migrants initially were racialised by being considered as 'not-quite-white' in the USA and UK in the nineteenth century, they used whiteness against blacks to improve their situation in the labour market (Ignatiev, 1995). However, there is an important difference between the US and the UK contexts regarding the Irish, who despite 'becoming white' faced high levels of discrimination in Britain until the 1970s and 1980s. This was manifested through the signs in pubs and lodging houses stating 'No Irish, No blacks, No dogs'. In fact, Cohen (1988: 14) points out that "Blacks and Irish were *interchangeable* as animal categories of racial abuse". Ryan's (2007) research about Irish nurses in Britain, who mostly migrated in the 1950s and 1970s, reveals the ambiguous position of these migrants as white and European insiders but, at the same time, as cultural outsiders. Similarly, based on her research of lived experiences of Polish nurses in Norway, van Riemsdijk (2010) argues that while in comparison to more visible groups, Polish migrants are considered 'like us', in other contexts they can be seen as undesirable outsiders. These examples show that whiteness can be defined as a category with shifting boundaries and internal hierarchies which can be crossed and climbed by certain groups in certain contexts (Dyer, 1997).

Gender is an important aspect of the construction of whiteness in terms of specific functions assigned to women as biological reproducers of the nation (Yuval-Davis, 1997). For instance, in the post-war period in the UK, Latvian migrant women were perceived as more desirable than other migrants due to their whiteness (McDowell, 2007). They were considered as potential wives and mothers of the future generation of British people. Nevertheless, while whiteness can include certain ethnic and national groups, it does so within limits, as mentioned earlier.

Following the EU enlargement in 2004, Polish migrants in Britain initially become recognised as a 'desirable' migrant group and have been labelled as 'invisible' because of their whiteness. *The Spectator* (January 28, 2006) states: "The New Europeans are hard-working, presentable, well educated, and integrate so perfectly that they will disappear within a generation". They were initially seen as unproblematic as they posed "few questions of cultural and racial difference from their host societies" (Favell and Nebe, 2009: 206). However, as Fox et al. (2012: 685) suggest, whiteness comes in shades and racialisation can upgrade and degrade. While Polish migrants were initially advantaged by the UK policy with the effect of making them white, as a result of British anxieties over uncontrolled European immigration and the Brexit vote, they have been degraded with the effect of making them less white and unwanted.

At the same time, many Polish migrants arriving in super-diverse Britain have become aware of their whiteness and they recognised it as an asset according to a belief that white minorities are treated better than non-whites (Eade et al., 2006; Lopez Rodriguez, 2010; Parutis, 2011). Some emphasise their whiteness/Europeanness and distinguish themselves from other migrants and ethnic minorities on the basis of skin colour and place themselves in the category of whiteness to assert their privileged position. Others may occupy an ambiguous position in between an assumed higher racial status of white Europeans and a lower social status as a result of low-skilled employment (Fox et al., 2015). Nevertheless, the presumed whiteness of these migrants in the UK has not exempted them from racism, violent attacks and discrimination, partly fuelled by negative discourses in the British media and politics.

In the Spanish and Catalan context, the issue of whiteness and migration is relatively under-researched. Whiteness in reference to Polish migration in Spain is hardly mentioned in the existing literature, possibly due to perception of it as a norm. Recent literature stresses the invisibility and the privileged treatment of

Polish migrants who due to their skin complexion are considered as *nórdicos* from the North, highly respected in Spain (Nalewajko, 2012; Ramírez Goicoechea, 2003). The 'invisibility' of Polish migrants is explained by the physical and cultural similarity of these migrants not only to other Central European migrants but also to Catalans and Spaniards themselves (Władyka and Morén-Alegret, 2013). Furthermore, they are rather considered as *extranjeros* (foreigners), a more neutral category in Spanish, than *inmigrantes* (immigrants) marked by negative connotations of inferiority. Polish migrants are seen as *próximos* (close) (González Leandri, 2003) with regard to alleged cultural, historical, political and religious proximity. Furthermore, in the Catalan context, Polish migrants, particularly those who speak Catalan, might be perceived as integral in the process of Catalan nation building due to their assumed whiteness.

While exploring encounters between Polish migrant women and the local population in both Manchester and Barcelona, it is important to consider how whiteness influences these encounters. This may also lead to a greater understanding of the shifting positioning of these migrants (Rzepnikowska, 2019).

The research

My research was inspired by my own interest in understanding the daily interactions and negotiations of difference in multicultural societies, especially in the context of Polish migration from a predominantly white society. This is particularly important at the times of increasingly diversified patterns of migration and divisive public discourses on migration and diversity. My personal experiences of living in Poland, Britain and Spain inevitably influenced the research process, including the design, data collection and analysis which I discuss in this part of the chapter. When I became familiar with the concept of conviviality around 2008, there was hardly any empirical research exploring this concept. I was inspired by Gilroy's idea of conviviality having the potential to make 'multiculture an ordinary feature of social life in Britain's urban areas and postcolonial cities elsewhere' (Gilroy, 2004: xi) on the one hand; and on the other, by the Spanish notion of *convivencia* with a rich historical context and multiple socio-political uses in contemporary Spain. This part of the chapter gives an overview of the approach taken to the fieldwork; explains why I focused on Polish migrant women and situated my research in Manchester and Barcelona; briefly discusses the methods of participant observation, narrative interviews and focus groups, as well as the longitudinal dimension; and my complex positionality in terms of ethnicity, gender, language and so on.

I decided to interview Polish migrant women because I was interested in the experiences of Polish migrants forming part of a large-scale migration since Poland joined the EU in May 2004, making it a particularly interesting and timely case study. At the time of designing my research, the narratives of migrant women, particularly coming from a predominantly white society, were largely overlooked. I was particularly interested in their experiences of encounter with difference in multicultural cities. My research recognised the plurality of women's experiences. It was guided by the intersectionality (Crenshaw, 1994) of social identities which does not simply look at intersecting axes of difference but also seeks to deconstruct social categories in order to challenge social inequalities. This approach demonstrates the importance of recognising the complex intersections between racialised, gendered and class identities and positions (Phizacklea, 2003).

It was clear to me that the best way to understand my research participants' experiences of encounters with difference in multicultural environments was through ethnography. I recognised the importance of using a comparative lens to gain a better understanding of the convivial experiences in the cross-cultural context. This was done by situating the research in Manchester and Barcelona. The fieldwork for this research was carried out in both cities between June 2012 and March 2013. It involved participant observation with various groups and organisations involving Polish migrants, narrative interviews and focus groups with Polish migrant women with a use of photographs. I maintained contact with most interviewees, particularly those still living in Manchester, and contacted them in 2017 and 2018 about their experiences after the EU referendum in June 2016. Initially, my research was not designed as longitudinal. As Ryan et al. (2016) point out it would have been difficult to plan a longitudinal study considering temporariness and uncertainty of Polish migrants' trajectories.

One of the most common questions at conferences and in discussions with my colleagues about my research was: 'Why Manchester and Barcelona?' The next section discusses the comparative approach to my research and the reasons behind situating my study in Manchester and Barcelona in more detail.

Why Manchester and Barcelona?

The cross-national comparative approach in European migration studies has played an important role in the development of migration studies as it has been significant in denationalising migration and challenging methodological nationalism (Martiniello, 2013; Wimmer and Glick Schiller, 2002). Stanfield II (1993: 25) has emphasised the importance of comparative research:

> The best social scientific work is comparative. This is because, whether we are trying to explain something about the world or to predict future trends and tendencies, our arguments are strongest when we are able to bring to the table evidence drawn from more than one case.

I follow Wise and Velayutham (2014) who advocate a less strict approach to studying ethnographic examples of conviviality in two different cities. They refer to Keith (2005: 10) who is cautious about too much emphasis on international comparisons because each space is shaped by multiple framings:

> Consequently international comparisons must look for a 'toolkit of concepts for conducting inquiries into contemporary world' in understanding a

history of a cosmopolitan present rather than assume it is possible to stand a rainbow comparison of experiences alongside one another.

Hence, this research does not aim to present a perfect set of comparisons between Manchester and Barcelona, although it is inevitable that some similarities and differences will be highlighted. Instead, it aims to advance a better understanding of conviviality and explore different ways in which it is experienced in two different cities, although historically similar in modern times, with attention to differences in social, political, cultural and geographic contexts. Furthermore, maintaining a strictly comparative angle would seem somewhat mechanical and perhaps unrealistic. Therefore, I adopt a use of a more flexible comparative lens to studying encounters with difference in two different urban contexts.

The experiences of Polish migrants have often been explored in the capital cities. However, migration increasingly affects all types of cities. I have chosen to situate my research in Manchester and Barcelona for several reasons. Both are intensively regenerated and post-industrial cities with a long tradition of immigration reception, although Spain used to be the country of emigration, and Britain has a longer immigration history. Both cities are characterised by an ethnically diverse population, mixed neighbourhoods and workplaces, making them ideal settings for studying convivial encounters with difference in terms of ethnicity, religion, class, age, gender and other social categories. The presence of migrants and ethnic minorities has profoundly changed the social landscape of these cities. Despite becoming urban locations of significant renewal in recent years, some parts of both cities are still characterised by deprivation and are shaped by class and ethnic dynamics. Both Manchester and Barcelona are cities with a migration-friendly narrative characterised by a wide support from the local governments. Under the banner of community cohesion[2] in Manchester and interculturality in Barcelona, a number of policies and initiatives have been developed with regard to ethnic diversity and migration. These policies and initiatives are usually characterised by a socio-cultural approach to migration and diversity. For instance, Barcelona City Council gives priority to campaigns and debates around the themes of diversity and living together (Council of Europe, 2011), as well as projects created to encourage dialogue and prejudice reduction, including an anti-rumour strategy to combat stereotypes about migrants and migration (Zapata-Barrero, 2014; Tarantino, 2014). Stakeholders, policy-makers, immigration officials and integration practitioners in Barcelona/Catalonia view Catalan society as open and tolerant towards newcomers and their ethnic and cultural differences (Hellgren, 2016). Manchester City Council gives importance to promoting good community relations and mitigating against possible tensions between established communities and newly arrived migrant groups by providing information on practical matters and promoting 'shared values', citizenship and common norms of behaviour (Manchester City Council, 2007, 2010, 2014a; Perry, 2011; Smith, 2010).[3]

Whilst the two cities share a number of similarities, there are nevertheless significant differences to be acknowledged. Barcelona is the capital of a Catalan nation without a state and with a strong discourse of Catalan independence. As mentioned in the introduction, during my fieldwork in Barcelona, a number of pro-independence street demonstrations took place, especially in the city of Barcelona on 11 September, the national day of Catalonia, *La Diada*. At the time of writing this book, the tension in Catalonia reached a recent peak, particularly in Barcelona, following the Catalan referendum in October 2017 which was rejected as illegal by the Spanish government. This was followed by the declaration of Catalan independence from Spain by the president of Catalonia resulting in imposed direct rule on the region by the national government in Madrid.

While in the UK context the Brexit vote in the EU referendum in June 2016 was closely linked with concerns about immigration and the free movement of EU citizens (see Chapters 1 and 5), the Catalan separatist motivations have not been based on anti-immigrant or anti–EU sentiment. Apart from Barcelona's location in Catalonia, characterised by bilingualism and national–regional identification, there is a strong discourse of *convivència* as part of the interculturalist approach to managing cultural difference at the policy level. Thus, Barcelona appears in the Intercultural City Index as part of the Intercultural Cities programme, a joint initiative between the Council of Europe and the European Commission (Council of Europe, 2011).[4] Catalonia's interculturalism strategy, providing the core framework for immigration, aims to set itself apart from the multicultural strategy of Britain (Barcelona City Council, 2010).[5] At the same time, as Conversi and Jeram (2017) suggest, Catalonia's interculturalism is closely linked with Catalan nationalism. Regional immigration and diversity policies have been constructed in opposition to those of the central state in Spain, while attempting to include migrants in subnational belonging and social cohesion (ibid.). However, these and other approaches often fail to engage with the actual lived experiences of encounter with difference in various city spaces. The lived experiences of migrants do matter because they enhance our understanding of *their* perspectives of living in multicultural cities and of migrants becoming important social actors in shaping convivial culture. This book stresses the importance of lived experiences of migrants in challenging the dominant negative discourses on migration and growing diversity of migrants and ethnic minorities, and it calls for the inclusion of the perspectives of migrants in the process of policymaking.

The fieldwork

I conducted the fieldwork between June 2012 and March 2013. It involved participant observation, narrative interviews and focus groups with Polish migrant women. Then, in 2017 and 2018, I contacted several research participants living in Manchester to ask them about their experiences in the context of Brexit in the UK. The epistemological framework of this research is grounded in the recognition that knowledge is situated and contextual (Yuval-Davis, 1997). Therefore, my study is contextualised under the feminist research framework which disrupts traditional ways of knowing to create new meanings. Even though feminist research does not offer a single methodology or framework, there is a "feminist mode of enquiry" that centres on the under-researched experiences of women (Maynard, 1994: 10). Feminist approaches to research break from the conventions of positivist research and scientific objectivity and seek new knowledge for new understanding that legitimises women as knowers (Harding, 1987; Mohanty, 1988). Furthermore, my research recognised the plurality of women's experiences, especially when considering the diversity of their identities, including the differences of class, age, religion, education level and so on. It follows the idea of research guided by the intersectionality of social identities which, as mentioned earlier, does not simply look at intersecting axes of difference but also seeks to deconstruct social categories to challenge social inequalities (Ali et al., 2004).

The following sub-sections focus on the research and analysis methods I used to explore the experiences of Polish migrant women living in Manchester and Barcelona.

Participant observation

The participant observation in Manchester was facilitated by the fact that I studied and lived there. I started my fieldwork by approaching various groups and organisations working with Polish migrants. I took part in various activities and projects in both cities organised by these groups, including family events, meetings, workshops, presentations, festivities, hiking trips, and so on. I entered the groups and organisations as a researcher and soon after I became an active member. I was invited to birthday parties and other events. This added a multi-sited dimension to my research. A multi-sited approach enables a better understanding of participants' positionalities in different locations (Falzon, 2009). I have spent many hours immersing myself in the field which enabled me to get to know my research participants, establish rapport, trust and obtain an in-depth knowledge and insights. This involved a constant negotiation of my multiple positionalities as a researcher and a participant. I entered the groups and organisations as a researcher and soon after I became an active member. I was expected to 'do' and 'think' as a member and not as a research scientist studying the groups. This is reflected in the email correspondence with the representative of one of the organisations, who wrote:

> My only request is that you do not look upon [the organisation] as an interesting experiment, as an external researcher might. ... The main question that I ask you to consider is the ambiguity of your role. ... It is one thing to juggle with multiple identities as a human being. That's life. It's something else when you have to deal with the overlapping boundaries and different priorities of two contrasting organisations – a huge academy with a commitment to excellence in its research standards and a very small, start-up voluntary organisation with a commitment to do the best that it can but with few written standards or traditions to speak of. That's where you have to engage with other peoples' lives and their expectations. How

will you deal with this role conflict? For example, if you are interviewing a member of [the organisation] one minute under your research hat and then have to work with them in the next minute in a practical way under your [organisation] hat?

(Research Diary, May 2012)

The task of negotiating multiple roles requires attention, especially in terms of shaping relations with the research participants through engaging in social activities together and developing friendly relations which often involved emotional experiences and running the risk of becoming too involved. Sociological and feminist debates have identified a need for reflexive research and the importance of emotion in the researcher's relationship to the researched (England, 1994; Gray, 2008). The practice of reflexivity, understood as the researcher's engagement with their own positioning in relation to the world studied and an awareness of the researcher's emotions, contrasts the idea of objective researcher who is able to shut off emotions. My participant observation required self-critical and self-conscious analytical scrutiny of my position as a researcher and careful consideration of the consequences of the interactions with those being researched.

The participant observation was important in conducting my fieldwork with the purpose of getting to know the research participants in their setting and gaining their trust. However, participant observation alone cannot always show why people do the things the way they do or what a particular activity means to them as it is difficult to access a person's own understanding and emotions (Darlington and Scott, 2002). Therefore, I combined this approach with other methods.

Narrative interviews

The opportunities for interviews arose mostly from the participant observation and field contacts. I conducted narrative interviews with 21 Polish migrant women in Manchester and 20 in Barcelona. The interviews took place at different locations, for instance, in cafes, pubs, university buildings, libraries and interviewees' homes. The interview site was likely to have an impact on the interviews and power relations. The interviews in my research participants' homes are a good example of that. In most cases, the interviewees would introduce me to their family members or flatmates. The introductions were usually followed by an informal and friendly chat with them which helped break the ice. The interviews with the informants usually took place in their kitchens or living rooms over a cup of tea which made the atmosphere much more relaxed, while the interviews in the pubs and cafes were often disturbed by the noise. Visiting the research participants in their homes also gave me a great opportunity to see the neighbourhoods they lived in. This made it much easier to understand their narratives about their neighbourhoods. I also conducted one walking interview. Julia in Barcelona asked me to accompany her on her daily half-hour walk from work to a bus stop in Barceloneta. This 'on the move' interview was ideal for understanding a part of Julia's daily routine. The go-along interview while walking side by side, as opposed to sitting directly opposite each other, helped to reduce the power imbalance and encouraged spontaneous conversation as talking become easier while walking (Kinney, 2017). The interview was conducted in a geographical location that Julia was familiar with which had the potential to put her at ease. To minimise the surrounding noise, I attached a small microphone to my digital recorder which Julia took hold off.

The narrative interviews formed the core of my research project. One of the main reasons I chose the narrative interviewing approach was because it elicits less imposed and more extended accounts. Encouraging research participants to speak in their own way shifts power in interviews. Despite the emphasis on research participants' constructions of extensive accounts in narrative interviews, I acknowledge my role in the interviews as the co-producer of data and my influence on what was said. As a researcher, I bring my own experiences to my research and decide what my research is about. This inevitably influences the research outcomes. As Salmon and Riessman (2008: 81) argue, storytelling happens relationally and collaboratively between speaker and listener in a cultural context where some meanings are shared. My research participants' narratives were a result of interaction with me. The co-construction is particularly visible in the parts of the interviews when the interviewees asked me to share my views and experiences. The sharing of my experiences with the research participants may help reduce the exploitative power balance between the researcher and the researched. This is particularly relevant in the research guided by the feminist mode of enquiry which aims to reduce the power imbalance between the researcher and the researched. Nevertheless, it is important to consider the shifting dynamics of power relations and that it is an impossible task of totally removing the power imbalance, particularly at the level of the data analysis when questions of power shift to the researcher.

Narrative interviews pose some important issues which require attention. Firstly, there is an issue of opening up and speaking at length about life experiences. As mentioned previously, participant observation allowed me to get to know some of the informants, establish trust and mutual respect. This has immensely facilitated opening up during narrative interviews. However, while some interviewees spoke at length, others produced brief accounts. Byrne (2003) points out that in her research on white mothers of young children living in South London, not all the respondents produced storied narratives of their lives in the interviews. She argues that "the production of different narratives depends on the respondent's positionality in terms of normative discourses of 'race', class and gender" (Byrne, 2003: 33). Furthermore, Byrne stresses that the storied narrative genre demanding the production of a coherent and whole self may restrict interviewees for communicating subjectivity. While most of my interviewees felt comfortable telling me about their experiences of migration and encounters with difference, several respondents expected me to ask more specific questions as they struggled with producing detailed accounts. In response to this, I tried to ask more precise questions and attempted to turn the narrative interview into a conversation which worked well. I also encouraged the interviewees to expand on their short answers. Also, there were a few who found it difficult to talk about encounters with non-white people. Several mothers of mixed-race children particularly avoided talking about race. This might be because the theme of mixed-race children has been a taboo topic not only in Polish migrant communities but also in Polish society. They were possibly concerned about being judged, since women are expected to play a key role in the ethno-national boundary maintenance and ensuring the continuity of their ethnic group (Anthias and Yuval Davis, 1992; Ryan, 2010). Secondly, there is a general issue in interviewing regarding the way the research participants construct their identities through storytelling, but at the same time they also construct how they want to be known, which raises some limitations. Informants often make assumptions about what the interviewer wants to hear. This required me to be aware that the interviewees might want to put themselves in a positive light with reference to events or people. For example, one research participant made an effort to speak positively about people from different cultures, but once the digital recorder was switched off, she freely expressed her ambivalent opinion about the issue of veiled Muslim women and security. Finally, what is presented in a narrative is constructed in a specific form and memories of earlier events may be influenced by the situation in which they are told. Nevertheless, all knowledge is partial and situated (Haraway, 1988). Furthermore, meanings of life events are not static, but change under the influence of subsequent events in the life of the narrator.

The sample for narrative interviews was chosen to be as varied as possible and it included Polish migrant women who entered Britain and Spain just before or after Poland joined the EU in May 2004. The interviewees were mainly recruited through the organisations I conducted participant observation with. Subsequently, I applied snowball sampling which enabled me to recruit harder to reach respondents, particularly those who were not members of the migrant groups and organisations. Snowball sampling enabled me to diversify the sample in terms of class, education level, occupation, age, marital status, religious beliefs and migration history. I recruited women who have been living in Britain and Spain for different lengths of time, but with a minimum of 6 months. In selecting interviewees, I also considered migrants' working status and area they lived in Manchester and Barcelona. Many were highly mobile and had lived, travelled or studied in different countries and areas in Britain and Spain. This research is not statistically representative of Polish women's experiences. On the contrary, it challenges the dominant regimes of representation of human agency and privileges positionality and subjectivity (Byrne, 2006).

Focus groups

The third research method I used was a focus group in each city made up of six Polish women in Barcelona and five in Manchester. Most were my interviewees.

Before the focus group meeting took place, the participants were asked to bring photographs reflecting everyday situations in multicultural Manchester and Barcelona. These photos were then used to stimulate group discussions. Some of them are included in this book. Each focus group participant had a chance to discuss the photographs which were then discussed by the rest of the group. The focus groups were used mainly as a supplement to cross-check and aid in the interpretation of data gathered through the above methods, but also to explore how the research participants discuss, negotiate and contest issues through interaction within a group context.

Using this research technique allowed me to observe how my research participants articulated and justified their ideas in relation to others through communication. It is also more power balanced between the researcher and the participants in comparison to interviews, as the researcher has less control over the data that emerge. The participants enjoyed participating in the focus groups and found them particularly useful as they had a chance to discuss issues important to them in a group setting:

> I feel that this discussion has taught me a lot and opened my eyes to questions I had no idea about.
>
> (Nikola, Manchester)

> I really liked it. It would be great if there were more opportunities for this type of discussions about different topics.
>
> (Aldona, Manchester)

Initially, I thought of including participants from different ethnicities and I also wondered how the presence of male participants would affect the dynamics of the focus group discussions. The reflections of my focus group participants about the possibility of presence of other ethnic groups and men mirror my concerns in terms of limitations, had I included those two groups:

> People from different cultures would surely have a huge impact. I suspect that we would not hear that many honest opinions which were expressed during the discussion, especially about people from different cultures.
>
> (Gabriela, Manchester)

> We were more open thanks to the presence of only women.
>
> (Julia, Barcelona)

With regard to the use of pictures during the focus groups, I follow Collier and Collier (1967: 5), who explored photography as a research tool: "The critical eye of the camera is an essential tool in gathering accurate visual information because we moderns are often poor observers". The authors pointed out that people have always used images to give forms to their concepts of reality. The non-verbal language of photorealism is a language that is most understood cross-culturally. Photographs can be tools with which knowledge can be obtained beyond that provided in direct analysis: "When native eyes interpret and enlarge upon the photographic content, through interviewing with photographs, the potential range of data enlarges beyond that contained in the photographs themselves" (99). During both focus groups, the photos triggered rich and stimulating discussions which often went beyond the content of the images but mostly were still relevant to the research agenda:

> It was a very good basis for the discussion, a point of departure for many statements.
>
> (Aldona, Manchester)
>
> The pictures gave us ideas to talk about and helped us express our opinions, in a way.
>
> (Nina, Barcelona)
>
> It was good to find out what other women saw in the pictures, especially considering that each of us looked at them in a slightly different way.
>
> (Julia, Barcelona)

Because the photographs were explored by the participants, they experienced less pressure from being the 'subject' of interrogation. Their role became that of experts leading through the content of the pictures and offering different interpretations.

Data analysis

The transcription of the interviews became part of the interpretation and analysis process. I transcribed all the recorded material. Although it was a very long and painstaking process, in the end it was valuable as I became very familiar with the material. After transcribing, the transcripts were summarised and then coded manually to identify the main themes. My point of departure is to acknowledge that my analytic interpretations are partial and alternative truths that aim for "believability, not certitude, for enlargement of understanding rather than control" (Riessman, 2002: 236). I chose narrative analysis because it allowed me to use a person and case-centred approach and concentrate on how the interviewees interpret and make sense of their experiences of encounters with difference. The narrative analysis approach draws on postmodern and poststructuralist schools of thought which involve an interest in the role language plays in social interaction and its place in structures of power (Griffin and May, 2012). Furthermore, narrative analysis allowed me to preserve the stories and treat them analytically as a unit instead of breaking them up and analysing fragmented chunks out of context. This is in accordance with Riessman's (1993: 4) argument that "narratives must be preserved, not fractured by investigators, who must respect respondent's ways of constructing meaning and analysing how it is accomplished". I employed a more thematic approach in concentrating on narratives about encounters with difference in various spaces of the cities. Nevertheless, in doing so, I analysed them in relation to the whole narrative.

In my analysis, I combined two different approaches to narrative analysis. Even though I mainly focused on what was said (the content), I also paid attention to the way a story was told. I firstly identified the themes, patterns and relationships which were common for various cases. Secondly, in analysing the chosen cases, I looked for different examples of conviviality, but also similarities and contradictions across the cases. Even though narrative analysis is case-centred, it can generate conceptual suggestions about social processes (Riessman, 2008). Finally, I used the data gathered through participant observation and focus groups to cross-check and supplement the data from the interviews.

I found it challenging to select specific cases for in-depth analysis, as all interviews raised important matters and were rich in data. One the one hand, I wanted to be comprehensively faithful to the material I gathered and do justice to my research participants who contributed to my research project. On the other, there was the need to leave space for detailed analysis. Therefore, I concentrated on several cases demonstrating various examples of conviviality and challenges posed to it. In doing so, I had to downplay some cases or use them as counter narratives, without going into too much detail about them.

Situating myself in the research

Feminist social researchers such as Stanley and Wise (1993) argue that we need to understand the role that we play as researchers in the research process. They have called for recognition of the importance of reflecting critically upon the multiple positionalities of the researcher and the ways in which various social constructions, including gender, sexuality, ethnicity, nationality and class, may influence and shape research encounters and processes (Hopkins, 2009; Ryan, 2015a; Valentine, 2002). The discussions in research literature about positionality of researchers are often limited to a conventional hierarchy – the researcher as western, white and privileged, and the researched as non-western and non-white (Kim, 2012). However, there is an increasing number of studies conducted on migrants by migrant or minority researchers (Ganga and Scott, 2006; Gawlewicz, 2014; Kim, 2012; Nowicka and Cieślik, 2014). When studying Polish migrant women, I needed to consider my position in relation to my research participants. As part of this exploration, I suggest a more nuanced approach to researchers' positionality beyond essentialised categories of difference.

When the relationship between the researcher and the researched is discussed in migration literature, there is an assumption that migrant researchers with shared national and linguistic background with their respondents have a deeper understanding of their research participants and are able to obtain better data. When I started my research project, I assumed my position as an insider researcher: a Polish migrant woman studying other Polish migrant women in the migratory context. My positionality as a Polish female facilitated entering the field and establishing contact and rapport with the informants and more balanced power relations. It also increased the sense of identification some of the women looked for. The discourse about a shared sense of belonging to the Polish nation was particularly significant during the focus group discussion in Manchester:

> I think that we as Poles, as our entire national group here in England, are disadvantaged by the fact that we are perceived negatively and because of that we can't focus on the positive aspects of our culture but we fight with this hatred.
>
> (Nikola, focus group, Manchester)

> It is up to us to gradually change this opinion from the basis and to somehow show our traditions and speak loudly that we are from Poland. Knowledge of own culture helps making good impression on people.
>
> (Patrycja, focus group, Manchester)

Getting a group of Polish women together in a room is likely to produce discussions of Polishness in a way that a group of mixed nationalities might not work in the same manner. Nevertheless, focusing on the similarities may reduce the differences that constitute different positionalities and identities of individuals. This clearly transpired during the focus group discussion conducted in Manchester, when after a long period of remaining silent, Celina found courage to say that she did not feel Polish in response to strong assertions of 'Polishness' and national pride by some participants:

> I don't know if I am brave enough because I am kind of *odd* [English word used] in this group ... because we are all from Poland, each of us is proud of it but I am not and will never be ... because I never felt Polish. Maybe that's why. I was born and raised there but ... [unfinished sentence]

The participant observation revealed similar tensions with regard to assumptions of national belonging and Polishness. Inka, an interviewee in Manchester, made interesting reflections about how the sense of cultural and linguistic familiarity can be sharply contrasted with different experiences and points of views. This supports Valentine's (2002: 122) argument that "many layers of sameness and difference can be operating at the same time with the participants and researcher simultaneously identifying and disidentifying with each other".

Furthermore, the positioning of the researcher as an insider in ethno-national terms might have an effect of the researcher appearing too close to informants and making them wary of sharing information (Mohammad, 2001). This became clear during the interview in Manchester with Karina, a Muslim convert married to a Muslim man. As a result of negative experiences with Polish people, she was very suspicious about the interview, despite her willingness to participate. She was particularly concerned about confidentiality and anonymity and did not want the interview to be recorded. I respected her wish and instead took notes, which she then checked thoroughly and asked to remove some data. She was possibly concerned that some Polish readers could identify her.

The assumption of being an insider as a result of common ethno-national background reproduces methodological nationalism (Wimmer and Glick Schiller, 2002) marked by traditional view of ethnicity and nationality as fixed. However, these categories are multi-layered and shifting, especially in the context of trans-national migration (Nowicka and Cieślik, 2014). It is undeniable that my transnational mobility and experiences of living in different locations of the world have also influenced my identifications which are shifting and filled with meaning contextually. Similarly, the identities of some of my research participants have been influenced by the experiences of living and travelling in various countries. These shifting characteristics and lived experiences are of crucial importance in the study of conviviality. I follow the argument that the understanding of insiders having better and 'truer' access to knowledge and a closer connection with the informants than outsiders is problematic, because it reproduces insider/outsider dualism obscuring "multiple positioning and (dis)identifications produced and reproduced during the course of an interview" (Valentine, 2002: 122).

There has been an assumption in feminist literature on interviewing that female researchers have a non-hierarchical woman-to-woman connection with female research participants (Oakley, 1981). When I entered the field, I was seen to have a multiple privilege of being not only Polish but also a woman. Some of my research participants told me that they found it easy to talk to me for this reason. Nevertheless, as discussed earlier, this privilege is complicated by structurally based and socially constructed differences between women in terms of their ethnicity, class, sexuality, marital status, age and other categories but also by being positioned in different moments of their lives. Therefore, assumptions that women interviewing women are automatically insiders obscure this diversity of experiences and viewpoints between and within various groups (Valentine, 2002). For example, one of the interviewees was reluctant to talk about her sexuality and her experiences related to it in the discussions on encounters with difference. Her partner, who was also interviewed, told me that this was because she feared of being judged and stigmatised because of her sexuality. Perhaps she was also concerned that since I knew people in her community through my research, they could find out that she was a lesbian.

My migration status could also be seen as a commonality with my research participants. However, my migration experience, in fact, differentiated me from some of my informants. My reasons for and experiences of migration were very different to those research participants who left Poland in search of work. I left Poland when I was 19 with an aim to study abroad and my experiences and relations with people have been affected by several years of studying and working in the academic context. Despite this difference, some research participants made assumptions about my migration experiences and class. For instance, Marlena in Barcelona thought I would be interested in a domestic job: "There is a flat. If you want you can do two hours for five Euros, two hours of ironing". Nevertheless, the interviewees hardly talked explicitly about their social class status. They did, however, openly talk about class when referring to British and Catalan people.

Conducting fieldwork in a shared native language carries assumptions of shared language experience between the researcher and the researched (Gawlewicz, 2014). It is argued that a shared language facilitates access and interaction with group members (Carling et al., 2014). However, when a common language is used, we tend to make the assumption that we know what the interviewees are saying, and alternative readings tend to be obscured or ignored (Riessman, 2002). In her empirical study of domestic workers and their employers in four European countries, Gutiérrez Rodríguez (2010) reflects on the presumed identity between her and her research participants as Spanish speakers. While she tried to establish a connection with her Latin American participants by presupposing that migration and Spanish language were a common point of departure, this was challenged by different positions influenced by historical, political and social contexts in Spain and Latin American countries. I also made assumptions about Polish as a common language with my research participants. However, some interviewees in both Manchester and Barcelona struggled to explain certain things in Polish and this was a source of their frustration, even though I encouraged them to speak English/Spanish if they preferred.

Another significant linguistic difference was the use of racialised language to describe difference by some interviewees. The feeling of detachment from some informants on this basis was also raised by Gawlewicz (2014), drawing on her research on migrant encounters with difference and the language of Othering. Would the informants use the same language of difference if they spoke to a non-Polish researcher? Gawlewicz (2014) argues that in a company of a fellow national, specific data is reconstructed as a result of the assumptions of shared language and migration experience. For instance, some of my interviewees used ambivalent and/or derogatory terms like *ciapaty/ciapak/ciapaci* and *Murzyn* (discussed in Chapter 3 and 4). It is very unlikely that these terms would have been used if the interview was conducted with a non-Polish speaking academic. Hence, even though researchers should avoid making assumptions about shared language, being able to speak and understand the language of the research participants can be beneficial.

To sum up, when exploring the relationship with informants, researchers should not rely on fixed categories. Furthermore, the insider/outsider binary prevents considering the complex and multi-layered identities and experiences (Valentine, 2002). Migrant researchers should not be simply labelled as insiders based on their ethnicity since migrant groups are very diverse with differences of class, generation, reasons for migrating, length of stay and so on.

Furthermore, encounters between researchers and researched are highly dynamic, as they negotiate their positions, instead of relying on the fixed notions of identity (Mullings, 1999). Valentine (2002) emphasises that connections and disconnections are about wider biographical moments. She reflects on sharing a sense of warmth and connection with some interviewees despite some fundamental differences. These similarities "go beyond the ethnic lens by illustrating not only that nationality, or ethnicity, is only one aspect of identity but also that it is highly contingent and constructed" (Ryan, 2015a: 55).

Notes

1 Whereas Abn al-Rahman III, the Umayyad emir in the tenth century who ruled the peninsula, pursued an ethnically and religiously inclusive policy, allowing complex interaction between the three groups, under Almoravid, Almohad and Christian rulers, *convivencia* was much more turbulent, ranging from some level of mixing to forced conversions, prejudice and violence (Gampel, 1992: 15).

2 The concept of community cohesion emerged from the government-commissioned report known as *Cantle Report*, following the 2001 race riots in northern towns in England (Cantle, 2001). It stressed the need to "develop some shared principles of citizenship" and "the promotion of cross-cultural contact between different communities" (11). It has been criticised for problematising cultural difference.

3 The emphasis on shared values emanates from the national level documents, for instance, the Commission on Integration and Cohesion report in 2007 entitled *Our Shared Future*, emphasising the importance of creating a shared vision for the future. This rhetoric is also present in the *Interculturality Plan for Barcelona* (Barcelona City Council, 2010).

4 The intercultural city is defined as a city of "people with different nationality, origin, language or religion/belief" where "political leaders and most citizens regard diversity positively, as a resource" and which, apart from actively combatting discrimination, "encourages greater mixing and interaction between diverse groups in the public spaces" (Council of Europe, 2011: 1).

5 In the British context, the policies of multiculturalism have been developed since the 1960s with the recognition of widespread racial discrimination (Modood, 2015) and they have been aimed to promote tolerance and respect for cultural difference in education, through supporting community associations and their cultural activities, monitoring diversity in the workplace, encouraging positive images in the media and other public spaces, and adapting public services including education, health and policing in order to accommodate culture-based differences (Verovec, 2007b). The backlash against multiculturalism has been fundamentally driven by anxieties about Muslims and fears among mainstream society that the accommodation of diversity has "gone too far" and is threatening its way of life (Kymlicka, 2012: 3). Trevor Phillips, the Chairman of the Commission for Racial Equality declared that multiculturalism is no longer useful as it fetishizes difference instead of encouraging minorities to be 'truly' British (Modood, 2005: 83). The former Prime Minister, David Cameron, proclaimed multiculturalism as failed and linked its failure with Islamist extremism. Nevertheless, the original multicultural framework and anti-discrimination legislation remain in place in Britain.

3 Conviviality in Manchester and Barcelona (and their environs)

Everyday convivial practices of the research participants developed through continuous border crossings as they go to work, college, places of worship, playgroups or visit friends across different urban areas. Neighbourhoods also emerged as prominent spaces of encounter with the local residents. Most research participants had a general perception of their neighbourhoods, although these perceptions do not necessarily match the actual ward or district delineations. While most discussed their immediate neighbourhood, blocks of flats, streets or estates, others referred to the wards and boroughs in Greater Manchester, and quarters and districts in Barcelona. They often constructed narratives about various activities in different places which did not necessarily take place in their immediate neighbourhood but extended through the city and beyond. Hence, the analysis of their narratives stretches outside their immediate neighbourhoods. I follow Çağlar and Glick Schiller (2018: 7–8) who abandon

> a nested concept of scale as encompassing a fixed hierarchy of bounded territorial units such as neighborhood, city, province and nation-state. Instead we trace social processes as they are constituted, noting their interconnections through both institutionalized and informal networks of differential economic, political, and cultural power.

This chapter explores examples of conviviality that exist in real, lived environments in various spaces of Manchester and Barcelona where individuals interact with one another. While there are tensions, conflicts and fear of the Other, this is not the whole story. The narratives discussed in this chapter illustrate multiple forms of convivial interaction in various spaces of the city. The particular empirical emphasis of this chapter lies in an exploration of the following questions: where and how do the research participants engage in daily encounters with the established population? What facilitates and what limits conviviality in various city spaces? How do the narratives of the research participants about encounters with difference contribute to the understanding of conviviality?

The research participants discussed in this chapter reveal their personal accounts of living in Manchester and Barcelona (and beyond). Although there are some common elements across the narratives, there are some important differences in their narratives about encounters with difference. Each account represents a unique story. In discussing each account, I also refer to the narratives of other interviewees and the data gathered during the participant observation and focus groups. The first part of this chapter focuses on the narratives of my interviewees living in Manchester and the wider area of Greater Manchester. The second part concentrates on the informants' accounts of living in Barcelona and beyond. The chapter also focuses on the lived experiences in Rusholme in Manchester and El Raval in Barcelona. Both are multi-ethnic neighbourhoods with a long history of working-class settlement and arrival of various migrant groups. Although both have experienced socio-economic decline, in recent years they have undergone major urban renewal. As Neal et al. (2018: 27) suggests, "situating the lived experience of multiculture in place makes it possible to materialise and ground conviviality". The final section explores motherly activities in the spaces for mothers in both Manchester and Barcelona, including nurseries, schools and children's centres where my participants meet others from different backgrounds.

Conviviality in Manchester and the wider area of Greater Manchester

Greater Manchester, a metropolitan county in North West England, includes ten metropolitan boroughs: Bolton, Bury, Oldham, Rochdale, Stockport, Tameside, Trafford, Wigan and the cities of Manchester and Salford. It mostly consists of urban areas as a result of urbanisation and industrialisation during the nineteenth century when the region thrived as the global centre of the cotton industry. The city of Manchester, one of the most culturally and linguistically diverse in Britain (Multilingual Manchester, 2013), is divided into 33 wards. Between 1991 and 2011, the ethnic minority population increased by 164 per cent in Manchester. Despite this growth, the White British ethnic group is the largest group in Manchester (59 per cent) and Greater Manchester (80 per cent). The largest ethnic minority groups in Manchester are: Pakistani (9 per cent), African (5 per cent), Other White (5 per cent) and Chinese (3 per cent) (CoDE, 2013: 2).

Polish migrants are dispersed across Manchester and the rest of Greater Manchester. Many research participants arrived in less advantaged areas with cheaper rent and poor housing. Along with their improved socio-economic situation and English language skills, some moved to more affluent residential neighbourhoods.

Conviviality through adaptation, co-operation and exchange

Krysia is 51 years old and she comes from a small town near Krakow. She arrived in Manchester in 2006 and moved to a studio in northern Manchester. Then, following the arrival of her son and a grandson, they moved to a house near Cheetham Hill, an inner city area in northern Manchester. Cheetham Hill is one of the most ethnically diverse areas in Manchester as a result of several waves of immigration to Britain. In recent years it has seen a steady arrival of migrants from Central and Eastern Europe. According to Census data from 2011, 44 per cent of those living in the Cheetham Ward were born outside of the UK. The majority of Cheetham Hill's residents self-identified as coming from only two ethnic groups: White British (29 per cent) and Pakistani (28 per cent) (for a more detailed analysis of the Census data for Cheetham Hill see Harries et al., 2018). I met Krysia in a Polish shop in Cheetham Hill. She was very keen to share her experiences of living in the area, and she invited me to her home she shared with a Polish male friend. Krysia's narrative demonstrates how convivial interaction in her immediate neighbourhood near Cheetham Hill develops over time from adaptation practices involving observing and following certain norms to instances of co-operation, interdependence, gift giving and exchange which are more meaningful forms of contact. Krysia mostly discussed her immediate neighbourhood in terms of "our street with 11 houses".

When Krysia moved to her new neighbourhood near Cheetham Hill, she found out that the previous tenants were Polish people who had frequent parties. Therefore, Krysia and her family did not receive a warm welcome from the neighbours. However, the residents changed their attitude when they noticed Krysia tidying up her garden. Her immediate neighbour offered to lend her a lawn mower and a ladder. She described this as the beginning of a 'pleasant coexistence'. This example illustrates how first encounters marked by stereotypes might be potentially transformed into something more convivial.

Despite her limited English, Krysia patiently observed her neighbours to understand the existing norms and customs in the neighbourhood and she then followed them:

> We adopted their ways, like the bins on the street. They have to be removed so that youths don't knock them down, because around the corner there is a youth institution. . . . It works like this: whoever is at home takes out all the bins and puts them back and everything is in order. I didn't know this at first, but I observed them doing it and we started doing the same. If there was something we didn't know, we observed the neighbours and adopted their customs. At the moment, it would be difficult to move into a different neighbourhood, even if I had better and more comfortable living conditions. My neighbourhood means a lot to me. I have very positive experiences of coexisting all these years that I have lived here.

This example demonstrates how the newcomers are required to adjust to the existing norms. While Harries et al.'s (2018) research in Cheetham Hill shows how bin practices are discussed through problematising ethnic difference, Krysia's narrative illustrates how shadowing the neighbours' bin practices leads to adopting common practices through which the residential area becomes a space of co-operation where neighbours work together in order to have a clean and peaceful neighbourhood. Furthermore, these common practices of residents show another facet of conviviality based on silent practices without actual interaction which enabled Krysia to fit in. Her strategy of following the neighbours' practices is a way of fitting in through not being different.

The littering issue is often part of the discourse on immigration in politics and in some media. The article in the *Daily Express* (18 September 2009) titled 'Exclusive: Another rubbish idea, lessons for immigrants on how to empty bins' is one of many examples portraying migrants as unable to comprehend the rules around recycling and bin collection. In November 2013, in an interview on *BBC Radio Sheffield*, former Home Secretary David Blunkett criticised Slovak Roma residents for littering the streets. This fits into a longstanding racialised discourse about hygiene. Nevertheless, Krysia became accepted by her neighbours as she lived up to the rules of cleanliness by following bin practices. In this instance it is the anti-social youth breaking the social order in the area by kicking the bins. Similarly, in Wessendorf's (2014a) study of Hackney in London, the residents complained about Hipsters and students littering the area. This moves beyond the tensions between white English majority and migrant minorities and it demonstrates that conflicts may involve practical matters.

Krysia's neighbourhood becomes the space of co-operation and interdependence where the residents come together to make their area safer. Krysia told me how neighbours prevented burglary of her home when she was at work. She was surprised that, despite being away from home, she could count on her neighbours. She quickly learnt about the home watch on her street. She now informs her neighbours when she stays at home alone and similarly, when the neighbours go away they ask Krysia to watch over their house. These practices demonstrate that neighbourhood can become a space of co-operation, care and trust. As Bridge (2002: 25) has suggested "the neighbourhood provides the realm of practical relations involving the exchange of small services as well as convivial relations that might contribute to a diffuse feeling of security and well-being". Nevertheless, co-operation between neighbours on a street might not be the same as co-operation in a larger territorial unit identified by city planners as a neighbourhood.

When Krysia's grandson arrived from Poland, her neighbours offered him gifts, including a golden chain with a cross. This was very reassuring for Krysia and her family. The offering of gifts by neighbours is an act of accommodating difference, a gesture of care and everyday recognition important not only in creating and maintaining ties but also in producing a sense of belonging (Komter, 2005; Wise and Velayutham, 2014). Komter (2005: 2) stresses that "the concept of the gift does not exclusively indicate certain material acts but has a wealth of cultural, social and psychological meanings as well, all referring to the abstract, symbolic functions of gift giving". Komter (2005: 7) perceives gifts as "tie signs" which reveal the nature of the tie between giver and recipient. In their case study of Sydney and Singapore, Wise and Velayutham (2014) explore the theme of intercultural gift exchange. They highlight that notions of hospitality and recognition are embedded in the practice of gift giving and are important in producing feelings of belonging and maintenance of ties.

A similar example to the gift giving is Krysia's exchange of flowers and plants with a black female neighbour. This practice takes place on a regular basis as they both share interests in gardening. The exchange of flowers has the potential of sustaining convivial culture through repeated practice. This example of conviviality demonstrates the possibility of shared interests between neighbours which deconstruct easy labelling of the 'stranger as enemy' and promotes new attachments (Amin, 2002).

Krysia's story reflects an 'un-panicked' low-key interaction in her immediate neighbourhood in everyday life, echoing Noble's (2009) idea of unpanicked multiculture. Her story shows how, in the words of Amin (2012), "slowly the strange can become familiar". While initially interaction with neighbours was limited possibly due to the temporary, transitory experiences and stereotypical perceptions, habitual contact with neighbours and various practices developed over time facilitated convivial culture in Krysia's immediate neighbourhood. At the time of the interview, Krysia had lived in her neighbourhood for about seven years. Hence, the temporal characteristic of the development of convivial culture in her neighbourhood must be considered. Over time, habitual convivial practices such as adjusting to the existing norms by following bin practices, watching over each other's homes, flower exchange and gift giving shaped Krysia's neighbourhood as a space of co-operation, trust and care. This made Krysia feel at home. In this example, convivial culture facilitates a strong sense of belonging to the neighbourhood. Krysia's experiences in the context of Brexit are explored further in Chapter 5.

From tensions to neighbourly conviviality

What was particularly interesting about the research participants' stories was how they often illustrated a journey through different neighbourhoods (as they changed accommodation quite frequently), where they experienced various forms of conviviality. This was particularly reflected in Paulina's narrative which shows a multi-layered account of living in close proximity with different groups and individuals. Paulina started telling her story about her experiences of encounter with two different groups: men of South Asian and Arabic origin and young white British men (also discussed in Rzepnikowska, 2016a, 2018b). These encounters were often characterised by fear and avoidance. However, as mentioned earlier, this does not tell the whole story. Later, her narrative reflected different forms of conviviality, from fleeting and superficial encounters in everyday interaction in the neighbourhood to more sociable forms involving socialising with neighbours in the space of the home.

Paulina is from a small town in northern Poland where she completed secondary education. At the time of the interview she was 27, married and had two children. Paulina arrived with her Polish husband in Manchester in 2006. She worked as a cleaner and a hospital attendant before giving birth to her first child. I first met Paulina at a family event during my participant observation. Then, I had a chance to get to know her a bit more at a garden party at the house of another interviewee. The interview with Paulina at her home revealed the complexity of her experiences of living in Manchester.

Paulina remembered her disappointment upon her arrival in Salford, a borough in Greater Manchester. Salford is a place of contrasts with regenerated areas, including Salford Quays attracting young professionals, next to some of the most deprived neighbourhoods in Britain. Paulina discussed her neighbourhood in Salford in race, class and gender terms. Like several other interviewees, she imagined Britain as a well-developed and safe country with well-mannered white middle-class people. Instead, after having moved to a shared flat in a high-rise block of flats in Salford with her husband and his friends from Poland, she perceived her new neighbourhood as unsafe and populated mainly by white British people. Paulina talked mainly about avoiding encounters with white British male youth she referred to as *kapturowcy* [hoodies]. She avoided going out on her own and she only used to leave the flat accompanied by her husband and the flatmates. Paulina restricted and modified her mobility in her neighbourhood because of fear. This reflects women's fear of male violence and how they perceive and use space as a result of it. Valentine (1989: 389) refers to it as a "spatial expression of patriarchy" (see also Bowman, 1993; Day, 1999; Koskela, 1999; Pain, 1991; Rzepnikowska, 2016a, 2018b).

Paulina not only experienced spatialised gender inequality in her local area in Salford, but also everyday racism:

> It was a very dangerous area … there were a lot of council flats, high-rise blocks and there were many people hostile towards us, Polish people. When they saw we had a car with Polish registration plates, they started harassing us, kicking the car or breaking the windows. This is how they manifested racism toward us. … In Salford there were many people from poor class. I would say that some of them, out of jealousy, instilled their children with prejudice against different nationalities. They were 15 to 17 years old or even younger and they were very hostile towards people with other nationalities.

Paulina's account shows how racism can be present and acknowledged in the interviewees' accounts. Hence, the discussion of conviviality must acknowledge not only the positive encounters but also the recognition of 'damage never being far away' (Neal et al., 2018). The car with the Polish registration plates becomes the marker of otherness. Even though Polish migrants often perceive themselves as white, they are racialised and constructed as the unwanted Other. Nowicka (2012: 116) emphasises that Polish migrants "disturb a certain invisibility of white immigrants with the legal equal status of European Union citizens". Even if the newcomers are white, they are imagined through the category of race because they are immigrants (Gilroy, 2006a), although their racialisation is more temporary compared to highly visible Others.

The interviewees often attributed racism and xenophobia to poor white British people with numerous families living in council estates. However, the actual attitudes of the local residents are unknown. This reflects a tendency in the UK of ascribing racism to poor white British people (Rzepnikowska, 2018b; Sveinsson,

2009). The dangerousness of the council estate is linked with a lower social class and racism in Paulina's narrative.

In the light of socio-economic deprivation of the inner city areas where many Polish migrants move into, some established residents perceive these arrivals as a source of competition for jobs, welfare services and housing. Popular anxieties over jobs and welfare are mobilised through hostility towards 'new strangers' (Amin, 2012; Valentine, 2008). The widespread negative political and media discourses about Polish migration further contributes to tensions by "constructing such new minorities as the main agents of the decline of established white British working class communities" (Garner, 2009: 48). Wimmer (1997: 31) suggested that xenophobic and racist perceptions of social reality should not be understood merely in terms of "a fight for scarce jobs or housing", but also in terms of 'the territorial dimension of the national community' which is:

> viewed as solidarity among the familiar ones who live in a borough or village that becomes a mini-model of the nation. The physical presence and visibility of foreigners in these social spaces, and especially their integration in local schools and communal institutions, nurture perceptions of invasion, inundation and existential rivalry.

It is also important to take into consideration the spatial dimensions shaping Paulina's experiences of street encounters. Amin (2002) argued that streets offer very few possibilities of conviviality between individuals as they are considered not as a space of interdependence and habitual engagement. They can generate "social pathologies of avoidance, self-preservation and intolerance", especially if the space is marked by uneven power dynamics (Amin, 2008: 11).

Paulina, like several other research participants in Manchester and Barcelona, spoke about gendered, classed and raced encounters with men of South Asian and Arabic origin (see also Rzepnikowska, 2016a, 2018a). She mostly encountered these men on the street on the way to college at the time when she was pregnant:

> I felt stressed when walking through that neighbourhood. People would accost me on the street and look at me in a strange way. I had blond hair then and those from *ciapaci* cultures would try to stop me and make inappropriate comments, so I felt uncomfortable. ... Their comments weren't nice. ... I felt really scared and uncomfortable.

Paulina, as several other interviewees, seemed unaware of the negative connotations of the terms *ciapaty/ciapaci/ciapaki* and why it was used. By the frequent and widespread use, these terms become normalised and often synonymous with the term 'Pakistani' not necessarily reflecting the actual ethnicity. While Paulina was unsure why these terms were used by some Poles, she linked it with race: "Honestly? I have no idea. Maybe they are mixed between dark, black-skinned people and us whites. This is just how we call them. I have no idea. I heard this word when my friend used it and I started using it". Paulina's account demonstrates the process of how racialised language is acquired from other Polish migrants. The term is raced because the main indicator is the skin colour tied to fixed characteristics. While, as many other interviewees, Paulina denied racism, she paradoxically associated the discussed group with kidnappings and rapes of women and with Islam: "I am not going to say that I am racist because many of them are at my courses and they are nice, but I have read so much about kidnappings and rapes of women and about their Muslim religion, totally different than mine, so I always have my concerns about these people". Paulina's narrative matches stereotypical portrayals of the sexually abusive Muslim men based on orientalist discourse (Said, 1995). Razack (2004: 129) calls social and political approach to Muslim men's violence against women as 'culturalist', meaning that "violence is understood as originating entirely in culture, an approach that obscures the multiple factors that give rise to and sustain violence". She argues that racism limits opportunities for effective anti-violence strategies and is likely to strengthen patriarchy.

Feminist geographers have concentrated on the racialisation of fear, highlighting that 'the problem of fear in public space is typically constructed from a white perspective' and that women mostly fear non-white men (Day, 1999: 307). The interviewees' perception of threat might be affected by a racialised schema. The experiences of street harassment shape ideas about the whole group as dangerous and oppressive to women, and 'race fear' sustains race prejudice (ibid). In Paulina's case the street encounter with men of South Asian origin elicited strong emotions of fear possibly having long-lasting effects. Leitner (2012: 832) stresses the importance of "the emotive nature of Othering and racialization" manifested by the strong emotions unleashed in encounters with difference. As a result, the gendered spatial practices of the South Asian men are understood by the research participants as racial practices.

Two research participants in Manchester contested the stereotypical perceptions of people of South Asian origin based on their everyday encounters. During the focus group, Nikola, a 31-year-old office worker in Manchester, reflected on convivial encounters with people of Pakistani origin which have the potential of breaking stereotypes and racialised categories:

> Look at the influence of the media, massive, because when you are in Poland, what experiences do you have with this culture? None. Apart from what you read and see, it's logical, is shaped by the media ... Pakistanis are like this and like that. When you arrive here you have some contact with this person. You go to a shop run by a Pakistani and you have a conversation and you think, blimey, they are not that bad ... and you start thinking differently. I have many friends with different religions and they opened my eyes ... and I realised that we know stereotypes and our knowledge is from newspapers, books and television, but it doesn't mean that this knowledge is accurate and real but it is transferred to us.

Nikola's narrative shows the importance of reflection and evaluation concerning religious and cultural difference. Her critical reflection echoes van Dijk's (2002: 152) argument that in countries which are less diverse culturally and religiously "the mass media are today the primary source of 'ethnic' knowledge and opinion in society" and "virtually all beliefs about the Others come from mass media discourse, literature, textbooks, studies, or other forms of elite discourse". Nikola's arrival in Britain and everyday encounters allowed her to reflect on this transmitted knowledge influenced by the Western discourses of colonialism and Orientalism, which can be challenged through convivial interaction. Her narrative illustrates how perceptions may change through the experiences of migration and convivial encounters. This example reflects Leitner's (2012) findings based on her study of white residents' responses to their encounters with new immigrants in a small town in rural Minnesota revealing that in some instances encounters with difference created moments of reflection that disrupted preconceived categories and boundaries. While it is argued that positive encounters tend to change negative perceptions about individuals and are rarely scaled up to the whole group (Leitner, 2012; Matejskova and Leitner, 2011; Valentine, 2008), Nikola's narrative illustrates a possibility of a shift in perceptions about the entire group. It also stresses the importance of the individual biographies, dispositions and values of the individuals which may shape encounters with difference (Valentine and Sadgrove, 2012).

Inka, a 28-year-old PhD student, contested the use of the term *ciapaki* when she became aware of its negative connotations:

> [W]e lived ... above a Pakistani shop owned by *ciapaki* ... I really don't like that this kind of word was used. In any case, I started using it because, as I said, everybody used it, so it was the easiest way and I automatically adopted it without thinking what connotations it had and to whom it referred.... I'm telling you now that it was a Pakistani shop, but maybe it wasn't Pakistani. Maybe the guy was from Bangladesh or India, I don't know but I know that he was of a darker skin complexion and that's why they used the word.... Later, I started wondering and I asked the boys [flatmates] why they called him like that and that it was not nice.

This reflects an important change of ideas about the Other over time and the possibility of becoming more conscious about the racialised expressions of difference. Everyday life in multicultural settings over a longer period of time serves as an experiential learning opportunity (Wilson, 2013b), leading to some changes in racialised perceptions.

Returning to Paulina's case, in contrast with gendered street encounters, she told me how regular attendance at an adult education course in a local college has led to friendly interactions with her course mates of South Asian and Arabic origin:

> I like the course a lot, so many people from different countries, a lot from Arabic countries, from Pakistan, but they are nice people. I have even better contact with them than with Polish people.

Figure 3.1 Aldona's photograph of the English class at the Trinity Welcome Centre in Cheetham Hill, Manchester

Habitual contact as a result of regular attendance at the course and the inclusive space at the course facility promote the establishment of social relations in a safe manner, free of fear and anxiety experienced on the street. This allowed Paulina to temporarily look beyond the ethno-religious boundaries. Several focus group participants in both Manchester and Barcelona also mentioned convivial interaction with course mates from a range of backgrounds during language courses. The focus group participants in Manchester discussed the image illustrating an English lesson (Figure 3.1).

> I took this picture and for me it carries a very positive message, because there are people from different cultures. It doesn't matter how they communicate, because this was a pre-entry level, so people can't really say more than 'good morning', but they are nice to each other. But the most important thing is that they leave home and have a chance to sit next to a Pakistani or Roma person, about whom they normally say all sorts of things.
>
> (Aldona, focus group in Manchester)

This example echoes Amin's (2002) argument that educational spaces bring together people from different backgrounds engaged in common activities. Convivial encounters at educational facilities allow migrants to get to know other students as individuals and these encounters have the potential of temporarily shifting stereotypical views about other groups.

Neighbourly conviviality

Despite fear and avoidance of the local white British youth in her neighbourhood in Salford, Paulina established a friendly contact with a male neighbour she described as a drug dealer who lived in the same block of flats:

> He visited us to borrow a hoover regularly. This is how I met him. He was very nice and when he saw that I was on my own he would do shopping for me and buy fruit so that I wouldn't have to leave home in fear.

Convivial interaction between Paulina and her neighbour occurred at a micro-scale of the flats. Lending the hoover to the neighbour who in exchange would do shopping for Paulina illustrates a quite developed form of neighbourliness based on trust and interdependency established over a period of time. There is a possibility of neighbourly conviviality beyond race, class and gender difference in a more intimate space of the flats. Everyday interaction with the neighbour interrupted social divisions. This example represents what Gilroy (2006a: 39) calls other varieties of interaction which "have developed alongside the usual tales of crime and racial conflict". It also reflects Back and Sinha's (2016) notion of the paradoxical coexistence of racism and conviviality. Paulina's multi-layered experiences in the neighbourhood reflect both "multi-vocality of place" (Grasseni, 2009: 37), which signifies the possibility of contradictory tendencies of both conviviality and tensions, and "multilocality", which conveys the idea that a single place, in Paulina's case her neighbourhood, may be experienced in different ways (Rodman, 1992: 647).

As their financial situation improved, Paulina and her husband moved to Didsbury, a prosperous suburban area in the south of Manchester with nearly 80 per cent of "all White groups" and just over 20 per cent of "all non-White ethnic groups" (Manchester City Council, 2012: 2). Paulina's journey from Salford to Didsbury is a good example of class mobility. Paulina described her new area as very quiet and safe. She was surprised that people in the park exchanged greetings even though they did not know each other. Wood et al. (2010) examined the association between the sense of community and aspects of the built environment, physical activity and neighbourhood perceptions. Their results emphasise the importance of convivial pedestrian-friendly areas regarding social interaction among local residents. It is argued that walkable environments increase opportunities for casual social interaction between people in their neighbourhood (Wood et al., 2010; Leyden, 2003; Lund, 2002). Paulina's activity of walking through the park in her new neighbourhood contrasts with her restricted movement in the previous neighbourhoods.

Paulina established positive relations with friendly white British neighbours who helped her and her husband when their car broke down and offered to

lend them a ladder to fix the bedroom window. This social interaction characterised by neighbourly help became an important part of everyday convivial
culture. The convivial character of the neighbourhood was established through
habitual gestures of civility, fleeting interaction and offering a helping hand.

Paulina also noticed the absence of the negative discourse about Polish
migrants in her neighbourhood in Didsbury, and she linked this with the
higher socio-economic status of the residents and the absence of competition
for jobs which she ascribed to class differences:

> They don't have this view that Polish people steal jobs.... I would say that
> this is a matter of class. They were the people from higher spheres who were
> not worried that someone would take their job because they had their own.

It might be the case that people with a different socio-economic background are
less likely to compete with each other (Lancee and Dronkers, 2011). Paulina
associated the higher social class of the residents (not discussed in racial
terms) in Didsbury with less prejudiced attitudes, in contrast with the perception
of poor white Brits living in more deprived areas as racist. However, it is important to keep in mind that the absence of racist rhetoric does not necessarily mean
the absence of racialisation or racism (Leitner, 2012).

After several months of living in Didsbury, Paulina and her husband moved to
a council house in a residential area in Baguley in South Manchester. The largest
ethnic minority groups in Baguley are identified as 'Other White' (3.1 per cent)
and Black African (2.5 per cent); Polish is the second most common language
spoken after English in the area (Manchester City Council, 2014b: 5). Even
though there was a degree of tension in Paulina's new neighbourhood as a result
of the cars belonging to several Polish neighbours being scratched by an
unknown perpetrator, Paulina described the relations with the local non-Polish
neighbours as positive. Everyday interaction in Paulina's neighbourhood included
courteous greetings and acknowledging each other: "An English neighbour, I
don't know his name, always waves at me and asks me how I am. He told me
that he is moving out and that he will miss us. So it is very nice that we are
here". The interviewees in Barcelona also emphasised the importance of "everyday
courtesy, exchanging *hola*, something not usual in Poland. It is a good start of a
conversation" (Daria, 31). This example of neighbourly conviviality is based on
often underestimated fleeting but regular encounters between neighbours allowing
them to become familiar, even if they do not know each other personally. As Heil
(2015) suggests, acts of greeting and mutually acknowledging the presence of others
illustrate an obvious example of the processes of conviviality. In Heil's fieldwork,
Senegalese migrants to Spain regularly emphasised the need to show respect to
and recognition of people they encountered by greeting them, even if it was just
a nodding of heads or an *hola*. Greetings reduced uncertain social situations.

Furthermore, based on her research on neighbourhood encounters in two cities
in the Netherlands, Nijmegen and Utrecht, Peters (2011) suggests that transitory
encounters lead to feelings of comfort, make people feel at ease and evoke

positive emotions. Despite some criticism in research literature of fleeting encounters like greetings, Vertovec (2007b: 33) challenges the expectation of
meaningful interaction and shifts attention to courteous but distant relations
between neighbours:

> Urban contexts are known to function through the lack of deep and mean-
> ingful interactions among city-dwellers; indeed, most people seem to be
> more than satisfied with maintaining cordial but distant relations with
> their neighbours and particularly with strangers. . . . We cannot and should
> not expect everyone in a complex society to like each other or develop
> numerous wide-ranging friendships.

While some neighbours have a need for a closer contact with neighbours, others
might have a preference of casual acquaintance as reflected in the saying: 'Good
fences make good neighbours', originating from the poem *Mending Wall* by
Robert Frost.

Valentine (2008) claims that fleeting encounters and taken-for-granted civilities do not automatically lead to respect for difference, as they might be characterised with ritualised codes of etiquette rooted in dominant western discourses
regardless of views and values. Nevertheless, Laurier and Philo (2006) argue that
low-level sociability should not be underestimated as it represents mutual
acknowledgement. Similarly, Boyd (2006: 872) discusses the importance of
civility in facilitating social interactions:

> As trivial as they may seem, then, casual signifiers of human respect such as
> 'please' or 'thank you', 'excuse me' or how's it going', serve to awaken a
> sense of sympathy and to breed an easy spontaneity among urban-dwellers
> whose primary interactions with others are both fleeting and superficial.
> Despite their evanescence, however, they are not devoid of moral signifi-
> cance. Insofar as they communicate to others a basic and elemental
> respect, these ritualised practices and everyday formalities are the cement
> that makes modern society possible.

The fleeting forms of neighbourly conviviality through greetings and casual acts
of kindness constitute an important element of convivial interaction which
Fincher (2003) calls small scale interaction in urban spaces. Bridge (2002: 3)
has suggested that relations in the modern western neighbourhood are largely
"neighbourly" entailing "non-intimate, convivial relations between people who
know each other to nod and wave to or engage in limited conversation".
These relations can also be conceptualised through Lofland's (1989: 469) idea
of "unpersonal relationship" which is

> simultaneously characterised by both social distance and closeness. Persons
> in these relationships may share little, if any, intimate information about
> themselves ... or if they share such information, they do so with the

understanding that no relational intimacy is implied. At the same time, the relationship is experienced as 'friendly' or 'sociable' – its emotional temperature as 'warm'.

In line with Lofland's (1989) argument that fleeting relationships can be transformed into more sociable forms, Paulina's narrative shows that fleeting encounters between neighbours may lead to more meaningful forms of contact and a sense of belonging as a neighbour which develop over time as the residents become more familiar with each other:

> I am still aware that I am an immigrant from Poland, but I definitely feel better here, because they don't treat me here like one but like a neighbour. This is very positive for me. When I invite them to barbecue, they eat Polish food, I tell them about Polish culture and they tell me about theirs, so we exchange experiences and it is nice. ... They don't judge me 'a Pole lives here, let's break the windows'. It is different, they don't judge me, and this is very important to me.

Habitual contact and familiarity developed over time are important factors influencing the intensity and nature of conviviality. Paulina feels acknowledged by the local residents as a 'neighbour', a more inclusive category she shares with other residents.

Paulina told me about neighbourly home visits for barbecues resulting in friendly relations and a sense of acceptance across difference. This illustrates a more intimate form of neighbourly conviviality in the private space of the home where difference is used as an important characteristic of interaction. Previous research demonstrates how traditional food is used to reinforce national identity (Bell and Valentine, 1997; Douglas, 1984; Rabikowska and Burrell, 2009). However, while Paulina's example of preparing and sharing Polish food and telling her neighbours about Polish culture may not only constitute the making of home and 'rooting her life' (Rabikowska and Burrell, 2009) in her new neighbourhood, but it also serves as an important aspect of interaction. Conviviality in this example permits the possibility of being different contrary to the assumptions that to be convivial requires sameness or conformity (Amin, 2008).

The narratives of both Krysia and Paulina showed a transition in encounters with difference from less convivial, fleeting, to more meaningful forms of interaction. Both Paulina and Krysia started their narratives by discussing first encounters in their neighbourhoods characterised by tensions. Then, their stories reflected various forms of neighbourly conviviality and finished with more meaningful forms of interaction. While initially their interaction with neighbours was limited possibly due to the temporary and transitory experiences, habitual contact with neighbours and various practices and interactions over time facilitated convivial culture in their current neighbourhoods.

The next story is different to accounts of Krysia and Paulina as it illustrates a connection with space and shows how concrete space can shape interaction.

Conviviality through connection with space in Rusholme

Maryla's narrative is different from the previous relational accounts since it introduces a different form of conviviality through connection with the space of the neighbourhood. Maryla, a 31-year-old teaching assistant from Krakow, converted to Islam before coming to live in Britain. She became fascinated with Islam during her visit to London where she saw many Muslim women on the streets of the multicultural city. She made the decision to move to Britain because she felt she was not fully able to practise her religion in Poland:

> Since my first visit I knew I wanted to live in England. I have always liked the fact that it is a multicultural country. In Krakow there are also people from other countries, especially foreign students, but not as many as in England's bigger cities. I particularly wanted to move here when I became Muslim in 2009. ... I made this decision, especially considering that in Poland there is a little awareness of other religions and cultures. I could not cover my head at work. This wasn't welcome and this was something I wanted to do so this was the main reason. I also wanted some change after so many years of living in Krakow.

After her arrival to the UK, Maryla moved to a shared flat in Rusholme, a suburban and commercial inner city area in Manchester with a succession of culturally diverse groups and students moving to the area. There has been a longstanding South Asian population within the area, and in recent years it has become home to new migrant groups from Somalia and Central and Eastern Europe. Rusholme is described as a reception centre for new migrants to the city (Manchester City Council, 2007). It has a rich socio-economic history, and like many other inner neighbourhoods in Manchester, Rusholme has suffered from economic decline. Until the 1960s, it was a suburban shopping district. The retail premises have been converted into a retail and consumer service centre for its South Asian/Muslim population, therefore largely serving halal meat and not serving alcohol. Although there is an increasing presence of North African and Arabic food, as well as kebab takeaway restaurants, the majority of restaurants along a section of Wilmslow Road, known locally as the 'Curry Mile', are run mostly by Bangladeshis but owned and operated by members of the Pakistani community (Barrett and McEvoy, 2006). Kalra (2014) considers Curry Mile as a diasporic space of interaction between majorities and minorities and it demonstrates an example of how people and place become linked.

Maryla was attracted to Rusholme because of its infrastructure suitable for her new lifestyle as a Muslim:

> There is the whole Muslim infrastructure, halal shops and shops with Islamic clothes and accessories, and so on. All this is very important to me, to live in a place where there are many halal shops, the mosque, Muslim people, restaurants where alcohol is not served. I am very satisfied with it.

Maryla's connection with her new neighbourhood shows how material conditions may underpin conviviality. Amin (2008) proposes a concept of conviviality as a form of solidarity with space. He argues that "human dynamics in public space are centrally influenced by the entanglement and circulation of human and non-human bodies" (5). This understanding of conviviality is not reduced to dynamics of interpersonal interaction. This form of experience involving the connection with space may lead to awareness of "belonging to a larger fabric of urban life" (19). According to Amin, 'empathy towards the stranger' emerges as a by-product of the convivial experience involving the connection between human and material bodies. However, it is hard not to notice that, to a certain extent, Maryla's connection with her neighbourhood is linked with consumption of culture, and she may share with other Muslims the same kind of rationale for moving to the area.

Maryla told me that she heard of a view that Muslim people tend to self-segregate and she recalled her Pakistani friend's labelling Manchester as 'Pakchester'. This corresponds with the assumption of self-segregating Muslim communities and the idea of 'parallel lives' in the light of 2001 disturbances in Northern English towns. However, Maryla explained that "it is inevitable that Muslim people prefer to live in an area convenient to them". This is also the reason why she moved to Rusholme:

> In Rusholme there is a mosque, so it is obvious that Muslims would move into this area, and if Muslims live here then there is a need for a Muslim infrastructure, halal shops, shops with clothes for Muslims. But some people think that Muslims live in ghettoes. In my opinion it is not creating a ghetto but making your life easier.

Maryla's narrative offers a counter-narrative to the existing research findings on Polish migrants in Britain distancing themselves the most from Muslims and less willing to include a Muslim person in their social network (Nowicka and Krzyżowski, 2017). Maryla's account about interaction with Muslim men is also very different to the perceptions of Muslim, Arab and South Asian men by my other interviewees. She interacted with people in local shops, bakeries and kebab restaurants where she received a lot of attention, especially from Muslim men. She assumed this was because of being white and wearing headscarf. This difference rather facilitated interaction than hindered it, since Maryla did not seem to be negatively affected by the attention she received. Her difference served more as an ice-breaker in casual conversations which usually evolved about the reasons behind her conversion to Islam often resulting in a sense of surprise that she did not convert because of a Muslim husband.

Another convivial space in Maryla's local area was the mosque. Glick Schiller et al. (2006: 626) stress current global turn to religion and spirituality bringing people together: "religion becomes more prominent as a pathway for becoming part of the locality, for newcomers as well as for native population of cities experiencing economic insecurity". Polishness and Polish migration are often linked with the Catholic religion, strongly associated with Polish identity, national culture (Trzebiatowska, 2010) and Catholic practices reproduced outside the Polish borders considered as a distinct marker of the Polish presence in Britain (Garapich, 2008; Nowicka, 2012). However, experiences of Polish migrants in other places of worship are largely overlooked in research literature. Maryla perceived the mosque as an open space allowing an inter-ethnic and inter-faith dialogue:

> When it comes to finding out about different cultures it should not be from the media. For example, most of the mosques I know organise at least once a year open days and anybody can come. ... There are sessions aiming to teach people about Islam to clarify some controversial issues. You can go to the mosque and just have a chat because they have open days and anybody can go.

Although many mosques have restricted access to women (Krotofil, 2011), in her local mosque Maryla meets other Muslim women of different ages, ethnicities and from different social classes. Once a week she attends lessons of reciting the Koran run by a woman from Syria. The contact with the women who attend these lessons is limited to the course, but Maryla stressed that "it is not because we don't like or don't understand each other but because we don't know each other very well just yet". Maryla explained that lack of close relations does not mean that people do not want to spend time with each other. She found it difficult to have a rich social life because of her busy lifestyle. She enjoyed the company of the women during the course: "The women who attend these classes are very communicative and it is not like they come and don't say anything. We always talk, and this is a group I like spending time with". Conviviality based on interaction and enjoying the company of others without a need for very close and intimate relations is a common theme discussed by the informants.

Having discussed the lived experiences of the research participants in various areas of Manchester and the wider area of Greater Manchester, the next section explores the interviewees' accounts of living in Barcelona.

Conviviality in Barcelona and beyond

Despite some similarities, the research participants' experiences of living in Manchester differed to those in Barcelona as a result of contextual differences. The city of Barcelona is divided into ten municipal districts (Ciutat Vella, Eixample, Sants-Montjuïc, Les Corts, Sarrià-Sant Gervasi, Gràcia, Horta-Guinardó, Nou Barris, Sant Andreu, Sant Martí) and 73 quarters (*barris*). Many neighbourhoods have undergone urban changes since the early 1980s, including restoration and rehabilitation of buildings, creation of new spaces and cultural facilities. These urban projects have been underpinned by a rhetoric promoting the everyday interaction between residents (Balibrea, 2001). In recent years, many districts have been influenced by the intercultural approach and have promoted reception plans and community actions to encourage 'peaceful coexistence' with a goal of intercultural dialogue (Barcelona City Council, 2010).

Polish migrants are dispersed across different areas of Barcelona and some live outside the city of Barcelona (Barcelona City Council, 2012b), although Władyka and Morén-Alegret (2013) identify a visible pattern of these migrants occupying mostly central areas. As in the case of Manchester, most of my research participants changed accommodation frequently and lived in different areas of Barcelona and beyond.

The narratives explored in this part of the chapter reflect the convivial character of Barcelona in various spaces of socialisation including the streets and squares. They also highlight the importance of convivial possibilities facilitated by Catalan partners and the role of language in shaping conviviality.

Convivial possibilities in Barcelona and beyond

Julia is 36 and she comes from a small village in south-western Poland. She was the first person in her family to go to university and to travel abroad, and she had lived in various countries. After several visits to Barcelona, she decided to move there in 2010 as she needed a change in her life. She is an office worker in an international company in the city of Barcelona. Julia's narrative focused mainly on observing interaction on streets and squares and it highlighted the importance of convivial possibilities facilitated by a Catalan partner. Julia firstly moved to a neighbourhood sharing the eastern border with the city of Barcelona and L'Hospitalet de Llobregat where her encounters with difference were limited to fleeting encounters with neighbours and observations of people on the street. L'Hospitalet has been a place of arrival for many migrants due to affordable rent. It is a municipality to the immediate southwest of Barcelona and is one of the most densely populated areas in Catalonia. In the 1960s and 1970s it experienced a population boom caused by migration from other parts of Spain, and subsequently from outside of Spain. Over a fifth of its residential population was born outside of Spain, mainly in Bolivia, Ecuador, Morocco, Pakistan and the Dominican Republic (L'Hospitalet City Council, 2013). The residential landscape of the neighbourhood reminded Julia of the blocks of flats in Poland built during the communist regime.

Positive but distant relations with neighbours

Julia described her neighbourhood as 'a dormitory of Barcelona' where people mostly sleep and from where they commute to work in the city. This also applied to Julia and it was one of the factors influencing her limited contact with the local residents. She spent most of the time in the city of Barcelona where she worked, attended a language school and gym and where her social life evolved. The interaction with neighbours was limited to fleeting encounters in a form of greetings and occasional neighbourly help. Several other interviewees in Barcelona expressed their preference of positive, fleeting, but distant relations with neighbours. This could be a result of not only preference of such relations and a limited time spent in 'dormitory neighbourhoods' but also a constant rotation of neighbours, mentioned by Julia, some of which might be international students and migrants who are highly mobile in Barcelona and beyond. Another interviewee, 33-year-old Klaudia emphasised a temporary character of migration to Barcelona: "People come here, do the Erasmus or doctorate and it's just for four years or so. You make many friends for several years and that's it". Other interviewees, especially those with families, simply favoured their intimacy over close relations with neighbours. This reinforces Wessendorf's (2014a) notion of 'being open but sometimes closed' with regard to living together in public but dwelling apart when it comes to private relations. This contrasts the more meaningful forms of contact with neighbours discussed in the context of Manchester. Based on her study on social relations in Hackney, UK, Wessendorf (2014a: 144) argues that private social spaces remain sites of separation and division: "people deal with diversity on a day to day basis in public and parochial space. But privately, at home and with friends, they want to relax and not deal with negotiations of difference". This particularly reflects the views of my interviewees in Barcelona, although there are some exceptions, especially in the context of home-based get-togethers of children from different backgrounds discussed in the section on motherly conviviality later in this chapter.

Observing street conviviality

Julia mostly observed the locals in L'Hospitalet on the way back from work. She would get off the bus one stop earlier to observe people spending time outdoors:

> I used to see people from India, China and from South America on the way from my bus stop to my home. There were many young people from South America, you know, you can tell because you see that they are a bit shorter and have certain face features ... you know, these were my everyday observations. I also often heard Catalan language and saw people dancing Sardana in front of the church ... I really liked the atmosphere in L'Hospitalet ... because I liked that people would come out on the streets. It's seven o'clock in the evening and elderly people sit down at a local square and talk, children run around, people don't sit at home ... I really like it and what caught my eye is this outdoor lifestyle.

Julia distinguished different groups in her neighbourhood by using categorisation based on visual characteristics along ethnic and racial lines. Peters (2011) argues that such categorisation is used because of lacking other frames to interpret other groups. Here, Julia used these categorisations to emphasise the racial mix in her neighbourhood. More importantly, Julia highlighted the specificity of the local areas in Barcelona characterised by public spaces of socialisation, including streets and squares at a particular time of the day. Julia's account, however, is different to other narratives discussed earlier in the way that it does not involve the actual interaction. However, not all encounters in the neighbourhood have to happen through practical activities. Peters claims that people-watching is a significant way of understanding what is happening in the local area as it provides a flow of information about others, for instance who they are, what they are doing and what they look like. She noted that in the public spaces of Lombok and Nijmegen people enjoyed watching the diversity of others because it was perceived as safe. Julia enjoyed the lively atmosphere in L'Hospitalet. Her gaze is central to the cosmopolitan consumption of the Other, and, at the same time, cultural and emotional detachment (Nava, 2002), as Julia's participation in convivial interaction was very limited. In the context of Barcelona as a tourist destination, this corresponds with Urry's (1995) idea of a tourist gaze and 'aesthetic cosmopolitanism' involving mobility, openness to others and consumption of landscapes, cultures and cities. Several research participants mentioned that following their arrival in Barcelona they were fascinated with the city and engaged in tourist activities. The tourist industry is an important characteristic of Barcelona which "turns into a lucrative, luxury, fun commodity that can be rapidly consumed by the tourist" (Balibrea, 2001: 189).

The debate about conviviality on the streets and squares of Barcelona also evolved during the focus group stimulated by Julia's photograph of a crowd of people gathering around street musicians and people dancing to their music in Barceloneta (Figure 3.2), a neighbourhood in the Ciutat Vella district of

Figure 3.2 Julia's photograph of street performers, dancers and the crowd in Barceloneta

Figure 3.3 Amelia's photograph of Capoeira and the crowd near Barceloneta beach

Barcelona attracting many tourists. Julia used to take a route through it on the way back from work. Amelia also brought a similar photograph to the focus group (Figure 3.2).

The photographs portray the convivial character of Barcelona, the outdoor life-style and celebratory character of the city also praised by other research participants. This example highlights the role of Barcelona as a leisure and tourist site (Balibrea, 2001). There is a very intensive use of public spaces in Barceloneta by both tourists and local residents. In line with the intercultural approach, the local government promotes intercultural mixing in public spaces (Barcelona City Council, 2010; Council of Europe, 2011). Nina, who described Barcelona as a "cultural melting pot", stressed that the street performances attract people from all over the world and "the boundaries between them become blurred" through dance and music "uniting the crowds". Several scholars have raised questions about celebration of ethnicised difference in public spaces. Amin (2002: 968) has warned about raised expectations from the uses of public space "for even in the most carefully designed and inclusive spaces, the marginalised and the prejudiced stay away, while many of those who participate carry the deeper imprint of personal experience that can include negative racial attitudes". Degen (2008: 25) in her work on the regenerated neighbourhoods in Barcelona and Manchester discusses how the urban experience is influenced through the sensuous lived experience of residents and visitors attracted to cities because of sensuous rhythms – 'sensescapes' of the areas. She suggests that these sensescapes are shaped by urban transformation of space orchestrated by regeneration processes attracting certain groups and rejecting others. Heil (2014) points out that although public gatherings are part of Catalan *convivència*, they do not necessarily lead to extended interaction. Despite these arguments, this street interaction demonstrates the emergence of conviviality based on negotiation of difference through dance, music and enjoyment. Dancing together allows crossing certain boundaries through touch, which might not be possible in other everyday encounters. Drawing on ethnographic observations of street performances, Simpson (2011) stresses the importance of the street performance producing moments of sociality and conviviality through fleeting interaction that emerges from momentary and transitory encounters between those who watch the performers.

Amelia raised the issue about who participates in these street gatherings by referring to the pictures during the focus groups, suggesting that while it is easy to make a connection with other migrants because of shared experiences of living in a foreign country, it is much harder to get to know native Catalans and establish longer lasting relations:

> But who asks you to dance? Where do the boundaries become blurred? . . . I can see here people of different nationalities who get together . . . I think that the blurring of boundaries will be between foreigners because they feel like they are strangers like us . . . what is really frustrating for me is that Catalans are very closed. I would like to get know this culture . . . it would be nice to get to know the [native] locals. They are going to stay here for longer.

The Catalan context is characterised by ambivalence and contradictions regarding Catalan identity and culture, and therefore it is very different from the British context. In the aftermath of the Franco dictatorship (1939–1975), during which Catalan identity had been violently repressed, Catalan language, culture, history and territory were recognised by the 1978 Constitution (Pujolar, 2010; Nogué and Vincente, 2004). Immigration to Catalonia has profoundly changed the social landscape of the region and questioned the cultural and linguistic characteristics defining its national identity (Pujolar, 2010). Nearly all my research participants were surprised to learn that Barcelona was part of Catalonia, a stateless nation in Spain with its own language and culture.

The construction of 'closed Catalans' mentioned by Amelia was a recurring theme in both interviews and focus group (see also Władyka and Morén-Alegret, 2013). Several research participants developed a perception of closed Catalans often associated with distinct language and culture, constructed in opposition to "open Spaniards" and "foreigners". This construction of closed Catalans is spatialised, as seen in Amelia's narrative. Similarly, Zofia offered her interpretations of Barcelona marked by clear ethnic divisions and described the Catalans as a closed collective in contrast to open and multicultural population:

> Basically, there are two Barcelonas. One is multicultural, Barcelona of tourists, foreigners, where you can speak to people in foreign languages . . . open

and multicultural, and the other closed, Barcelona of Catalans, Gaudí, monuments and Catalan culture where the stereotype of the open Spaniard, who after the first 'hola' becomes your best friend does not apply. ... It was a huge shock for me in the beginning that these two groups coexist next to each other.

Zofia's narrative illustrate Simonsen's (2008: 145) idea of "the multiple faces of the city" based on difference. Catalanness is constructed as a spatially embedded 'otherness' which produces boundaries between different groups. It is possible that the stereotypical idea of Catalan 'closedness' has been influenced by the hegemonic view from other parts of Spain (Denis and Matas Pla, 2002; Alén Garabato, 1999), often repeated in media representations. An example of these representations can be found in the article 'Cerrados, hedonistas e individualistas: así son los catalanes' [Closed, hedonistic and individualistic: this is what Catalans are like] (*El Economista*, 13 November 2009). Nevertheless, the stereotypical construction of closed Catalans is challenged through actual convivial interaction.

Convivial possibilities in the Catalan context

While the interviewees initially discussed the difficulty in establishing connections with Catalans, several narratives demonstrate the possibility of transcending the linguistic barriers and the discourse of Catalan closedness. This was certainly the case of Julia. Even though she initially found it hard to interact with the native local residents, a relationship with a Catalan man opened some opportunities for conviviality. After four months of dating, Julia and Jaume moved in together to his home town near Barcelona, described by Julia as a "proper Catalonia". At first, her lack of knowledge of Catalan language constituted a barrier in communication with the locals, but as a result of habitual contact over time, a sense of familiarity has developed which enabled the emergence of convivial culture. Through her Catalan partner, Julia became part of *colla*, a grass-roots community group which she described as a group of friends from the same region with family-like bonds, something that she thought she would not have a chance of experiencing in the city of Barcelona. She started participating in regular group meetings:

I am invited to a baby shower by one of the girls who is pregnant. I have known them for five months and they all speak Catalan. You know, they change to Spanish when they talk to me, but in a larger group, you know, I am new ... they end up speaking Catalan and I switch off. I try to understand something. It is frustrating and tiring but ... I see that this language is alive here.... In Barcelona it is a bit different because [Catalan] people may be forced to speak Spanish. I am thrown in at the deep end ... I know that I am the one from the outside and I have to adjust. It is a new experience for me.... For now, I actually start feeling like I am part of it, you know? ... I think I start connecting with these people. This is just the beginning, but I think that they have accepted me. For now, they have no choice because I am with Jaume, but I know one thing. If right now I disappeared from his life I would disappear from their life too.

Julia's narrative demonstrates the complexities of conviviality not free from tensions and ambivalence. Despite some linguistic limitations, Julia felt partly included in the group. There is a clear tension in her narrative in terms of belonging and not belonging to the group also influenced by the pressure to adjust. This tension demonstrates a dynamic and fragile character of conviviality.

The role of the Catalan partner in facilitating convivial possibilities within the group is significant here (see also Rzepnikowska, 2018a), and it was highlighted by most interviewees in inter-ethnic relationships. Julia owed most of her acquaintances with Catalans to her partner who became a gatekeeper to convivial relations between Julia and his family and friends. The partner becomes a transversal enabler (Wise, 2009), facilitating cross-cultural connections. As a result of the relationship with Jaume, Julia discovered new convivial possibilities. She got to know his family, friends and neighbours and she learnt why Catalan language and culture are important to them. This has resulted in more interest in Catalan culture and empathy manifested through comparing Catalan historical struggles to the Polish ones. Julia and several other interviewees tried to make sense of perceived Catalan closedness and pressure to speak Catalan by explaining it in terms of oppression of Catalan language and identity during the Franco regime and by comparing the Catalan situation to the Polish historical context of the loss of independence during the partitions starting in 1772 by Russia, Prussia and Austria. This shows the emergence of commonality between Polish migrants and Catalans.

> For a very long time, they [Catalans] could not use their language, and we have our stories, you know, how the Russians and Germans were trying to force us to speak their languages. Polish officially did not exist for over 100 years, and they [Catalans] had this for 300 years, they got that language back only 40 years ago. This is such a natural reaction [to want to speak Catalan]. If you really have someone who comes to you and tells you that you have to speak Spanish because this is Spain, it will be an automatic reaction ... so you know, their emphasis on Catalan results from the fact that they have been heavily forced to speak Spanish for a long time, and now a lot of non-Catalan people simply say no, because they feel like they are pressured to speak Catalan.
>
> (Julia)

The empathic interest is an important element of conviviality (Morawska, 2014). Empathy is crucial to respect and relate to others, and it becomes characteristic of interaction where people connect with each other. Leadbeater (2014: 14) stresses the importance of social capabilities which "depend on the shared capacity for empathy among citizens who want to bridge their differences". He describes empathy as a capacity to connect with others who are different, to find common ground and understanding of one another.

Most interviewees mentioned that Catalans frequently shared with them humorous anecdotes that Spaniards refer to Catalans as *polacos* [Poles] which often brings the interviewees and Catalans closer. This is illustrated in Weronika's account:

> In terms of Catalan culture, many times people react sympathetically when they find out that I am Polish. You probably heard that outside of Catalonia, Catalans are called *polacos*, so this is the moment for jokes and it breaks the ice.

During my participant observation, several Catalans also told me that *we* have something in common as *we* are *polacos*. This shows how a derogatory term emphasising 'Catalan otherness' in Spain is used in a positive context. There are many different theories regarding the explanation of the word *polaco* as a term ascribed to Catalans. The most common, often mentioned by my informants, refer to the perceived linguistic parallels between Polish and Catalan language and historical parallels between Polish and Catalan histories of oppression. There are also several other explanations, including the parallels made as a result of Poles fighting alongside Catalans during the War of Spanish Succession between the years 1700–1714, and Polish soldiers participating alongside the Republicans in Catalonia during the Spanish Civil War (1936–1939). The Francoist troops understood Catalans as little as the Poles. The use of the term was popularised as derogatory, referring to the Catalans and their language, as it was difficult to understand. Despite the derogatory nature of the term, it has been given much playfulness and humour.

Finding a common language

In the informants' discussions about relations with Catalans, the issue of Catalan language was frequently mentioned, as seen in Julia's narrative (see also Rzepnikowska, 2018a). This requires examining the current situation of Catalan language in Barcelona and its importance in Catalan politics. The Catalan immigration approach has become strategically linked to its language policy which has gone some way towards reducing the "ethnic closure of Catalan" (Woolard, 2003: 86) by making it *llengua comuna*, "the vehicular language of immigrants'" to be commonly used in the public sphere, as part of the national building project (Climent-Ferrando, 2012). While the Barcelona Interculturality Plan (Barcelona City Council, 2010: 33) recognises Catalan and Spanish as official languages, it places special emphasis on encouraging the "learning of the Catalan language, as a language in itself and as a factor of social cohesion and generator of opportunities". Furthermore, Catalan language as a marker of Catalan identity plays a part in the discourse of Catalan independence. This socio-political context is important in understanding migrants' encounters with the native population.

Julia told me about a negative experience involving Catalan language. Nevertheless, she later realised how important it was for her to learn Catalan and how her relationship with a Catalan partner would facilitate this:

> It happened to me that a Catalan woman in a shop in my neighbourhood, nearly attacked me for learning Spanish and not Catalan. It was a crack and I can tell you that this is still in my head ... she said it in an unpleasant way ... she said that I am in Catalonia and I should learn Catalan ... it was an unpleasant experience.
>
> I don't know how to tell them why it is wrong the way they try to promote their language, because I don't believe that everyone who comes here doesn't want to learn it, but many foreigners say that they don't like the way they are pressured to learn it. I don't know, we will see. I will learn it, but not as fast as they would want it. ... After some time of living here I realised that if I move outside of Barcelona I will have to learn Catalan. When I met Jaume I knew I would learn it, but I'm telling you, he is a fierce Catalan, a separatist. He wants Catalan independence. I have been indoctrinated for the past half a year ... I will learn Catalan whether we will be together or not. If we will be together this will help me to learn. I understand why this is so important to them.

Interestingly, Julia and her partner negotiated their linguistic differences by communicating in common languages: Spanish and English.

For Zofia, being able to communicate in Catalan facilitated deeper bonds and a sense of belonging with her partner and his family:

> They accepted me from the beginning and they didn't make me feel that I am different or inferior. ... I started learning Catalan from my own will, not because of pressure from Catalan society. ... When I wanted to pass the national exam, we switched with my partner from Spanish to Catalan to practise and it remained like this. I speak Catalan with his entire family ... I did a reading in Catalan at his family baptism and it was important for me because it meant that I am part of the family.

This example of conviviality is situated at the partner's family home which becomes a common place of interaction where Zofia is able to communicate in Catalan, although later she told me that her partner's mother preferred to speak with her in Spanish. This experience is also situated at a particular time of Zofia's migratory experience, contrasting with her earlier encounters with Catalans upon arrival in Barcelona discussed in terms of Catalan closedness. Zofia also became part of a Catalan association aiming to promote Catalan culture outside of Spain:

> It means a lot to me. ... I was invited to become a part of it and I became an executive member. This was an honour for me because I am the only foreigner there. ... Sometimes when we are away at an event, for example,

the Italians ask what we are doing and where we are from, I then feel like part of the group and I say, "Our culture is like this and like that ...". I also feel like this is my culture, my language and my family.

Sharing accommodation also brings the interviewees closer with their flatmates, as transpired in Amelia's narrative:

Laia [previous flatmate] is from Catalonia. She is very *cabeza cuadrada* [squarehead], supporting Catalonia, strongly, but she is the most open. This is what is interesting. Sometimes she speaks to me in Catalan but it doesn't bother me, because I like her and I know that it is not intentional. ... So Laia is the only person, who suggested, "if you like this", for example, "I will cook it for you on Sunday", "Do you feel like, I don't know, go to the beach, I want to have a beer, whatever, or go to la Rambla, do you want to join me?" ... I also think that it is because she feels isolated, for her own reasons, isolated from society. She is a type of a loner, but she would also like to have friends. So here we are. I am from Poland, she is from here, both in the same situation. We both search for someone, so that we have someone, apart from work, to go out, I'm talking about friends. And because she lived with me, she felt at ease, because you know ... so she wanted to have a good relationship with me even more. And this is very interesting. I realise that this is not only the culture or upbringing. ... Just now I realise that it is not only a matter of cultural difference.

Being able to get to know her flatmate reduced ethno-national and linguistic boundaries, and has led to establishing friendship. The feelings of isolation and otherness which both Amelia and Laia have in common bring them closer. This example also shows that the meanings of life events are not static. They change not only under the influence of subsequent events in the narrator's life, but also when telling the story during the narrative interview. Through telling the story of the relationship with her Catalan flatmate, Amelia realised that cultural differences become less significant. She realised that Catalan language, initially perceived as a barrier, does not constitute an obstacle to establishing a meaningful connection. The language of friendship becomes more important.

While many interviewees in this research discussed a significant pressure to speak Catalan (see also Władyka and Morén-Alegret, 2013), other studies illustrate some contrasts. For instance, Pujolar's (2010) research on Catalan language delivery for Moroccan and West-African women in Northern Catalonia shows that even when migrants want to learn or speak Catalan, the locals switch to Spanish. While language policies identify Catalan as facilitating social cohesion, this is contrasted with contradictory linguistic practices in everyday life in various settings whereby newly arriving migrants are expected to "treat Catalan as a fully functional public language while large sectors of the local population still treat it as a minority language not adequate to be spoken to strangers" (Pujolar, 2010: 229).

Eliza (32, office worker), as many other research participants, wanted to learn Spanish upon her arrival to Barcelona. She was an au pair living with a Catalan family. Initially she wished she went to Madrid where she thought she would learn Spanish more easily and she regretted moving to Barcelona: 'I came here to learn Spanish and I could mainly hear Catalan: at home Catalan, on the street Catalan and with my foreign friends we spoke English'. After some time, she passed what she called a 'rebellious phase' and she started to understand and respect Catalan language and culture:

> I started understanding it after several years and I started to establish friendships with Catalans and I started to learn Catalan language. I realised that it is an asset. If I was in Madrid I would only learn Spanish and now I know both Spanish and Catalan, and I became more open and now I don't regret it. I have two in one, and I respect their identity and the need to have their own country.

Eliza took part in a voluntary Catalan language learning project (Voluntariat per la llengua). She was matched with a retired Catalan man with whom she practised Catalan on a weekly basis. This resulted in a friendly relationship across linguistic, cultural and generational differences. It is argued that the situation of using Catalan functioned as an in-group language only used among those categorised as 'Catalan' is gradually changing due to the contemporary conditions of mobility and access to language and "implications for ethnic ascription are open to negotiation and contestation" (Pujolar and Gonzalez, 2013: 139). Nevertheless, it is important to acknowledge different social classes, gender, linguistic and ethnic backgrounds of migrants with regards to access to language classes and other linguistic possibilities and their relationship with dominant discourses about language. As Pujolar (2006: 3370) stresses, "speaking Catalan is socially experienced not as a cognitive skill, but as a component of the performances that embody the cultural capital of the middle classes". Therefore, in terms of learning and speaking Catalan with the locals, the experience of educated and white middle-class Polish women will be different to that of illiterate or near illiterate black African women from a poor background in Pujolar's study (2006). The local government's efforts to promote interaction in Catalan considered as a factor of social cohesion should take into consideration the intersection of race, gender and class shaping interaction between migrant women and the local population.

Conviviality in El Raval

El Raval, a neighbourhood in Ciutat Vella district of Barcelona, was frequently mentioned by the research participants and discussed in terms of a contrast where street conviviality intersects with fear of harassment and mistrust. Like Rusholme in Manchester, El Raval is one of the most ethnically diverse neighbourhoods in Barcelona. Its migrant population amounts to nearly half of its population. The most numerous groups are from Pakistan, Philippines, Bangladesh, Morocco, Italy and India. Until recently, El Raval was one of the most densely populated urban areas in the world. In the past centuries, El Raval with its industrial origin was one of the most deprived areas of Barcelona. El Raval, informally known as '*Barri xinès*' or '*Barrio chino*', has a long history as a working-class neighbourhood and shelter for poor and marginalised people (Tremblay and Battaglia, 2012). The southern half of El Raval was infamous for prostitution and crime. Nevertheless, it has changed significantly in recent years due to its central location and ongoing regeneration schemes. It is experiencing gentrification processes determined by a regeneration policy aimed at urban redevelopment, with the construction of students' residences, office blocks, galleries, fashionable restaurants and bars, especially in the north part of El Raval. Nevertheless, the socio-economic status of the population in El Raval is the lowest in Barcelona, having strong social inequalities. Nevertheless, it has a high number of services and local organisations aiming to meet the needs the needs of its residents.

As part of my observations, I attended the 10th edition of Festival de Cultura del Raval in November 2011. This annual festival explored different facets of El Raval with an aim to foster links between cultural organisations (some of which face challenges with financial sustainability) and people living in El Raval through joint cultural activities. Different venues hosted an extensive programme of free events organised by various organisations and groups, including street shows, tours, workshops for children and adults, and visits to cultural institutions. One of the themes was *convinencia*, including activities that promote equality, solidarity and conviviality. This involved a forum theatre play in both Spanish and Catalan titled 'Mustafa és al repla' [Mustafa is in the landing] about everyday racism, stereotypes, and prejudice about immigration by Pa'tothom Forum Theatre, supported by Pla interculturalitat [Interculturality Plan] and Network Anti-rumours Barcelona. The audience took part in finding a solution to the problem of stereotyping and prejudice. Firstly, the audience answered some questions about the nature of the problem, and secondly, some of them took part in the theatre play trying to show a solution. The conclusion was that the attitudes of prejudice and stereotyping can be contested by finding things people have in common, getting to know each other and establishing a common dialogue. The audience was multi-ethnic and many different views enriched the discussion about coexistence of people from different cultures. Wilson (2013b) argues that at a time of economic and social insecurity, community organisations and projects of intervention that deal with diversity-related tensions are essential. These types of events contribute to the development of new forms of social learning. Nevertheless, while these types of structured cultural events are important, less attention is paid to everyday convivial interaction from below in various parts of the cities where migrants become important social actors in shaping convivial culture.

The existing research highlights outsiders' representation of danger and fear in El Raval and scapegoating racialised migrants for the negative reputation of El

Raval (Degen, 2008). Several research participants in my research who mentioned El Raval in their narratives described it as a Pakistani neighbourhood, and some heard of its more recent racialised nickname: *Ravalistán*. Others perceived it as an area populated by deprived ethnic minorities: "People from Africa and Asia in Raval are poor. ... Some have their own small shops" (Hanna, 30). Daria, a 31-year-old photographer referred to a graffiti on a wall she once saw in El Raval with a phrase 'No Pakis, no party' reflecting reliance on South Asian migrants selling alcohol on the streets and, at the same time, reinforcing the racialised, classed and gendered stereotype of Pakistani street vendors. This Otherness is spatialised with reference to the locality of El Raval. In a way, both El Raval in Barcelona and Rusholme in Manchester are perceived in a stigmatised way.

In contrast, there were two participants who lived in El Raval and discussed it in a very different way based on their lived experiences. Hanna described El Raval as a popular neighbourhood, ethnically mixed, with many bars and cafes, but also a place where migrants move into because of cheaper rent:

> I think that in neighbourhoods like Raval there is a mixture of people. There are people who love this neighbourhood and there are those who live there because it is cheap, so there are many immigrants from various places ... It is a mixture. Barcelona Bohemia.

Ada, a 28-year-old marketing specialist, lived in El Raval for two years with her Italian partner. She was aware of the common description of El Raval as dangerous, possibly due to its past. This corresponded with several narratives in both Manchester and Barcelona labelling some deprived and ethnically diverse areas as unsafe. Nevertheless, Ada's fear was more linked with crime in general terms without any references to ethnicity. The fact that El Raval was alive day and night made her feel safe:

> This neighbourhood was totally different from the previous one because there are many more migrants and it is also known as relatively dangerous, although I felt safe because there are people on the streets 24/7.

Previously Ada had lived in Sant Antoni (located in Eixample district of Barcelona) for several months where she shared a flat. She described it as a Catalan neighbourhood, peaceful, with hardly any migrants, partly because the flats were more expensive. Nevertheless, Ada preferred living in El Raval where she was able to establish connections with neighbours from various countries and of a similar age:

> In the building where we lived, there were many shared flats and mostly young people lived there, so we had frequent contact, especially when they organised party they invited us or we saw each other on the balcony when spreading the washing. There were many more opportunities for contact. The neighbours often changed. They were many different nationalities.

Ada's narrative highlights not only the importance of shared accommodation and similar age of the neighbours, but also the specificity of the building where she lived which facilitated possibilities of contact through shared spaces:

> In terms of the residents in our building, we have somewhat more opportunities for contact because we have a shared veranda with all the residents so our neighbours have to pass our window to enter their flats so there is no way not to see each other. That's why we know well our neighbours.

Ada preferred living in a neighbourhood like multicultural El Raval populated by other migrants who shared similar experiences of living in a foreign country:

> I prefer it [El Raval] to a typical Catalan neighbourhood. ... Most of my acquaintances are people from other countries because we are here in a different environment. We know less people. That's why I prefer more mixed neighbourhoods like El Raval.

In comparison to Maryla's narrative of connection with space in Rusholme, Ada's account is rather relational. Nevertheless, both narratives reflect Gilroy's (2006a: 40) idea of how people from different backgrounds "dwell in close proximity", but their racial, linguistic and religious differences are considered as not obstructive to conviviality. They show how social divisions can be disrupted through making urban life habitable (Neal et al., 2018). Even though difference can be place defining, it is not problematised; it becomes ordinary. Ada's silence about any specific ethnic group in El Raval may also reflect "civility towards diversity", which, according to Lofland (1989: 464):

> specifies that in face-to-face exchanges, confronted with what may be personally offensive visible variations in physical abilities, beauty, skin colour and hair texture, dress style, demeanour, income, sexual preferences, and so forth, the urbanite will act in a civil manner, that is, will act 'decently' vis-à-vis diversity.

Instead, Ada prefers to focus on commonalities rather than differences (see also Glick Schiller et al., 2011). Hence, El Raval becomes a 'space of commonality' (Hage, 2014: 236). Nevertheless, these commonalities are often established with people with a similar age and socio-economic position.

The final section in this chapter explores the connection between motherly activities, space and conviviality. It raises the importance of spaces for migrant mothers in shaping convivial culture.

Motherly conviviality in Manchester and Barcelona

After becoming mothers, women start using their local areas more intensely than before and seek other mothers to spend time with (Byrne, 2006; Fenster, 2005;

Ryan et al., 2009; Wessendorf, 2014b). This section discusses the importance of a connection between motherly activities, spaces for mothers and conviviality in various areas of the neighbourhoods in both Manchester and Barcelona, including nurseries, schools and children's centres where parents and children meet others from different backgrounds (see also Rzepnikowska, 2018a). The interviews with Polish migrant mothers emphasised the significance of spaces for mothers and families, as well as family activities in facilitating conviviality. Several interviewees established strong links with other mothers from various backgrounds on the basis of shared experiences of being migrant mothers. The interviews shed light on mothering practices which are not only gendered but also raced and classed in some instances. Several examples also show how migrant mothers create opportunities for cross-cultural interaction between those from various backgrounds.

Judyta and Paulina: spatialised practices of motherly conviviality in Manchester

At the time of the interview, Judyta lived with her partner of African origin and their son in a suburban residential area of Salford in Greater Manchester. Paulina lived with her Polish husband and two daughters in Bagley, South Manchester. When both Paulina and Judyta became mothers, like many other informants, they made a lot of effort to get to know other mothers in their local areas. While Paulina, at first, struggled with the language barrier and therefore interacted less with non-Polish mothers, Judyta started attending various activities, including baby-friendly screenings, local breastfeeding clubs and playgroups, which became part of her everyday routine. Byrne (2006: 113) describes these daily activities as "a strategy for relieving the intensity of full-time care of young children, allowing both parent and child to have other company".

While Byrne's (2006) study reveals the social segregation between middle and working class women forming separate groups evolving around classed activities, Judyta's narrative indicates separate clusters of white British women and migrant mothers of different origin at the breastfeeding club and mother and toddler group. She mostly identified with other migrant women who shared similar experiences of motherhood and migration. In her narrative about activities with other mothers, she focused on those commonalities that intercut the dimensions of fixed identity and difference:

> All these women from different countries, who came here like me, they need it, because they don't have families here, they don't have many friends, and we all need to meet people, establish friendship, so they are more open. And maybe this is what brings us closer, because for example, there is a mother who came from Zimbabwe . . . she misses home too and she is able to understand that someone may feel homesick, so this is what brings us closer. . . . We meet up together with our kids, or we visit each other for a cup of tea or coffee.

The participation at the support groups for mothers and their children, establishing relations based on common experiences, illustrates an example of motherly conviviality. It is described as motherly because it is situated at a space particularly for mothers who get to know and can get support from other mothers. In this instance, motherly conviviality is experienced by migrant mothers from a range of backgrounds. This finding confirms D'Angelo and Ryan's (2011) argument that despite the initial shock about ethnic diversity in Britain, some Polish migrants establish stronger links with other migrants on the basis of shared experiences. According to Glick Schiller et al. (2011: 404), "the process of engagement with others is always going to be with particular individuals with whom one may want to identify or share moments or spaces of 'conviviality'".

Another reason why Judyta wanted to spend more time with the mother from Zimbabwe might not only be a shared experience of migration but also possibly the fact that Judyta's child is mixed-race. Judyta expressed her fear of racism in the context of her son's interaction with white Polish children. She wanted to take her son to a Polish Saturday School, but she feared he would face racist comments. As Byrne (2006) suggests, mothering practices are not only gendered but also raced. Judyta and her child's socialisation with a black mother and her children possibly relieved the pressure from the Polish collective expecting her to fit to a role of the cultural reproducer of the nation (Yuval-Davis, 1997), and it offered a sense of security away from the Polish dominant gaze and stereotypes.

Judyta also raised the issue of isolation of migrant mothers with young children without family support networks relying on other migrant women for company. She set up a group 'Mother and I' in Salford for migrant mothers and their children to tackle isolation, something she experienced when she first arrived in Manchester and had a child:

> These [migrant] women have similar problems, usually isolation. They simply have nobody to talk to, go out with or invite home.... It's monotonous because you don't work, you have children on your shoulders, little support from your man, so you have to somehow organise your time.... This isolation is the main problem here, because as they [mothers] say, they attend English classes but despite that there is lack of integration with the local community. There is this barrier all the time and even if it is not a language barrier there is a cultural one and it is hard to change it.

Here, isolation is influenced by linguistic and cultural barriers, constituting an obstacle to conviviality. Hence, there is the need to address this issue by creating an opportunity for migrant mothers to establish new connections with other mothers. Judyta's initiative, which created a platform for inclusion and a kind of convivial space, is another example of fostering motherly conviviality which raises the importance of the 'transversal enablers' (Wise, 2009; Wise and Velayutham, 2014) in facilitating interaction across difference. According to Wise (2009: 24), transversal enablers are those who create connections between culturally different people, opportunities for cross-cultural interaction, and spaces of intercultural care and trust.

While Judyta socialised with mothers from a range of different ethnic backgrounds, Paulina mostly interacted with Polish mothers and, when her English improved, with white British mothers. She became friends with Jenny, a white British woman, as they both did a course at the adult education college, and it turned out their children went to the same school:

> With Jenny we meet up for a cup of coffee. She visits me and I visit her or we go together to town and to do shopping. She has a child in the same school my child goes to and we always see each other at school and we have a chat there.

Paulina's account raises the importance of schools in facilitating contact with other parents. In their study on Polish parents and children in London schools, D'Angelo and Ryan (2011: 239) discuss "schools as sites of socialisation where newly arrived migrants encounter the host society in complex and varied ways" (see also Neal et al. [2016] who describe schools as sites of collaborative sociality, friendly interactions and as connective conviviality sites). Wilson (2013a: 102) stresses that in Britain schools are considered significant in the strengthening of community relations: "Repetitive interactions of everyday school life shape the capacities of parents to live with difference". Interaction through school encounters may also permit migrant mothers to develop new forms of social learning. Despite English language difficulties, Paulina developed practical competencies over a period of time which allowed her to interact with non-Polish mothers.

Paulina's narrative highlights the multi-sitedness of encounters. It involves interaction with Jenny at the adult education college, at the school gates and at home. This interaction takes place in different but connected spaces. Motherly conviviality transcends a single place of interaction and it reflects interconnection of different spaces. The proximity of Paulina's residential area with the school and the college, and the same spaces being used for the same activities by different individuals facilitate this interconnection (Neal et al., 2016).

Marta and Emila: conviviality in the local family spaces and beyond in Barcelona

After finishing her studies in Poland, Marta returned to Barcelona and when she had a baby, she moved with her Mexican husband to the Sants district in the southern part of Barcelona. This is a post-industrial and mainly a residential area and a tourist hub populated by people from different backgrounds, mostly from South American countries, Italy, China and Morocco (Barcelona City Council, 2012a). Marta moved with her family to Sants in order to have better access to schools and family-friendly areas where she subsequently was able to establish contact with other parents. As in Judyta's and Paulina's cases, Marta's narrative highlights the connection between family spaces and conviviality:

> Because we have a small child, it is important for us to have access to schools, parks, and different sorts of attractions for children, family spaces and workshops and in this neighbourhood there is plenty of it so generally we are happy.... I have managed to establish relations with quite a lot of people since my daughter was born. I have acquaintances from the nursery, preschool, park, workshops and extracurricular activities.

As in the British context, nurseries and schools become key sites of encounters for parents, although the Spanish/Catalan context offers a more complex picture of socialisation in the school environment influenced by the wider sociolinguistic dynamics and ambivalence about language and class (see Alarcón and Garzón, 2013). Through Marta's experiences of mothering, she learnt that school activities lead to acquaintances with other parents and allow getting to know them better, contrary to fleeting and superficial encounters in other public spaces:

> Quick situations in shops, café, hairdressers or bars do not allow getting to know people closer.... We can talk about getting to know others when we meet each other at parents' evenings, school events or when we collect children from school. I would say that in these situations I can meet somebody better. I wouldn't call it a relation when buying veggies or having coffee in a bar, but something superficial, a contact between a service user and a service provider.

Regular contact at school or nursery facilities goes beyond casual greetings and it may lead to more friendly and sustained relations across difference (Wessendorf, 2014b). Marta's narrative reflects some geographers' argument that spaces of superficial and chance encounters are not spaces where people engage with each other in a more extended way (Amin, 2002; Valentine, 2008; Matejskova and Leitner, 2011), although Lofland (1989: 469) offers a more complex picture of fleeting encounters in public spaces and argues that "fleeting relationships" are being "constantly transformed into more sociable forms", just as any space may be transformed as the time goes by.

Schools can also be sites of tension where Pakistani parents and the number of Pakistani pupils are perceived as problematic:

> It could be that ... if my daughter went to a school ... it depends to which public school, she would have a majority of friends from Pakistan and India. We wanted to avoid this, not because I am against these cultures, but in groups where there is a vast majority of students from Pakistan, from 70 or 80 per cent. Unfortunately, their parents hardly get involved in the school routine and it is very difficult to maintain classes because they don't pay basic money, they don't bring materials for PE or Arts, don't

collect children on time, don't know the language, form separate groups and ghettoes and sending a child to this kind of ghe ... not to a place where there are equal groups of immigrants from Asia, Africa and Latin America. In places where the local community is totally dominated by South-East Asia, problems arise, and these schools are marginalised. Unfortunately, this is how it is. So, we avoided this by sending our daughter to a different school ... Whenever there are problems in schooling resulting in lack of involvement of parents from certain ethnic group, I would say they would be from Pakistan. Other groups, for example from China, Latin America or Morocco function in the same way as the locals. At the moment, my daughter is in a different school dominated by Catalans, so this year I don't have contact with people from other cultures, but last year when she was in a public school, there were people from Dominican Republic, Morocco, Latin America, China and other groups.

Marta's narrative shows carefully chosen expressions which indicate possibly some awareness that what she is saying may be seen as discriminatory. Pakistani parents are perceived as failing to conform to acceptable norms and, therefore, are portrayed as problematic. The discourse about Pakistani parents not caring about their children's education and schools disproportionately populated by Pakistani pupils reinforces the ideas of class and race. Similarly, in Wilson's (2013a) study on parent encounters with difference in a Birmingham primary school, Asian parents were also considered by the British parents as refusing to get involved in the running of the school and its extra-curricular activities. However, it seems like neither Marta nor the British parents in Wilson's study considered the reasons for not contributing, for instance, potential language barriers, socio-economic differences and other forms of exclusion.

The problematic group of Pakistani students is set in opposition to other ethnic groups, for example, Chinese, Latin American or Moroccan migrants who are constructed as 'model minorities' in the context of schooling. According to Reay et al. (2007: 1049), a section of the ethnic minority children represent the

acceptable face ... of ethnic/'racial' difference as they are the children who are 'exceptionally bright and very nice', 'are doing the best', those who are a paler shade of dark, and come from families 'where the parents really care about education', 'have high aspirations' and 'are really ambitious for their children' – the 'model minority'.

They are accepted because they share the normative white middle-class values.

The discourse about schools overpopulated by Pakistani students is contrasted with Marta's idea of schools with "equal groups of immigrants from Asia, Africa and Latin America". This idea of equal groups of certain ethnicities illustrates what Byrne (2006: 120) calls "the right mix" or the right balance desired by some white English mothers in her research, defined as the equal proportion of the raced groups from the 'global South'. "Getting the mix right", according to Byrne (2006: 120), represents openness to difference, as long as there is not too much of it – this represents the discourse of being outnumbered by the classed and raced Other. As Reay et al. (2007: 1050) suggest, the gains from social mix only are seen to work if there is a majority of white and/or middle-class students. Similarly, even though Marta expressed her openness to difference throughout the interview, she prevented her daughter from going to a school with too many students of Pakistani origin. Therefore, Marta's narrative illustrates "simultaneity of openness and boundary maintenance" (Glick Schiller et al., 2011: 410).

Marta's categorisation of Pakistani people forming ghettoes constructs a "spatially embedded otherness" (Simonsen, 2008: 147) of 'Pakistani community' isolated and fixed in the ghetto. Pérez-Rincón et al. (2012) points out that there is a high concentration of Pakistani migrants in the central districts of Barcelona and in some peripheral areas, mainly as a result of affordable rent and transnational social networks. Even though there is evidence that the level of concentration of these migrants decreases as they disperse to different areas of the city, certain spaces remain perceived in a stigmatised and racialised way. The representation of the neighbourhood populated by migrants as a ghetto feeds a negative mythology in which the discussed migrant group is seen as problematic. It is likely that in Marta's case the ambivalent construction of Pakistani people serves to justify her choice of a private school for her daughter. However, it is not only the ethnicity but also class which may be considered as the most important concern when thinking about who parents want their children to socialise with (Byrne and de Tona, 2013). It is not that Marta does not want her daughter to interact with children of Pakistani origin. However, education in a private Catalan school may serve as a so-called "social elevator" generating upward social mobility for the children of migrants through Catalan immersion (Alarcón and Garzón, 2013: 109). Nevertheless, Marta's choice of school not only plays a part in determining her daughter's future and her social position, but also shapes her child's experience of encounters with difference.

In contrast, Emila expressed a strong desire for interaction with mothers from other ethnic backgrounds and she wanted her children to establish closer contact with their children. Emila is 35 and she lives with a Polish husband and their three children who were born in Barcelona. Emila's case illustrates a tension between her desire for conviviality and some difficulties in getting to know other mothers. Her narrative also highlights the role of mothers in facilitating conviviality.

After several years of living in Barceloneta, Emila and her family decided to move to Les Roquetes in the Nou Barris district located in the northern part of the city. It was the place of arrival for labour migration from Spain in the 1950s and 60s. In the first decade of the twenty-first century, it has become one of the areas with the strongest presence of migrants from outside of Spain, including Hondurans, Ecuadorans, Pakistanis, Moroccans and Romanians (Barcelona City Council, 2012a). This has given Emila the opportunity of contact with people from different ethnic and religious backgrounds. School also became one of the main places of encounter with difference. Although she appeared to be happy that her children had the opportunity to live in an ethnically and religiously mixed environment, she voiced her concerns about the headscarf worn by Muslim girls:

> This is a great neighbourhood populated mainly by people from South America. You notice it when you take children to school. But there are also people from Romania and Pakistan. I think that people from Pakistan are amazing, nice, delightful. They bring children up very well, although I feel sorry for those girls wearing headscarves later on. ... My daughter has a friend who is now twelve and they put a red scarf on her head. She is very nice, and her parents are too. When I see it ... this is not a barrier for me, but I just feel sorry that at some point the doors will be closed for her, she will not do further studies, at some point they will prohibit her for religious reasons. That's why I feel sorry for the child. As a mother, I would fight for my child to enjoy childhood for as long as possible, while they put an end to it with their free will.

At first, Emila's praise of parenting by Pakistani people contradicts Marta's concerns. However, later her narrative is based on stereotypical assumptions about Muslim women oppressed by their parents and religion. The rhetoric of the veil in the informants' narratives in Barcelona may have been influenced by the frequent media, political and public debates in Spain considering the veil as a symbol of Islam and a sign of backwardness and oppression. The favoured discourse of *convivencia* in Spain is contradicted by the influential media framing of Muslim women in a problematic way, promoting negative attitudes (Román et al., 2011).

Emila's narrative about her daughter's veiled friend continued for some time. She mentioned an encounter in a local shop with the veiled girl and her mother offering an opportunity for interaction:

> She was very embarrassed to go out for two weeks and I told my daughter to tell her that she looks very nice in her headscarf and one day I met her in the shop. She was with her mother. She was embarrassed to even say *hola* [hello]. First, her mum said *hola* to me and she told her daughter to say *hola* too. I told her that she looked beautiful in her red scarf and later she again started going out to the park with my daughter and other girls.

This encounter is not only limited to the exchange of civilities but there is an element of empathy and affection in Emila's narrative as recognition, accommodation and negotiation of difference expressed through praising the girl's look contrary to Emila's perceptions of the practice of veiling.

Emila expressed her desire of establishing convivial relations with Moroccan and Pakistani women who, like Emila, gathered in front of the school gates:

> If we could become more open and get to know a woman from Morocco or a man from Pakistan, if we could become their friends, I would love that. I

kind of need it because there are groups of people in front of the school: women from Pakistan in one group, women from Morocco in another and this woman from Poland totally on her own. These groups are a totally natural thing. Anyway, it would be great if we could have a chance to get to know them and be invited to their home, where they all wear veils, and to taste the delicious food. We have a chance, because we live in a country where there are many people from different countries.

Beneath the fascination about getting to know veiled women through being invited to their homes and trying their food, there is an expression of loneliness and a desire for closer and more convivial relationship with other parents. This narrative reflects the argument shared by several other research participants in Barcelona who highlighted the difficulty of mixing despite living in a multicultural city. These obstacles illustrate some challenges with regard to the Catalan discourses of interculturality and *convivencia* premised on the principle of interaction. Although it is claimed that schools in Barcelona involve parents from migrant and ethnic minority backgrounds in daily school life (Council of Europe, 2011), there might be a need for creating more opportunities for parents to break down some barriers and for coming together to reduce loneliness and isolation. Furthermore, Ryan (2015b) suggests that accessing new relations requires not only opportunities for contact but also reciprocity and mutual willingness to make the effort. She claims that not sharing a common language, interests, lifestyles or beliefs may lead to more effort needed to get to know others. Nevertheless, Ryan also argues that the basis of shared interests may change over time.

Emila's desire for convivial interaction was partly fulfilled by creating opportunities for interaction between her children and their friends from different cultural backgrounds. Emila is passionate about bringing up her children as tolerant and open to cultural differences. This is manifested through her role as a mother encouraging her children to maintain bonds with their friends from different backgrounds. Furthermore, as Byrne (2006) suggests, children may also play an important role in bringing their parents into contact with people from various backgrounds in terms of race, ethnicity, culture and class, who might be different to those they usually meet at work or in their social lives.

What is different about Emila's case in comparison to Marta's is the fact that her narrative did not include the discourse of her children being outnumbered by the Other. Instead, Emila discussed the actual examples of conviviality facilitated by her and experienced by her children. She allowed home visits and organised birthday parties. While Emila earlier mentioned that she preferred convivial interaction outside of her home space, she allowed get-togethers for her children which had the potential to generate interaction across difference in personal geographies (see also Neal et al., 2016). One example Emila discussed in more depth is her daughter's birthday celebration discussed during the interview and the focus group. Emila brought some pictures to the focus group illustrating her children interacting with their friends from different backgrounds and used the images to discuss these examples of conviviality (Figure 3.4):

> We can see children from different countries. This girl is from Pakistan, here there are four sisters from Morocco. Here is a boy from Brazil and this boy is from Pakistan. Listen, there are no barriers for children, these barriers don't exist. Look. Let's learn from them. There are completely no differences. They play, they are celebrating birthday. What difference does it make that this girl is from Poland? It is her birthday, and everybody is having fun. There are no differences. A bunch of kids playing together. There are no class or national differences ... they have a language in common – Spanish, although the girls from Morocco sang happy birthday in English. We made *piñata* and filled it with sweets and the kids played all together.... Together with my husband we sang happy birthday in Polish.

This narrative constructs the children's interaction during the birthday celebration as blurring ethno-national boundaries. Even though Emila tried to make difference invisible, she gave examples of different cultural elements included in the birthday celebration. This account also stresses the importance of convivial practices in convivial spaces of the neighbourhood. The open space seen on Emila's image and the spatial layout of the neighbourhood facilitate outdoor gathering and birthday celebrations. This convivial space is inclusive and enables interaction. This again raises the importance of urban planning in

Figure 3.4 Emila's photographs of her daughter's birthday party and home visit (Barcelona)

facilitating conviviality. Fincher (2003: 8) argues that "spaces can be planned to make such encounters more likely, more pleasant and unaccompanied by anxiety".

Conclusion

The narratives in both cities have illustrated different and often multi-layered encounters within various sites of the cities. Furthermore, the narratives have demonstrated some of the complexities of social realities marked by local tensions and avoidance of contact, as well as different forms of interaction based on boundary-crossings. While initially encounters are often marked by tensions and stereotypical views, there is a potential for conviviality to emerge as a result of habitual encounters and interaction over a period of time.

The narratives have also revealed many different factors influencing the experiences of conviviality, including the length of stay, commonalities and shared experience, urban infrastructure and so on. They also raised the importance of more and less convivial spaces, the former facilitating interaction and accommodation of difference and the latter reinforcing fear and avoidance. Following from Lofland (1989), it is important to distinguish between encounters on a street where passers-by do not know each other, as it was in the case of street encounters between Paulina and men of South Asian origin on her way to college; and a street where inhabitants know each other as neighbours, as it was in Krysia's case. Habitual contact over an extended period of time in shared spaces is likely to generate familiarity and lead to possibilities of interaction across difference as well as more meaningful forms of contact. Conviviality is generated at specific times and places and by different individuals; therefore, it cannot be explored outside of the context in which it occurs. Thus, it is more suitable to use the term situated convivialities, specific to the local and national contexts and influenced by encounters at a particular time, personal circumstances and other factors.

The focus group discussion shed light on the outdoor lifestyle and shared spaces facilitating interaction on the streets and squares of Barcelona. Nevertheless, a valid question was asked about who participates in this type of street conviviality. Even though most interviewees (re)constructed the image of closed Catalans, Julia's story has shown that conviviality can be facilitated by a Catalan partner who enabled her to become part of a Catalan community group. Her example allows understanding conviviality as a dynamic and ongoing process without any guarantees, since her group membership is conditional. Inter-ethnic relationships and being able to speak Catalan, combined with empathy, facilitated deeper and more sustained forms of living together.

The narratives highlighted the importance of neighbourly conviviality based on fleeting but habitual encounters between neighbours, including greetings and acknowledging each other, casual conversations and neighbourly help which often formed an important part of everyday convivial culture in the neighbourhoods. They also showed how fleeting encounters between neighbours can be transformed into more meaningful neighbourly relations. Krysia's narrative has illustrated that neighbourly conviviality may generate more meaningful forms of engagement with neighbours where contact goes beyond casual greetings and fleeting encounters. This has transpired in the examples of interdependence, gift giving and neighbourly support which generate a culture of care and a sense of inclusiveness and belonging. These forms of convivial culture develop gradually and over a period of time between the neighbours who become familiar through habits of everyday interaction. Maryla's narrative, on the other hand, has portrayed conviviality reflected as a form of connection with her neighbourhood facilitating convivial encounters across difference.

It is important to highlight some differences between the two contexts with attention to positionality of my interviewees. In Manchester, the Polish women discussed in this book are older (Krysia) or have children (Paulina and Judyta) and they settle into relations with their immediate neighbours (mostly in inner city residential areas) with this positionality. In Barcelona, the interviewees are younger, more mobile, some partnering with Catalan men (Julia and Zofia) and some are mothers (Marta and Emila), often living in flats in various parts of Barcelona (characterised by street life) and beyond. As I mentioned in Chapter 2, my research did not aim to present a perfect set of comparisons between Manchester and Barcelona and I argued that maintaining a strictly comparative angle would seem somewhat mechanical and unrealistic. Nevertheless, it is important to keep in mind that my participants' gender, age, maternal and spousal status, the area where they live, and the length of time are important factors influencing their experiences of encounters with difference.

The narratives of Judyta and Paulina in Manchester, as well as Marta and Emila in Barcelona, have shown the possibilities of motherly conviviality. Schools, nurseries and support groups for mothers become important spaces of encounter between mothers from different backgrounds. While for some convivial relations crossed ethnic and racial boundaries, others found these difficult to overcome. Common experiences of migration brought Judyta closer with other migrant women. In Paulina's case, motherly conviviality was characterised by certain kinds of activities which reinforced classed and raced positions. Marta's narrative has demonstrated both openness to difference and boundary maintenance. This openness has been limited by the discourse of being outnumbered by the classed and raced Other. Emila's case has also illustrated certain ambivalence between stereotypical perceptions of veiled Muslim women and a desire for convivial relations with them. Emila's and Judyta's accounts also raised the importance of mothers facilitating cross-cultural interaction between mothers and children.

The next chapter continues investigating diverse encounters in the workplace in Manchester and Barcelona, including the lighter touch and playful forms of interaction characterised by the interplay of language and humour; and more meaningful relations by concentrating on the workplace friendships. These forms of conviviality are contrasted with the example of conviviality characterised by forced encounters.

4 Conviviality in the workplace

Workplaces have become increasingly diverse as a result of migration and other socio-economic changes in Europe but also due to legal obligations of organisations with regard to equality legislation (Valentine and Harris, 2016). Furthermore, employers are under pressure to find employees who are not only technically proficient, but who have the ability to work effectively with individuals from cultural backgrounds different from their own. British Council (2013) sets out the value of intercultural skills in the workplace, raising the importance of developing these skills and sensitivity to differences. These skills include the ability to understand different cultural contexts and viewpoints and demonstrating respect for others. As Fong and Isajiw (2000: 252) note, "the workplace is the most natural place for people to meet, make friends, and develop social networks". Estlund (2003: 3) also suggests that "typical workplace is a variable hotbed of sociability and cooperation, of constructive and mostly friendly interactions among co-workers day after day, and often year after year".

Many Polish migrants are in workplaces where multiculture is an everyday lived experience. Much attention in Britain has been paid to the lower end of the labour force and it has been argued that mixing of Polish and other Central and East European migrants with co-workers of different ethnic or national backgrounds is "the exception rather than the norm" (Cook et al., 2011a: 11). Furthermore, studies of the workplace encounters between these migrants and established communities tend to focus on negative experiences (Fox, 2013; McDowell et al., 2007; Parutis, 2011), while the examples of positive mixing at work are described as "largely superficial encounters" which hardly facilitate genuine integration or challenge prejudice (Cook et al., 2011b: 732). There is some evidence that the workplace has the potential to be an important site of prejudice reduction and can promote meaningful encounters with people who are different in terms of ethnicity, religion, sexuality and disability. Nevertheless, it is argued that the relationships established at work rarely translate into spaces beyond the workplace (Harris and Valentine, 2016).

In Spain, social relations between Polish migrants and the local population at work are under-researched. The study conducted by Colectivo Ioé (1998), focusing on construction workers of Polish and Moroccan origin in Madrid and Barcelona, highlighted limited contact between these migrants and the native workers as a result of preference for their own national group, language barriers, stereotypes and suspicion based on assumed cultural differences and discrimination. More recent literature stresses that, while interaction between Polish migrants and the native population is often described in terms of cultural proximity, encounters with other migrant groups are referred to in terms of distance and prejudiced views influenced by negative rhetoric about non-white and non-European migrant groups in Spain (Nalewajko, 2012).

The narrative interviews conducted with my research participants in Manchester and Barcelona reveal much more complex realities of contact with difference at work demonstrating various forms of conviviality which can take place in both voluntary and involuntary contact situations (Neal et al., 2013). This chapter demonstrates how the interplay of language and humour facilitates playful interaction between co-workers. It also explores more meaningful social relations by concentrating on workplace friendships, largely overlooked in research, which provide migrants with support and a sense of inclusion and belonging transcending the space of the workplace, contrary to the research findings revealing that relationships formed at work hardly translate into spaces beyond the workplace (Harris and Valentine, 2016). These meaningful relations are contrasted with the example of forced encounters used as a survival strategy. This chapter also illustrates how conviviality may be limited by negative discourse about Polish migrants, exploitation, prejudiced views and ethno-stratification of the labour market.

This chapter draws attention to the importance of exploring conviviality at the workplace as a possible frame for interaction across difference with an emphasis on lived experience. It does so by focusing on the narratives of selected research participants in Manchester and Barcelona. I have carefully chosen the research participants' stories which demonstrate a range of encounters at work. The experiences of each research participant are shaped by different employment sectors, social positions and personal histories. I continue exploring conviviality as a spatial, temporal and a highly contextualised process which needs to be studied with consideration of geographical, socio-economic and personal circumstances.

Conviviality at work in Manchester

Encounters with difference at work should be studied with regard to the context of Polish migration in Britain. Previous research shows that the majority of A8 migrants in the UK work in the lowest segments of the labour market in poor quality, low-skilled and manual jobs, often below their qualifications and for a minimum wage (Anderson et al., 2006; Cook et al., 2011a), also referred to as 3D jobs (dirty, dangerous and dull). Nevertheless, there is also evidence of Polish migrants' labour market upward mobility (Kershen, 2015; Ryan, 2015c), also manifested in my research, and a growing number of highly skilled professionals settling in Britain. Since many Polish migrants have been considered as overqualified for the jobs they undertake in the UK, some of these migrants believe themselves to be 'worse off' than other ethnic minorities

(Cook et al., 2011a). It is argued that such views arise because "many A8 migrants see themselves as whites in a largely white country and expect to not suffer discrimination or even be in a privileged position in the job market" (McDowell, 2009: 30). It has been argued that Polish and other East European migrants benefit from the racially and ethnically stratified labour market in the UK due to their assumed whiteness and Europeanness making them more desirable than non-white and non-European migrants (Fox et al., 2012; Nowicka, 2018; Salt and Okólski, 2014). Nevertheless, Polish migrants have been represented in some media, political and public discourses as an economic threat and, therefore, they have been blamed for job shortages, unemployment and strain on social services. In the context of Brexit, debates continuously returned to immigration and reducing the numbers of EU migrants in the UK (see Chapter 5).

This part of the chapter explores the narratives of three interviewees in Manchester discussing their experiences at work. Bogusia's account shows a light-hearted and playful form of conviviality beyond language barriers, highlighting the importance of language and humour, as well as a form of 'forced conviviality' in situations of interaction with her supervisor as a form of strategy to get by in a new environment. Krysia's case offers a narrative of encounters in cleaning and domestic work marked by care, affection and empathy crossing ethno-religious boundaries. Finally, Lucyna's account illustrates how anti-immigrant rhetoric disrupts conviviality and negatively influences relations with co-workers.

In-between light-hearted and forced convivialities

Bogusia is 37 and she arrived in Manchester in 2009 with her daughter to join her husband, who already lived and worked there. Bogusia got a job in the same hotel as her husband as a housekeeper. Upon her arrival in Manchester, she did not speak English, and this prevented her from establishing relations with the local people in everyday situations. The workplace became her most significant place of interaction with people from different backgrounds.

Bogusia's narrative about encounters at work begins with a description of positive relations with mainly white British co-workers. She told me with pride how much they liked a Polish cake prepared by her and her husband for parties and gatherings at work:

> English people at work are fascinated with a Polish cake, *karpatka*. Whenever there is a party planned, they ask if there will be a Polish cake, they love it! Last time we brought one to a farewell party when a colleague was leaving and the first question was, 'Will you bring Polish cake?', 'Yes, we will'. They don't have to ask us anymore. We know we have to make it.

The Polish cake becomes a symbolic material element in the context of gatherings and parties at work. The narrative also highlights the importance of social events in shaping conviviality at work. This convivial sociality facilitates familiarity and enables co-workers to interact, get to know each other better and bond through interaction during work events.

Some of Bogusia's co-workers used Polish words and phrases. This demonstrates openness, negotiation and accommodation of difference:

> They learn silly Polish words so to speak, not only swearwords but useful Polish phrases too. For example, when I arrive at work I don't hear 'please' and 'thank you' in English but they say it in Polish. ... My husband teaches them ... it is nice that they want to learn and try to communicate with us. They know I find it hard to get to know new people, not mentioning those from other countries who speak different languages. But the more time I spend with them, the more I feel at ease. I would like to have these kinds of relations with my neighbours, but there is no way because I think that they don't really want it, because they think 'They are Poles'. I can feel the difference in the way they treat us.

Bogusia makes a clear distinction between encounters at work and in the neighbourhood, where encounters with neighbours might be limited by the negative discourse about Polish migrants. By contrast, positive relations at work characterised by some work colleagues adopting Polish phrases forms an integral part of everyday convivial culture, making her feel welcome and included. This narrative demonstrates how communication between Bogusia and her co-workers is facilitated by language-accommodating practices, acknowledging a minority language. Adopting phrases from a different language in everyday speech "legitimates differences between people and their languages as part of everyday conviviality" (Heil, 2014: 8). Thus, cultural differences may become important resources for convivial interaction at the workplace, facilitating positive relationships across difference. While in other contexts foreign language can be seen as a burden on local services, as seen later in Lucyna's case (see also Alexander et al., 2007; Byrne, 2017; Harries et al., 2018), and a foreign accent can become a marker of Otherness, Bogusia's example demonstrates that the minority language can also serve as a bridge between people.

Similarly Milena (34), who worked in Manchester as a mechanical engineer before having children, recalled convivial banter at work and her co-workers' efforts to teach her colloquial English phrases: "Our desks were joined together and my workmates taught me different phrases and words. They swore at each other in a humorous way. They would use one new word a day so that I could remember it well". These examples show routine ways in which cultural and linguistic diversity is negotiated in everyday work.

The interplay between language and humour constitutes an integral component of everyday interaction among workmates and help them feel included. Previous research highlights the importance of humour at work (Graham, 1995; Holmes, 2006; Holmes and Marra, 2002; Wise, 2016). One of the primary factors which emerged from Graham's et al. (1992) study of functions of humour in conversation was positive affect. Graham's (1995) later analysis of the impact of humour on relationship development revealed that a high sense of humour facilitated a reduction of social distance between people taking part in the interaction. Based on their research on communication in New Zealand's workplaces, Marra and Holmes (2007: 153) argue that humour may serve as a form of relational practice by creating team, building in-group solidarity, collegiality and good relations between workers. They describe it as "the glue that holds groups together and helps people feel included" (154). Furthermore, they suggest that humour plays a function of providing relief from repetitive work and making relationships more enjoyable. They also mention that swearing and jokes contributed to creating unique team culture and positive relationships within the team. However, jokes and banter, particularly in relation to foreign accents, have been reported as examples of racism at work (Ashe and Nazroo, 2017). Nevertheless, my research findings show how humour and language differences became integral components of conviviality at work, facilitating more amusing but, most of all, inclusive and bonding interaction with co-workers beyond language and cultural barriers. The interplay between humour and language serves as "the lighter touch, 'cooler' qualities of conviviality that enables exchanges to happen through and across difference" (Neal et al., 2013: 316).

Bogusia stressed that despite working as a housekeeper, she interacted more with the kitchen staff because they created a space with a "family-like atmosphere" where she felt accepted. The family-like bonds are an example of a more meaningful form of sustained and deeper social relations: "They are not just friends, it is one big family". Nevertheless, Bogusia felt she was stuck somewhere in-between: "[other workers] don't know which category to pin me in because I don't stick with Czech girls, but I am not English ... so they don't know which group I belong to and I am in-between". The 'in-betweenness' may be arising from the idea of not feeling quite Eastern European but, on the other hand, being perceived as 'not-quite-European' (van Riemsdijk, 2010) with a lower status position of a room attendant. The sense of being 'in-between' may reflect a sense of belonging split between different groups and between Poland/Central and Eastern Europe and Britain, reflected in several other narratives.

Apart from discussing relations with peer co-workers, a substantial part of the interview involved a narrative about Bogusia's relations with a black male supervisor which sharply contrasts her experiences discussed previously:

> There is one *Murzyn* [black/Negro man – ambivalent term] at work ... I work with him and I have a feeling, not as a result of his or my racism, but I am his slave. This time I am black and he is white ... he makes me work hard ... I partly allow him because he is above me ... from him I only get orders and this is when my racism comes out ... I am telling you, I have nothing against him but I feel like I am his slave. ... That snotty-nosed brat is not going to keep on at me to do my work. He is so lazy.

The perception of black people through the prism of race is closely linked with the term widely used in contemporary Poland, *Murzyn* (Ząbek, 2009: 170). This term appeared in the Polish language in the fourteenth century derived from the same root as the English word 'Moors' – *maurus* in Latin, and it indicates a black person (Ząbek, 2007). Although in the opinion of many Poles and scholars it is not an offensive term, many people of African origin do not accept this word because of its pejorative connotations influenced by negative stereotypes and ambivalent translations as 'Negro' or the highly offensive term 'nigger', both echoing the context of slavery and colonialism (Karpieszuk, 2009; Piróg, 2010). In the survey of social perception of verbal abuse and hate speech, 68 per cent of respondents considered the word inoffensive (CBOS, 2007: 13). In contemporary Polish language, the word *Murzyn* has largely negative social connotations. Many popular sayings or idiomatic expressions have racist undertones referring to a situation in which somebody is a servant, a slave, a cheap work force or backward (Ząbek, 2007).

Bogusia's narrative reflects previous research findings revealing that relations between Central and Eastern European interviewees and black supervisors often lead to tensions and demonstrations of power (McDowell et al., 2007; Parutis, 2011). This narrative illustrates how uncomfortable Bogusia was about finding herself in a subordinate position to and being given orders by a black supervisor. This positioning clashed with the idea of whiteness associated with a position of dominance and privilege. She considered her lesser position as synonymous with blackness. It is possible that her narrative has been affected by the racialised discourse in Poland. Terms such as *Murzyni Europy* [Negroes of Europe] and *biali Murzyni* [white Negroes] have been used in some Polish media, social networks and even in politics with reference to white Poles and Europeans who are underpaid, work long hours in difficult conditions, and/or receive a low wage, often in the context of migration.[1] This racialised discourse makes a direct link between blackness, slave-like conditions and low status.

Bogusia also reinforced preconceived notions of blackness associated with slavery and laziness. This demonstrates how deeply rooted racialised notions of blackness and whiteness can be in some migrants' consciousness. It is possible that conflicting relations have led to a sharpening of difference and racialisation (Fox, 2013). The gender dimension is also important in shaping these encounters. Based on their research on migrant workers in the hotel industry, McDowell et al. (2007: 20) argue that "racism mirrors the extreme segregation between jobs and makes solidarity at work harder to achieve", and they emphasise that the ethnic and gender divisions of labour are reinforced by limited contact between different groups in the hotel.

At the same time, Bogusia was expected to fit the stereotype of the hardworking Polish room attendant, even when she was ill. She was not allowed to go home until she had a very high temperature and nearly fainted. The same evening, she received a phone call from the supervisor asking if she would come to work the next day, with little regard for her well-being. Bogusia told me she has repeatedly refused to report discrimination because she was afraid of being accused of racism.

As a result of her conflictual relations, Bogusia felt reluctant about interaction with her supervisor:

> He sometimes tries to say something funny to keep the conversation going, but for me this is forcing a conversation, forcing a smile. ... If there is nobody to talk to, he comes to me, but I don't need to talk to him. I am nice, and I say 'Hello, how are you?', but I don't start a conversation.

This narrative shows that humour does not always work. More importantly, it also illustrates an example of forced conviviality which I define as a form of coexistence marked by "involuntariness of interaction" (Estlund, 2003: 4) within the workplace. This means that people have little choice with whom they work and they can be "forced to get along – not without friction" (ibid). As seen in Bogusia's example, forced conviviality is characterised by superficial and limited involuntary interactions which are strategic. She has developed strategies in a form of everyday performances of forced encounters in order to get by (Datta, 2009). These strategies are particularly important in the context of the legal frameworks of equality legislation in the workplace which "shape encounters through performances of civility" (Valentine and Harris, 2016: 918).

Forced conviviality is specific to particular workplaces where workers are "forced to get along and get things done together not where we choose to do so" (Estlund, 2003: 5) and where certain norms of behaviour are expected. These norms are not as clear-cut in the neighbourhoods. Furthermore, in Bogusia's example, forced conviviality is influenced not only by gendered and raced dynamics of power but also by poor labour conditions and exploitation which is common in the hospitality sector. This form of interaction at work between Bogusia and her supervisor contrasts with the playful and light-hearted forms of interaction experienced with the kitchen and restaurant staff which facilitate sociality, a sense of belonging and inclusion. In fact, in line with previous research, Bogusia's peer relations may become closer as co-workers turn to each other for support when confronted with supervisors perceived as unfair (Sias and Cahill, 1998).

Meaningful conviviality in domestic work and beyond

Krysia is the oldest research participant (51) with a lower level of education and very basic English language skills. Her narrative about encounters at work reveals rich and diverse interactions. For Krysia, the workplace also became one of the main sites of interaction with difference in terms of ethnicity, religion, class and age. When Krysia worked as a cleaner in the local cinema, her co-workers from various backgrounds were younger than her. She was surprised that her age and limited English language skills did not prevent her from establishing convivial relations. Despite the language barrier, Krysia and her workmates at the cinema used humour as a strategy of communication. This fostered a positive and convivial atmosphere:

The supervisors were English women, but there were also two black men, an Argentinian man, people from Spain and few Poles. The atmosphere was nice. I didn't speak the language. There were two Polish women and they translated for me. It was a kind of cooperation. ... There were always jokes and laughter when we didn't understand each other. Somebody would say something, and another person would do a different thing and we turned it into a joke.

Previous studies suggest that the language barrier constitutes one of the main obstacles of forming social relations with people of other ethnicities, and that Polish migrants with poorer language skills, especially those who are older and working in low-paid jobs mostly depend on strong co-ethnic networks and 'stick together' with other Poles (Pietka, 2011; Cook et al., 2011b). Positive workplace encounters have been usually attributed to Polish nationals who have good English language abilities and higher levels of education. Nevertheless, Krysia's case challenges these arguments by demonstrating that humour can be used as a strategy to overcome language and communication barriers. Humour is used in Krysia's example to deflect attention from misunderstandings at work. This example contributes to my earlier discussion on the importance of the interplay between language and humour at work.

While Bogusia's narrative demonstrated the possibility of socialising at work, Krysia's story illustrates an example of mixing with workmates beyond the workplace:

The manager of each group organised activities outside of work hours. There was a social fund for workers so we used to go to different restaurants and we had nice food or we used to go out for coffee or beer, and because it was usually in the afternoon, everybody tried to make it and it was fantastic! For a laugh, everybody spoke to each other in their own language, but it was so special and nice, really nice. I would never allow myself to go to a restaurant. I have never done it in Poland and I wouldn't do it here ... but this was a chance for me to see this life here, the pubs at weekend, because they love it here, it's their tradition, and the restaurants from different countries. I would never go on my own. This was a chance for me to see this life from a different side, not only evolving around work and home. This is a very nice memory.

Conviviality transcends the setting of the workplace through after-work activities which facilitated interaction and bonding between co-workers, allowing the disruption of monotonous everydayness. What is significant about this example is that difference does not have to be dissolved or disappear to facilitate conviviality. In contrast, different languages were used by co-workers in a humorous way, demonstrating the emergence of convivial culture across ethnic, linguistic and age differences. As in Bogusia's case, language difference is used in a positive way to allow self-expression and to engage in playfulness with languages. The pubs and restaurants become spaces of interaction between co-workers. In her study of everyday cosmopolitanisms experienced by East European construction workers in London, Datta (2009) explains that while a highly controlled and hierarchical environment at work did not provide the physical conditions for socialising, the pubs after work became the extension of social interactions with English colleagues and supervisors.

When Krysia became a self-employed cleaner, she mainly cleaned people's homes and offices. During the interview at her house, Krysia pointed to a framed picture on the living room wall illustrating a Jewish family she worked for:

> Can you see this family? ... I got this picture for my fiftieth birthday.... It was very nice of them. It is a Jewish family.... When I left the hospital, they called me and texted me. I don't remember how many 'get well' cards I received from them. It was very nice. I was in tears when I was receiving the cards, because it was hard to believe that they would treat a cleaner like this. Yet, you can still be appreciated. I wasn't well with my injured arm, I couldn't do anything, but when I heard the 'get well' wishes, that the children missed me and asked when I would return, I felt better. I also received greetings from others. They were also Jewish because the family told their friends about me and I got their trust. They used to leave me the keys and it was ok. Jewish people have Shabbat and their own customs as in any other religions and I have always respected it. ... I try to respect and adjust to their hours, because the Shabbat starts on Friday night and lasts until Saturday night at a particular time.

Domestic work is often associated with exploitation of migrant workers and the feminised and racialised character of its labour force (Gutiérrez Rodríguez, 2010; Jayaweera and Anderson, 2008). As the demand for domestic workers in the EU increases, migrant women from Central and Eastern Europe and the 'global South' are employed to do the housework and they are likely to be subjected to precarious conditions. According to Jayaweera and Anderson (2008: 40), domestic workers are particularly vulnerable not only for the reasons of gender and migration status but also because of working in the private household, where employers can exercise and abuse power over workers. However, Krysia's narrative and the framed picture on the wall of the Jewish family she worked for illustrate a strong bond. According to Komter's (2005) theory of giving, the function of the picture from the Jewish family on Krysia's living room wall may be the creation of a bond between Krysia and the family, and the maintenance of this bond. The motives of gift giving may involve the desire to express gratitude not only for her work but also for forming ties with the children and respect for religious practices.

Through domestic work, a private household becomes a space of contact with individuals from social groups with which Krysia previously did not have any connection. Gutiérrez Rodríguez (2010: 10) stresses that although migrant domestic workers and their employers come from different backgrounds and live in different neighbourhoods, "in the privacy of the households, these two women meet and share moments of unprecedented intimacy. Moments of worries, anxieties, fears and joys are exposed, expressed and exchanged instating the affective encounters between these two women". Krysia's narrative confirms Gutiérrez Rodríguez's portrayal of domestic work as affective labour involving the creation of emotional bonds and relational complexity within private households. Parutis (2011: 274) describes private households as facilitating 'personal interaction' and 'friendly relations' in comparison to other workplaces. During interaction in private households, house owners express interest in the lives of the domestic workers beyond the workplace and this helps migrant women feel they are seen as individuals and even friends.

Krysia's example of conviviality characterised by affection transcends the convivial space of the domestic work through gestures of gift giving, phone calls, text messages and get-well cards which demonstrate Krysia's employers' sensitivity, compassion and affection in response to her illness. These gestures affect Krysia by leaving an impact on her body and mind. Her feelings are linked with a body reaction demonstrating her emotions, appreciation and improved well-being. Her narrative illustrates the capacity to be mutually affective and establish meaningful convivial contact with the members of the household contrary to the perception of domestic workers perceived as robots and subjects of exploitation (Gutiérrez Rodríguez, 2010).

Krysia's respect for different religious practices was also manifested in encounters at work with Muslims:

> I also cleaned an office where Pakistani people worked. I think they were Pakistani. I worked in the afternoon and they had their ritual prayers. For example, I walk in, take the litter and suddenly a man with a smile greets me and puts a rug on the floor and kneels, then I know that this is the time for prayer and I have to respect it and I say 'sorry' and leave. They would apologise and thank me. They always seemed happy with me and offered sweets and asked if I wanted to have something to drink. At first, I was surprised, but I apologised and said I would return in fifteen minutes. ... We worked very well together. The women were there too and even though I couldn't understand the language, the atmosphere was nice and they were lovely.

The surprise about different religious practice was followed by adaptation, familiarity and acceptance as a result of regular contact which promoted co-operation and positive atmosphere at work. This example demonstrates how habits of accommodations may be acquired. Through daily encounters, Krysia gained awareness and the ability to accommodate difference.

After discussing encounters with people at work, Krysia reflected on her perceptions of difference upon her arrival in Manchester and the way she views it now, illustrating a shift in perceptions of difference as a result of habitual encounters with difference:

> When I came here I was closed and shocked, because everybody looked different and used a different language and then suddenly you encounter people with different nationalities and everybody has their own customs and a different way of being, but this has passed and now everything is ok. These differences are less important. We are all human. . . . This has taught me to respect everybody and every culture.

Migrants' attitudes towards other ethnic minorities may shift over time as they become more familiar with difference which becomes commonplace (Wessendorf, 2014b) and part of everyday life. The existence of commonplace diversity and 'un-panicked multiculturalism' can be considered as influential factors in shaping more meaningful forms of conviviality understood as a process of regular encounters leading to respect for difference. By referring to meaningful conviviality in Krysia's case, I follow Valentine's (2008: 325) notion of 'meaningful contact' which "changes values and translates beyond the specifics of the individual moment into a more general positive respect for – rather than merely tolerance of – others". As a result of living and working with people from different cultures, Krysia's attitude translated into acceptance and respect for different groups and individuals and their cultural and religious practices.

While the narratives of Bogusia and Krysia illustrated various forms of conviviality characterised by the absence of negative discourses on Polish migrants, Lucyna's discussions of workplace relations mainly focused on how relations at work have been negatively influenced by prejudiced perceptions of Polish migrants.

The impact of anti-Polish discourses on relations at work

Lucyna is a 34-year-old interpreting coordinator and a part-time PhD student who came to Manchester in 2008. Like many Polish migrants, Lucyna started from low-skilled and low-paid jobs in the catering sector, despite her high level of education and work experience. She worked as a kitchen and canteen hand and later in a sandwich shop. Her next job at a nursery finally matched her work experience gained in Poland. Lucyna also worked as an interpreter for the National Health Service (NHS). I interviewed Lucyna in 2012. Her narrative about experiences at work are very different from earlier accounts discussed in this chapter as it mainly focused on how the negative discourse about Polish migrants in Britain influenced her relations with her co-workers. She believed that the negative perceptions about Polish migrants have been adopted across social classes and ethnic groups. Lucyna told me how she has been subjected to prejudiced comments by medical staff while working as an interpreter:

I personally heard these types of comments from people from all classes and from different groups. For example, I had to deal with doctors when I worked for some time as an interpreter and they asked: 'How much do you earn?', 'Those Poles come over here and they don't learn English', 'I don't need you here, why did you come here? How much is the hospital spending on you?'. Especially when the economic crisis started, these situations became so notorious that I decided to quit that job.

While language differences became integral components of interaction at work in earlier accounts, in Lucyna's example Polish language is perceived as a burden on local services (see also Alexander et al., 2007; Byrne, 2017; Harries et al., 2018). The doctors' hostility echoes the discourse on the costs of providing language translation/interpreting services to Polish patients.[2] These attitudes are voiced despite the workplace being regulated by diversity and equality regulations under the Equality Act 2010, which aims to ensure that the workplace environment complies with the law (see also Valentine and Harris, 2016). Ashe and Nazroo (2017) argue that racism remains a persistent feature of work life in Britain which disadvantages ethnic minority workers, and they emphasise the inconsistency in the promotion of equality, diversity and fairness in workplaces (see also McGregor-Smith Review, 2017).

Several interviewees offered a counter-narrative to the stereotype of Polish migrants as 'stealing jobs', as seen in Patrycja's quote:

> I have never felt that I was taking somebody's job. Even when I looked for a job and I went to the job centre, I was in a queue, there were three of us. One was a skater, dressed totally like … with a big chain, and next to me a seventeen years old girl with her cleavage out and those earrings, and I was dressed modestly. If an employer came, who would he choose?
>
> (Patrycja, a 28-year-old full time mother)

Patrycja emphasised the visual difference of the two youngsters at the job centre manifested through inappropriate clothing and appearance in opposition to her modest look of a 'model migrant' (see also Nowicka, 2018). She implied that their visual Otherness was the reason of failure in securing a job. This encounter is characterised by social distance marked by the classed and racialised difference. While Patrycja might have been perceived as an Eastern European migrant taking local jobs, she viewed the visually different youth as the classed Others. Maryla (31) showed me a picture of a banknote she was given as change in a supermarket with a scribbled note "Brit jobs for Brits, not Polish":

> I'd like to show you something funny. When I lived in Scotland, I went to a supermarket to buy something and I was given some change. I took a picture of it and showed it to everyone. I had a good laugh. It said, 'Brit jobs for Brits, not Polish' and it is underlined, so somebody must have been very frustrated and angry [laugh]. … I showed it mostly to Scottish people and

they said it was horrible, racist, and I said, come on, this is so funny because it doesn't make any sense. I don't think I'm taking anybody's job.

While Lucyna experienced discrimination in the workplace in Manchester, Maryla had a different experience. She told me how her experiences of discrimination at work in Krakow, Poland, where she worked as a teacher of English in a private school and she was not allowed to wear a headscarf, differed from her experiences in the UK. At the time of the interview, Maryla worked as a teaching assistant in a Church of England school in Rusholme and she described her workplace as an inclusive place where ethnic and religious difference is respected.

In contrast, Lucyna's account shows how the presumed whiteness has not exempted Polish migrants from discrimination (see also Fox et al., 2012) in some workplaces. The privilege of whiteness disappears once they start speaking. While whiteness allows a certain level of invisibility, Lucyna's foreign accent marked her as the Other:

> It sounds sad but if you don't speak, then everything is alright, because people are not entirely sure if you are Polish, or maybe English, because I am white. But it is obvious that as soon as I start speaking, you can tell that I have an accent and people straight away know and always ask this question: 'Where are you from?'.

This confirms Frankenberg's (1993) argument that whiteness is always situated and temporary (see also Rzepnikowska, 2019).

Lucyna's narrative illustrates how the negative discourse about Polish migration affects relations in a wider multicultural spectrum in the context of the workplace and leads to inter-ethnic tensions between some established groups and Polish migrants marked by dynamics of competition and conflict over jobs and resources. Lucyna told me she mostly experienced discrimination and prejudice by established ethnic minorities. She gave an example of how the negative rhetoric about recent Polish migrants affected her relations with female workers of South Asian origin who:

> questioned whether Polish people should be here. Before they were exploited ... and now they are trying to show me that they have been here longer than Poles and this allows them to be treated better, and now 'you have to go through what I have been through, and you will see how it is'.

According to Solé and Parella (2003: 134), prejudiced attitudes

> reflect the image and the perception of foreign immigration not only as a socio-cultural threat ... but also as an economic threat: real competition in the job market in a society that has a welfare state, which must, it is assumed, give priority to 'those from here' over 'those from abroad.

This reinforces the rhetoric of the 'deserving' established population and 'undeserving' recent arrivals. The presence of assumed competition between the established population and the new arrivals undermines conviviality in Lucyna's example.

Lucyna believed that these strained relations between the British and the Poles and other migrants result from the "media manipulation of the image of the Poles ... and this badly influences relations between people". The negative media rhetoric may lead to tensions between settled ethnic minorities and Polish migrants at work. This is also reflected in Renia's accounts focusing on Brexit narratives discussed in Chapter 5.

Having explored the research participants' workplace encounters in Manchester, I will now move on to discuss workplace relations in Barcelona.

Conviviality at work in Barcelona

As discussed earlier in the book, Spain did not open its labour market to the new accession countries until 2006, and the Polish migration since this period has been characterised by the arrival of mostly young and educated migrants from bigger cities. Their employment often matched their qualifications or served to improve them, sharply contrasting the disadvantaged labour market position and deskilling often experienced by Polish migrants in Britain. They have often been referred to as a model of a well-integrated migrant group into Spanish society (Hellermann and Stanek, 2006; Nalewajko, 2012) and good workers. Polish migrants in the Spanish/Catalan context have hardly been associated with anti-immigrant rhetoric, contrasting the negative discourses about Polish migrants in Britain. This, however, does not mean that the rhetoric about immigrants as 'intruders' who take native jobs, decrease wages and make working conditions worse does not exist in Spain (Solé and Parella, 2003).

It is also important to stress the significance of the Catalan context. Catalonia represents a new immigration region and it has been experiencing severe consequences of the economic crisis, alongside the rest of Spain. High levels of unemployment rates characterise almost all the Catalan municipalities (Rodon and Franco-Guillén, 2014). However, immigration in Catalonia has not become as politicised as in Britain and in the rest of Spain, where it has been used as a political tool for mainstream political parties (Escandell and Ceobanu, 2009). Immigration has decreased in importance and general concerns have been focused on the state of the economy, and in more recent years on the issue of Catalan independence. The Catalan political discourse towards immigration adopted a particular approach based on the respect for diversity and belonging to the Catalan community (Rodon and Franco-Guillén, 2014). However, while there is emphasis on respect for difference in Catalonia with a strong discourse of *convivencia*, the issue of socio-economic inequalities experienced by non-European migrants and minorities was raised by some of my interviewees.

This part of the chapter explores three different narratives of encounters at work in Barcelona. I begin by exploring the case of Eliza who worked for an international organisation and developed friendly relations with co-workers. Eliza's narrative stresses the importance of under-researched friend-ships developed in the workplace. Irena's narrative stresses the importance of working together as equals and the limitations of contact with difference as a result of ethnic stratification of the Spanish/Catalan labour market. Finally, Dorota's case draws attention to women's friendships established at work as a way of distancing herself from the previous experiences of a housewife.

Openness to difference and workplace friendships

Eliza is a 32-year-old office worker who comes from a small town in northern Poland, where she previously had no contact with people from different cultures. When Eliza arrived in Barcelona in 2005 she experienced difficulties in finding a job as a result of restrictions imposed on the new EU members in 2004. When the restrictions were lifted in 2006, she realised that she had many more employ-ment possibilities enhanced by her English and Spanish language skills. She then got a job at an international charity organisation and worked there for five years as an office worker. She established positive relationships with people at work, although she stressed that these relations were not 'typical' as they differed from everyday relations with people in Barcelona:

> My position at work was not typical and it does not illustrate the situation in Spain because the organisation was very international, multicultural. ... My Spanish friends were always telling me that I live on a rose-tinted planet, that what happens at my work does not take place at a normal workplace.... There were people from all over the world speaking different languages. There were Spaniards and Catalans, but there also were people from South America, France, Italy, some from Africa, Ghana, Argentina and the relations between us were very good because there was a strong emphasis on team work and positive work climate, and there were hardly any negative situations.

Although little is known about the organisational factors that impact social rela-tions at work, Eliza's narrative shows that the environment and the type of workplace are important characteristics shaping relations with co-workers. By joining the charitable organisation she worked for, employees were expected to commit to its values and principles and follow their professional code of ethics with respect for the cultural traditions and religious beliefs of others. By employing people from different ethnic and cultural backgrounds and emphasising the importance of teamwork and a positive working atmo-sphere, the supranational organisation facilitates an environment that fosters workplace relationships. The positive relations and work climate discussed by Eliza differ from the hostile working environment experienced by Lucyna in Manchester.

Eliza's narrative demonstrates the absence of stigmatisation of migrant workers in her workplace, contrary to Lucyna's case:

> I often used to go to work with a smile on my face and I have never felt that I was an immigrant, and that because of that I earned less or that a Spaniard was better treated than me. Sometimes it was quite the opposite. I thought that I received a preferential treatment.

Favoured treatment of Polish migrants by Spanish employers compared to other migrant groups is also reported by Nalewajko (2012) who claims that it is a result of assumed cultural proximity between Polish migrants and Spaniards, which makes them more welcome than other groups. Nalewajko (2012) and Ramírez Goicoechea (2003) stress the invisibility of Polish migrants and suggest that in the Spanish imaginary they are not considered as a problem in contrast to other groups, including *gitanos* (gypsies), or as Eliza noticed, South Americans, who paradoxically are culturally closer to Spaniards, although the colonial nature of this cultural similarity should be kept in mind. Solé and Parella (2003) also highlight the new phenomenon of preference of EU workers over native ones in Spain, especially in multinational firms. The authors suggest that this tendency is linked with an imagery of the EU workers having a greater professional capacity simply because of coming from abroad.

Like some other interviewees in Barcelona, Eliza was aware of discrimination experienced by other ethnic minorities and their absence in public positions contrary to the super-diverse workforce in Britain:

> I realise that there is a lot of discrimination, even in Barcelona, because I have many South American friends, who were discriminated in employment.... In Great Britain you can see an Indian doctor or a bus driver from Pakistan, but in Barcelona, Pakistani minorities ... don't have access to this kind of public positions. The Catalan language is an additional barrier.

Eliza's narrative illustrates how certain migrant groups labelled as 'outsiders' tend to be pigeonholed in marginal spaces of the labour market. These dynamics result in a segmentation of the labour force based on ethnic criteria and often intersecting with gender, regardless of non-EU migrants' education levels, skills and work experience (Colectivo Ioé, 1998; Solé and Parella, 2003). Despite the anti-discriminatory legislation in Spain, the discourse of 'preference based on nationality' is still present. In this case, the Others are often non-white and non-European from the South. In contrast, the whiteness and Europeanness of Polish migrants in Spain become an advantage. This is contrasted with their experiences in Britain where they can be perceived as 'less white'. Although the interviewees in Barcelona were aware of this preferential treatment and privileged position, most of them did not explicitly discuss whiteness; possibly because it was considered as something natural and taken for granted (Ryan, 2010).

One of the most significant aspects identified in Eliza's narrative about encounters at work are workplace friendships:

> Until now, some of my good friendships were made at work and I always was able to count on them. For example, a year ago I moved to another flat in Barcelona … it was unfurnished and I only asked at work if anyone had some furniture, and they started bringing everything they had from their homes, of course, after having asked me: 'Eliza, do you need a blender?', 'Eliza, I have some spare chairs and a table', 'I have pots I don't use'. So basically, everybody offered some kind of help.

This example raises the importance of friendship as a possible outcome of conviviality at the workplace. Previous research highlights the importance of the workplace friendships (Rawlins, 1992; Sias and Cahill, 1998) characterised by 'voluntariness' since they develop by choice (Ryan, 2015a). This distinguishes workplace friendships from forced conviviality marked by obligatory ties as described in Bogusia's example. While workers mostly have little say in choosing their peer co-workers, they choose which co-workers they befriend (Sias and Gallagher, 2009). Even though Eliza's discussion of friendships made at work does not focus on any particular group, she made it clear during the interview that her work colleagues were from diverse backgrounds. Furthermore, she made these connections with people who share not only a convivial environment at work but also a similar age, lifestyle and openness to difference. Similarly, Klaudia, a 32-year-old store manager assistant told me that it was easier to make friendships at work with other migrant workers: "We were a big group of friends from different parts of the world. They didn't know many people here, so we stuck together, did things together, organised parties and trips". Klaudia strongly believed that:

> foreigners are more open, they don't have families here so for them, just like for me, a friend in a foreign country is like a family, because I can cry on their shoulders, borrow money or anything else I need, or when I need to find a room, a place to live I know I can stay with them. They are like a family.

Both accounts show that life events influence workplace friendships. This finding is consistent with previous research suggesting that co-workers often become a valuable source of support when individuals deal with important events in their personal lives (Ryan, 2015b; Sias and Cahill, 1998; Sias and Gallagher, 2009). The practical support of friendly co-workers transcends the workplace setting and demonstrates the blurred line between the workplace and personal life. This interpretation is similar to that of Sias and Gallagher's (2009: 79) who argue that "the common occupational interests and experiences co-workers share make the workplace a somewhat natural 'incubator' for personal relationships that extend beyond the professional boundary". Therefore, workplace friendships are sources of support crucial not only for helping employees to deal with organisational life but also to cope with personal life events.

Working together as equals

Irena is a 28-year-old part-time PhD student and product engineer who grew up in a city in southern Poland. Although Irena had some contact with people of different ethnicities in her home city in central Poland prior to arrival in Barcelona, she stressed that "it was strange to see a black person because in Poland immigration is not very high". When she arrived in Barcelona in 2009, Irena was very surprised with the super-diverse population. She compared her fascination with difference to that of a child visiting a shop with sweets for the first time.

Irena lived with her Spanish partner in three different areas of Barcelona, but her contact with neighbours was very limited. For Irena, neighbourhoods in Barcelona were not places of interaction. Instead, her narrative mostly focused on acquaintances made at the workplace, considered as the main place of everyday interaction in comparison to other places of encounter:

> Most of my acquaintances are from work. ... We sometimes go out for a beer after work ... I've had this job since May, this is not a very long time, so I can't say yet that they are my best friends. Sometimes we go for a dinner, but nothing other than that. When I worked at the university we used to go out together. It was a larger circle of friends. ... You spend eight hours with a person from a different culture you have no idea about. At work you don't always work, you talk, go for a coffee or do other things. This gives you the opportunity to get to know the other person and if not at work then where? You can sign up at a dance course or a gym, but I go to the gym and I don't have any acquaintances from there. Sometimes I talk to somebody, but I have no idea about them, so if not at work, you don't have a chance to get to know the person.

The length of time of working together becomes a significant factor shaping Irena's experiences of conviviality at work and beyond. She stressed the importance of time spent with co-workers and socialising over coffee or lunch as a way of getting to know them as individuals. This socialisation takes place at work, during breaks and outside of the workplace. The theme of work-based relations not being confined to work-based activities runs through all the narratives.

Habitual contact at work allowed Irena to look beyond ethno-religious differences of her co-workers:

> If you can see that I work shoulder to shoulder with a Muslim man or woman, and she does exactly what I do, and she is treated exactly the way I am, I start treating her the same way too. ... You see, she wears a burka, or however you call it, but she works with me. She is a scientist.

> She is a normal human being like you and me. I am not saying that before I worked with her she was not normal, but I didn't know [her] ... this is a chance to get to know her and her culture.

The theme of veiled Muslim women was frequently mentioned during the interviews and the focus group in Barcelona, while this issue was hardly mentioned by the research participants in Manchester. Some interviewees were fascinated by veiled Muslim women, while others discussed the veil as a symbol of oppression by the Islamic religion and culture. However, Irena's narrative illustrates how boundaries along ethno-religious lines become blurred through everyday interaction at work. It shows how familiarity and habituation can lead to "unfixing" of essentialised ethnic categories (Neal et al., 2018: 27). The construction of Otherness based on assumptions that the Other is 'not quite human' (Harris et al., 2017) is deconstructed through everyday workplace interaction. Irena realised that she shared a common humanity with her co-worker who initially was perceived solely through an ethno-religious lens. Furthermore, as Irena noticed, they both are scientists and they perform similar work. It is the perceived similarity which can have a profound impact on relationship development at work. This example demonstrates an emergence of workplace relationships encompassing both similarity and difference. Irena told me that even though her co-workers have different values and lifestyles, she learnt to respect these differences. Conviviality here involves the process of learning about difference, resulting in respect for it.

Like Eliza, Irena stressed the specificity of her workplace in comparison to low-paid and low-skilled jobs often occupied by non-European migrants. Irena was aware of the limited possibilities of contact with people from different cultures at the workplace as a result of inequalities in employment based on ethnicity:

> Today, if you see that people from South America mostly work in bars ... and in grocery shops you usually see Pakistani or Chinese people [pause] then they are not seen in the same way. Also, you can't see them in politics and in public offices. There is a lack of possibility to work with them and to get to know them. The first step is for the employer to treat everyone equally, and then you have a chance to get to know others. ... These people are not treated fairly; they are not given equal chances to get a better job.

While anti-discrimination law is considered as the UK's greatest area of strength, it is one of Spain's weakest policy areas (Niessen et al., 2007). In 2011, The Council of Europe (2011: 5) suggested that a specific recruitment strategy should be implemented in Barcelona "to ensure that the ethnic background of public employees reflects the composition of the city's population". The results of Intercultural City Index analysis for Barcelona in 2017 shows that nothing much has changed: "The ethnic background of public employees does not reflect the composition of the city's population, the municipality does not foresee any recruitment plan nor encourages diverse workforce in private sector enterprises" (Council of Europe, 2017: 21). This calls for an effective strategy addressing the issue of lack of wider ethnic diversity in public sector jobs.

Women's friendships

Dorota is 36 and completed secondary education in Poland. Before she got divorced, she was limited to the domestic domain as her husband wanted her to adopt traditional gender norms, to be a housewife and look after the family. After the divorce, Dorota had to find a job to support herself and her son financially. The workplace became a place of new acquaintances and friendships with co-workers. Dorota mainly talked about convivial relations with Spanish and Catalan female co-workers. She was not only fascinated by their lifestyle, but she also identified with them. This was reflected in her discussion of liberation from her oppressive husband, and of contemporary Spanish women freed from the past of the oppressive Franco regime:

> I started going with them to parties ... I saw how they think and, as they say, *las españolas llevan los pantalones*, that it is the Spanish woman who wears trousers in a relationship, that it is the Spanish woman who decides whether she wants to get married, have children or not, that she will do whatever she wants, and so on. Today the Spanish woman doesn't want to have anything to do with the past of her mother or grandmother who was kind of imprisoned by the Franco regime.... In the meantime, when I worked there when I was a divorcee, when my husband could not gag me at home [laugh], I went out to people with freedom, as I am, because he wanted a quiet, a kind of woman who wouldn't talk or laugh too much ... but after the divorce my situation changed. I got a job and started interacting with Spanish women. It was a new world for me.

Dorota's identification with Spanish and Catalan women underpins the processes of workplace relations formation, a possibility of experimenting with a new lifestyle and a way of distancing herself from the previous experiences of a housewife. Furthermore, convivial workplace relations with the local women were also shaped by the nature of her workplace with roles that are still gender-specific.

Several other research participants highlighted the importance of friendship with other women. Ryan (2015b) also points out that in her research on network formations of highly qualified Irish migrants in Britain most of the women had largely female friendship groups. For Dorota, socialising with female co-workers was possibly a way to challenge social control (O'Connor, 1992). This contributes to the argument that women's friendships may serve to challenge patriarchal practices (Andrew and Montague, 1998).

While in the British context workplace relations with the native population were sometimes marked by tensions resulting from the negative discourse about Polish migrants, as seen in Lucyna's case, Dorota's narrative illustrates that her ethnicity was not an obstacle in forming workplace relations with Spanish and Catalan women. It is not only a perceived cultural proximity between Polish migrants and Spaniards/Catalans, but also the importance of gender shaping these relations.

Even though Dorota was made redundant and had to look for a job elsewhere, at the time of the interview she was still friends with some women from work. As in Eliza's case, ongoing mobility does not necessarily lead to breakdown of friendships made at work.

Conclusions

As illustrated in this chapter, migrants spend a large proportion of their time at work and one cannot avoid interacting with others. The narratives revealed complex encounters with difference at work demonstrating various forms of conviviality not always free from tensions.

Humour and language differences may become integral parts of convivial culture at work, facilitating not only playful but also inclusive and bonding interaction. Ethnic and cultural differences become less important in the context of more meaningful workplace relations and friendships based on deeper social bonds, care and respect for difference. Nevertheless, the workplace can also be a place of conflict and tensions between different groups and individuals, characterised by hostility, prejudice and racism (see also Chapter 5 on Brexit narratives). While a small number of interviewees openly spoke about their whiteness and expressed prejudice (particularly in the British context), most participants hardly mentioned it in discussions about workplace relations. This could be due to a different profile of Polish migrants in the two cities. Nevertheless, as Ryan (2010) argues, whiteness might not be explicitly discussed because it is assumed as natural and therefore taken for granted. Leitner (2012: 837) stresses that "more educated and well-off whites are better able to control forms of racial signification than are working-class whites".

Despite conflict and tensions, migrants may use survival strategies to get by, as manifested in examples of 'forced conviviality' characterised by involuntary and superficial interaction. Workplaces usually have rules and regulations with regard to diversity and equality. Therefore, employees are expected to be convivial, although they may hide prejudiced views in fear of disciplinary action (Valentine and Harris, 2016).

The type of workplace and equal status may influence relationships with people at work. Equal status shared between co-workers in a non-competitive working environment seems to aid conviviality at work, while power hierarchies, especially between the established ethnic minorities and new arrivals, may result in tensions, as seen in Bogusia's case. The time-varying factor plays an important role, since the longer the time of employment, the more opportunity there is to get to know co-workers and establish friendships. The narratives of Krysia, Eliza, Irena and Dorota stressed the spatio-temporal character of conviviality, with possibilities of establishing more meaningful relations over time and beyond the workplace. The role of gender was particularly important in the narratives of Bogusia and Dorota. While in Bogusia's case, gendered divisions of labour combined with racialised discourses negatively impacted on relations with a black male supervisor, in Dorota's example, convivial workplace relations with Spanish and Catalan women were partly shaped by the gender-specific nature of her workplace.

Experiences of interaction at work are highly contextual. In the British context, the portrayal of Polish migrants as invaders stealing jobs and as a burden to local services, as discussed in Lucyna's case, may seriously harm their relations with the local population likely to adopt opinions and stereotypes repeated over a long period of time. In the light of Brexit, this may lead to further divisions along ethnic lines and discourage minority groups from actively interacting with others who use a discriminating rhetoric. As highlighted in McGregor-Smith Review (2017: 6), employers play an important role and "need to act fast and ensure that outdated and offensive views or behaviours are not tolerated". In contrast, in the Spanish context, there is an absence of such negative discourse about Polish migrants. They are seen as skilled, well-educated and culturally close to Spaniards and Catalans. Nevertheless, the narratives illustrated that ethnic stratification in the Spanish and Catalan workplaces may lead to limited contact with non-whites and non-Europeans. Occupational segregation affecting ethnic minorities is not unique to Spain/Catalonia. Hence, there is a need for a more representative workforce and more inclusive workplaces.

Notes

1 A populist Polish MEP Janusz Korwin-Mikke, in his speech in the European parliament in 2014 used the term "Negroes of Europe". The article titled "Murzyni Europy" in *Gazeta Finansowa* (26 August 2016) makes a direct reference to Polish migrants in various European countries, including the UK. Also see various discussions on a Polish forum mentioning the term 'biali Murzyni' (Gazeta.pl Forum, 2018).
2 The article in *The Telegraph* (26 December 2012) 'NHS spends £11 million on interpreters' highlights that the highest cost for face-to-face interpreters covers services for Polish-speaking patients.

5 Brexit narratives

Conviviality under threat?

On 23 June 2016, the UK voted to leave the EU by 52 to 48 per cent. Leave won the majority of votes in England and Wales. While Manchester had the strongest remain vote in the North West, the majority of Greater Manchester boroughs were characterised by the majority leave vote. The EU referendum choices were strongly linked to views about immigration in the UK: "opposition to immigration on any measure strongly predicted support for 'Leave', while those with positive views of migration leaned heavily towards 'Remain'"; and class, education, ethnicity and location were also significant components (Ford, 2018). An IPSOS Mori (16 June 2016) poll showed that immigration was the top issue for British people voting in the EU referendum. The wave of post-Brexit vote hostility revealed the extent of racism and xenophobia which affected not only Polish nationals but also other migrants and settled ethnic minorities, including British citizens (Burnett, 2017; Komaromi and Singh, 2016; Rzepnikowska, 2018b). Nevertheless, recent study findings show a positive shift in attitudes since Brexit vote across the political and social spectrum (Ipsos MORI, 2017; Ford, 2018). They show that while the majority of people still want immigration reduced, people have become more positive about immigration in the last few years.

In the previous chapters, I focused on different forms and degrees of conviviality in various city spaces and in the workplaces by exploring the narratives of Polish migrant women in Manchester and Barcelona who were interviewed in 2012/13. Conviviality explored in this book reflects the everyday process of how people live together and how they negotiate their differences. Now, I am turning to look at how people live together in the context of Brexit, as it seems more relevant than ever because of continued attention to immigration, identity and nation raising questions about conviviality. By drawing on the interviews conducted with Polish migrant women after the Brexit vote, this chapter explores the influence of Brexit on everyday lived experiences of my research participants. It illustrates the importance of the interplay between the media and political discourses, race and ethnicity, class, place and time in shaping relations between Polish migrant women and the local population. It argues that conviviality is a highly dynamic process influenced by spatio-temporal characteristics revealing the coexistence of conviviality, tensions and racism. It also shows that while Brexit poses challenges to conviviality, there are instances of thriving and sustained convivial culture that endures despite exclusionary anti-immigration rhetoric.

This chapter focuses on the narratives of mainly three research participants re-interviewed after the Brexit vote. I contacted ten of my interviewees in 2017/18 to find out the impact of Brexit on their everyday experiences. They told me how shocked they were about the Brexit vote and how anxious and uncertain they started to feel following the EU referendum in 2016. They were aware of anti-migrant sentiment in the run up to the EU referendum and in the aftermath. Several felt fearful of post-Brexit racism and xenophobia they heard about in the media or from family and friends. Nevertheless, going back to Poland was not considered a good option because they felt settled in the UK or felt discouraged by the current situation in their country. A strong sense of continuing uncertainty about the future in the light of Brexit has bred further anxiety and distress. In this chapter, I mainly focus on the narratives of Renia, Krysia and Oliwia. Their complex experiences in the context of Brexit have been very much influenced by the areas where they live and interact with the local residents.

"Everything changes"

Renia (age 62) was one of my interviewees who was very keen to tell me about her experiences after the EU referendum in June 2016. Renia experienced both conviviality and racism on her street before and after Brexit in Ashton, Tameside, Greater Manchester – a former mill town with 11.5 per cent of the local population from an ethnic minority group. In Tameside, 61.1 per cent voted to leave. All the wards in Tameside, including Renia's, had a majority leave vote. The leave vote was associated with a longstanding frustration over immigration in more deprived parts of Greater Manchester (BBC News, 24 June 2016).

In the first interview in 2013, Renia told me that despite having experienced harassment by white British youth, she had good relations with her immediate white British neighbours of similar age. She described one of her neighbours, a retired 75-year-old white English man, Ed, as an "ideal neighbour: friendly, and watching over her flat, although a bit reserved when sober". After the EU referendum, amicable relations with Ed remained unchanged. Nevertheless, the local white British youth resumed harassing both Renia and her husband:

> After our conversation [in 2013] they gave us a break. I didn't have any prob-lems. But after the referendum it started again. We are quiet. We don't mess with those kids. Their aggression towards me is not out of nowhere. It started happening just after the referendum and it stopped about six months ago. When the caretaker heard all the insults directed towards us he intervened. He took care of it so well that since then we've had no troubles.

Even though the harassment stopped, Renia noticed that her relations with other neighbours were not the same after the Brexit vote in 2016. She noticed that a close neighbour, a white British woman, was no longer as welcoming and friendly as she used to be:

> Everything changes. It constantly fluctuates. A neighbour who has been living here for several years, always used to talk to me, you know, she asked 'how are you, how is it going, is everything OK?', and everything was fine. Now, when I see her, she turns her head away and pretends she doesn't see me. I think that there starts to be a tendency of negative sentiment towards migrants because of Brexit. I can't tell you that this is hundred percent the case, but I have this feeling based on people's attitudes.

This narrative shows how dynamic conviviality is and how it can be limited by specific events at certain times and places. It illustrates how daily encounters are marked with tensions. As Neal et al. (2018) point out, "conviviality speaks to the unpredictable experiences and responses to urban multiculture". Therefore, "static conceptions of how multiculture is lived" (38) should be avoided.

Renia's account illustrates interviewees' awareness of anti-migrant sentiment in the context of Brexit. Ford and Goodwin (2018: 21) point out this anti-immigration sentiment is not new:

> British immigration debates have long been intertwined with public anxieties over race and identity, with public hostility in earlier decades directed at black and South Asian migrants from former imperial territories in the Caribbean and the Indian subcontinent, who began arriving in large numbers from the 1950s onward. Yet starting in 2004, the focus of anxiety moved to the large new flow of migrants from EU states in Central and Eastern Europe. As a result, anti-immigration voters came to see migration (and the social changes that it brought) as an issue closely bound up with Britain's EU membership.

As discussed earlier, the physical presence and visibility of Polish migrants became the issue in the run up to the EU referendum. The perceptions of a 'Polish invasion' have been reinforced by the populist tabloid press (ECRI, 2016) with a highly negative stance on migration, fuelling anxieties about the perceived effects of migration on public services, welfare and identity (Ford and Goodwin, 2018; Rzepnikowska, 2019). For instance, the *Daily Mail* article on 6 May 2016, titled 'A rapist protected by the police and the mining town that turned into little Poland' makes a clear reference to the visual and audible difference of Polish presence with several images of Polish stores, bakeries and beauty salons. Furthermore, it uses the phrase 'Polish invasion' and comments on the perceived lack of integration of Poles within the community with attention to Polish language seen "as a barrier to stay separate".

Renia does not work because of health issues, but she was particularly concerned about and affected by her husband's experiences at his workplace after the Brexit vote in June 2016. Renia told me about an incident at her husband's workplace, a meat processing plant in Greater Manchester, the day after the EU referendum. She described the incident as if it was a theatre play:

> I want to tell you about the incident in which my husband took part on Friday 24 June last year [2016]. It was the first working day following the Brexit referendum.
>
> Time of action – morning after the referendum around 6 AM.
>
> Place of action – pork cutting hall at the meat processing plant.
>
> People – about 30 employees, of which 50 percent have English nationality.
>
> The atmosphere like never before. You can hear laughter and loud manifestation of joy, not so much from the referendum victory, but because of the belief that from the next Monday the migrants will miraculously disappear from the company.
>
> John, Jack, Connor shout: 'No more Polish Vermin!'
>
> John approaches Marko, a Slovakian gypsy and shouts: 'Go back to Poland!'
>
> Connor: 'In a week time don't show up here.'
>
> John to Marko: 'And you, you have three days to be out of here, and if not, then ... '
>
> John puts his right hand in the shape of a pistol ... he aims at Marko's chest and you can hear loud bang, bang, bang. The hall is filled with loud laughter. Marko lowered his head, slicing the meat with his knife, though his hands were shaking.

The racist slur of 'No more Polish vermin' seems to originate from the racist incident in Huntingdon, Cambridgeshire, where laminated cards in English and Polish with the words 'Leave the EU/No more Polish vermin' were left outside primary schools and posted through letterboxes of Polish people (Cambridge News, 25 June 2016). This shows how racist and xenophobic rhetoric quickly spread across the country. According to Komaromi and Singh (2016), over 6,000 racist hate crimes were reported to the National Police Chiefs Council (NPCC) within the four weeks after the Brexit vote. The wave of post-Brexit vote hostility revealed the extent of racism and xenophobia which affected not only Polish nationals but also other migrants and settled ethnic minorities, including British citizens (Burnett, 2017; Komaromi and Singh, 2016; Rzepnikowska, 2018b). It did not matter to the perpetrators whether their targets of xeno-racist violence were black, brown or white, as they all were seen as a threat to Englishness (see also Virdee and McGeever, 2018). Even though racism and xenophobia were not new to Renia and her husband, they had not experienced it in such potency before the Brexit vote. Anti-migrant sentiment in the context of Brexit illustrates "a more complicated racial stratification than is sometimes acknowledged ... Eastern European whiteness in a Western European context carries with it further, emplaced, geopolitical racial connotations" (Botterill et al., 2019: 3).

Renia told me that the employers responded to the incident by organising a staff meeting and explaining that similar behaviour would not be tolerated. However, Renia's husband told her that "although everything is ok, nothing is the same as it was before the referendum". Renia recounted the incident as if she were there. She relived the story told by her husband by creating her own narrative in the form of a dialogue to give me a better idea of what happened:

> I put this scene in the form of dialogue to better illustrate the course of this incident. It really happened. This shocked me in an unbelievable way. Not only because English workers behaved in a certain way. Yes, or even worse, people of every nationality would have behaved in a similar way to the media-inspired Brexitism.

Renia told me that there have always been some divisions at her husband's workplace, particularly between Polish workers. Nevertheless, she gave clear examples of workplace conviviality which was later disrupted by hostility and further division triggered by the Brexit vote. This has clearly affected both Renia and her husband:

> The production hall is divided into two parts, one for English workers and the other migrant workers. It wasn't like this before. Before, the supervisors told Polish workers that everything should be done together. Now the production line is reserved for the English workers. I don't work there but I'm affected by this. ... They were always told to integrate. There was never such a huge division. My husband was better integrated with the British workers than with the Poles. He had unpleasant conversations with other Poles. ... He distanced himself from them. He preferred working with the Brits.... He preferred to sing with them on Friday, an unforgettable English tradition. When Friday was approaching they were so happy at the production line. He preferred to goof around with them. He felt better in their company. Then Polish women would approach him and scornfully say that he thinks he is English. Now he feels some discomfort because he feels that he works the way he did before, but they [the English co-workers] don't want him anymore. He returned to the 'Polish side', if I can call it this way. They no longer sit together at the canteen. The relations changed completely. Everything changes.

Renia's narrative illustrates the fragile and temporary character of conviviality disrupted by social inequality, exclusion and anti-migrant sentiment. It also highlights the emotional impact of Brexit on changing relations between migrants and the native population which triggered feelings of being unwanted and rejected in a very short space of time. Furthermore, the recent research shows that non–UK EU citizens feel anxious (Guma and Dafydd Jones, 2019), undervalued and disempowered by the prolonged Brexit negotiation process (Sigona, 2018), or even feel treated as "second class citizens and betrayed" (Duda-Mikulin, 2018a), experiencing emotional insecurity and finding themselves in limbo, uncertain about how Brexit will affect their lives and their futures in the UK (Botterill and Burrell, 2018; Duda-Mikulin, 2018b; Trevena, 2018).

Renia linked xenophobic attitudes of some British people with the rise of right-wing populism in the UK:

> I think politicians for their own or party interests, for these unfortunate 'bars of popularity', are able to do everything. For example, to tell British people that the only remedy for Britain's return to the nineteenth century super-power is the expulsion of immigrants. And then it will be a land flowing with milk and honey. . . . Honest and professional journalism is a dying species. Now the media is governed by the audience. The Brexit example clearly shows that the populists are better off than those who can reliably present the results of the decisions which were made.

Renia, as well as several other interviewees were aware about intensifying racialisation of political and media debates and growing nationalist orientations in the UK which have constituted a challenge to conviviality. Burnett (2017) argues that based on the examination of over one hundred cases of racist violence after the EU referendum there is a clear link between the language and behaviour of perpetrators and populist discourse.

Renia does not want to return to Poland as she became disappointed by the current situation in her country of origin following the electoral victory of the Polish populist Law and Justice Party (PiS) in September 2015, and intensifying xenophobia, aggressive nationalism and intolerance (Fomina and Kucharczyk, 2016). Similarly, Nowicka's (2018) recent research on Polish migrants in the UK also revealed that her interviewees also felt discouraged from going back to their country due to the current situation in Poland. Renia was aware of anti-migrant sentiments in both Poland and in the UK and this affected her sense of not-belonging. Like many other EU migrants, she felt "unwanted" as a result of the Brexit vote:

> I can't escape to Poland because when I look at Kaczyński [PiS leader] . . . I get angry and I am scared to go to Poland to sort out things. I'm scared of those people. I'm scared of those hooligans, I'm scared of ONR [*Obóz Narodowo-Radykalny* – English translation: The National Radical Camp, a far-right movement in Poland]. I'm scared of this mad house over there. Neither in Poland, nor here, because they don't want me here.

While Renia's account shows how racism and xenophobia have intensified in the context of Brexit and disrupted conviviality, Krysia's narrative demonstrates resilience of convivial culture.

"Nothing much changed but we are closer than before"

When I contacted Krysia in 2018, she continued living in the same area near Cheetham Hill (see Chapters 3 and 4 on a detailed discussion of Krysia's experiences in her neighbourhood and in the workplace). In contrast to Renia's experience, Krysia's relations with neighbours were not affected negatively by the Brexit vote, although she was aware of anti-Polish sentiment at the time of the EU referendum in 2016. In fact, she felt that these relations became even stronger in recent years:

> Nothing much changed in our neighbourhood. God, I would wish everyone to have neighbours like ours. We are closer than before, and I can count on them. . . . They aren't happy with Brexit at least those who live next to us. They don't approve of it. They voted against it. We have been living here for nearly 12 years, so we can talk about everything. We like each other. They like us. . . . We saw stuff about Poles on the Internet, in the newspapers; we heard about it [anti-Polish sentiment]. We were saying all the time with my [Polish] friend [living with Krysia], 'Jesus, thank God we live in this neighbourhood which is different to what you hear', it's a neighbour-friendly area. Even a bit further away in the shops [people are friendly]. We don't feel discriminated. We didn't experience it at the time when the anti-Polish sentiment was more intense.

To put Krysia's narrative into context, Manchester had a strong remain vote (60.4 per cent). According to Krysia, her neighbours were among those who voted remain. In her narrative, she makes an indirect connection between the unchanged attitudes of her friendly neighbours and their remain vote.

Krysia's narrative about her neighbours is very similar to that five years ago, discussed in Chapter 3. It reflects an un-panicked multiculture (Noble, 2009) marked by peaceful low-key interaction between neighbours, trust and small acts of care and kindness:

> It's important that I can count on my neighbours, that they keep an eye on my house and I keep an eye on their when they are away. There is this, you know, neighbourly trust. This is very important. It is a different kind of con-viviality [*współżycie*] between us and the English neighbours. It's not like some Poles who go from one house to another and then spread gossip. You won't find it here. We go out to the garden, greet each other, ask if everything is fine, about health, I make a cake. . . . Our neighbour's wife died about three years ago so when I make some food I share it with him. When his daughter comes with children he brings us some cake. We are not interested in what goes on in their homes. You don't offload your prob-lems onto your neighbour, there is no gossiping . . . but if any help is needed, we help one another. . . . When an ambulance arrived to take Mirek [Krysia's friend and housemate] to the hospital when he was ill, I couldn't speak [English] properly because of nerves . . . so both neighbours came to help.

Conviviality in Krysia's immediate neighbourhood is socially and spatially constituted. She has developed an affectionate relationship with her immediate neighbourhood and to people who inhabit it (see also Neal et al., 2018). It offers her a safe haven and a strong sense of belonging not affected by Brexit. Everyday relations between Krysia and her neighbours play a crucial role in building this sense of belonging which is "a dynamic emotional attachment that relates people to the material and social worlds that they inhabit and experience. It is about feeling 'at home' and 'secure', but it is equally about being recognised and understood" (Wood and Waite, 2011: 201). Krysia's narrative is a good example of a thriving convivial culture that endures despite exclusionary anti-immigration rhetoric. In fact, it is possible that paradoxically these exclusionary discourses strengthen the existing conviviality. In this example, stronger bonds are formed in response to the challenges of Brexit.

"Feeling safe in a migrant neighbourhood"

Like Renia and Krysia, Oliwia, who has been living with her husband and three children in Rusholme since 2010, was aware of anti-immigrant sentiment in the run up to and after the EU referendum:

> While two weeks before the EU referendum I was convinced that the result would be to remain in the UK, a few days before the referendum I realised that it was highly likely that the result would be to leave the EU. This was based on the poll results announced on the radio, BBC Radio 4, and largely on the anti-Polish or anti-immigrant profile of the broadcasts I listened to. ... I think that anti-immigrant attitudes were prominent also before Brexit. However, the referendum has led to many discussions on this topic, including nationalist stances and tacit approval of racism.

The results of the referendum triggered a sense of fear and uncertainty about the future, feelings shared by several other interviewees:

> When the results were announced I was a bit afraid and I started to feel uncertain ... I started to think what would change and how quickly changes would happen. For the first few days I had to get used to this new and uncertain situation. I was wondering if the welcoming England would change for the worse.

In contrast to Renia's experiences, Oliwia did not experience racism or xenophobia. In fact, she told me how surprised she was when her acquaintances apologised for the referendum results and reassured her that Britain was still her home and she was welcome to stay. Nevertheless, Oliwia told me that it was important for her to hear this in the context of increasing hostility towards Polish people after the referendum. Despite some fear of anti-migrant hostility, Oliwia felt safe from racism and xenophobia in her ethnically mixed neighbourhood in Rusholme (discussed in Chapter 3) she called a 'migrant neighbourhood' – in a previous interview in 2013 she referred to it as a 'Pakistani neighbourhood'. It is worth pointing out that ethnicity was crucial in some areas of the UK, with ethnic minority areas generally more likely to vote remain in the EU referendum (Rosenbaum, 2017). Furthermore, due to its proximity to the universities, Rusholme has a large student population. Education levels have a strong link to views of migration (Ford, 2018).

Oliwia assumed that she did not experience anti-Polish sentiment possibly because she thought she did not 'look Polish'. She pointed out that because of her darker skin complexion she has often been perceived as Spanish, and sometimes as South Asian. She felt that she blended in well in her ethnically mixed area where she lived. She was much more concerned about going back to Poland because of the growing hostility to ethno-national and religious minorities in Poland (ECRI, 2015; Kornak et al., 2016). Oliwia thought she would not feel safe in Poland because of her darker skin complexion.

Not only ethnically diverse areas were considered as safe from post-Brexit racism and xenophobia. Two other research participants, Nikola and Celina, told me that they have not been negatively affected by Brexit and they felt safe living in Didsbury and Chorlton, more prosperous suburban areas of Manchester. On the contrary, they both experienced racist and xenophobic violence several years before Brexit in other parts of Manchester. This confirms my earlier argument that racism and xenophobia manifested towards Polish migrants was well-established before the Brexit vote (Rzepnikowska, 2018b). Different local contexts and temporalities may influence experiences of migrants and their relations with the local population. While the neighbourhoods with social housing mostly populated by less affluent white Britons were perceived as dangerous and marked by fear of racism, diverse and more affluent areas seemed to offer protection against racism.

Conclusion

This chapter reflected upon the narratives of three research participants who recounted their experiences of living alongside the local residents in Manchester and the wider area of Greater Manchester in the context of Brexit. Even though there are some similarities in their experiences, including the feelings of uncertainty, awareness of anti-Polish sentiment and fear of racism and xenophobia at the time of the EU referendum, there are important differences. Renia's narrative illustrated coexistence of conviviality, tensions and racism in her immediate neighbourhood situated in Greater Manchester characterised by a significant leave vote. As discussed in Chapter 3, conviviality is a dynamic and ongoing process without any guarantees. The current crisis in Brexit Britain has been marked by racism and insular nationalism (Virdee and McGeever, 2018). Renia was particularly affected by post-Brexit xeno-racism at her husband's workplace. Her case highlighted how less visible minorities can become racialised and experience racism and xenophobia, which were well-established before the Brexit vote. Racism and xenophobia were mostly discussed in the context of specific places occupied by specific people, mainly deprived neighbourhoods mostly populated by less affluent white British people (Rzepnikowska, 2018b). This highlights the importance of place, race, ethnicity and class in the discussions on conviviality and Brexit, and it raises questions of inequality and hierarchies. If convivial culture is to be sustained, it is necessary not only for individuals, but for British society as a whole to address inequalities along the lines of race, ethnicity, class and gender to facilitate new ways of thinking in the context of developing relations across difference.

In contrast, Krysia's and Oliwia's accounts reflect an "un-panicked multiculture" (Noble, 2009) marked by mostly peaceful coexistence. Krysia's narrative shows a great example of a sustained neighbourly conviviality resisting racism and xenophobia, characterised by peaceful interaction between neighbours, trust and acts of care and kindness. Her account shows the possibility of maintaining social connections and belonging in the context of Brexit. Furthermore, the example of convivial culture in Kryia's case challenges the divisive public political discourses in the Brexit era, linked with the racialised politics of English nationalism (Virdee and McGeever, 2018), which hinder the constructive engagement with difference (Heil, 2015). It shows a more resilient form of conviviality able to thrive in uncertain times. This contrasts Heil's (2015) argument that conviviality only emerges as "fragile and changing and only able to lead to *minimal* forms of sociality". The accounts discussed in this book reflect not only changing and fragile fleeting nature of conviviality, but also more meaningful forms which can be sustained over time.

The three contrasting cases discussed in this chapter show the situatedness of conviviality within the geographical, social and temporal contexts. As discussed in Chapter 2 and illustrated throughout this book, situated conviviality is: local and specific", "not something that can be replicated in a programmatic way" (Wise and Velayutham, 2014: 425). Hence, this and the previous empirical chapters contribute to the existing literature on encounters with difference by recognising the spatiality of social relations influenced by dynamics of race, ethnicity, gender and class and other categories which often intersect.

The empirical chapters in this book confirm Gilroy's (2006a 40) argument that "recognising conviviality should not signify the absence of racism" (see also Karner and Parker, 2011; Neal et al., 2018; Nowicka and Vertovec, 2014; Valluvan, 2016; Wise and Velayutham, 2014). Different forms of lived experience discussed in this book remind us that alongside racism, conflict and practices of classed and ethnicised avoidance, there is a clear evidence of often overlooked convivial cultures evolving as the time goes by, despite Brexit uncertainties. Krysia's narrative shows the possibility of building up resilience to everyday racism and anti-migrant discourses in the context of Brexit and of everyday-boundary crossings which have the potential to break through racialised and classed discourses at the local level.

6 Conclusions
The future of conviviality in Manchester and Barcelona

This book focused on convivial experiences of Polish migrant women in two cities, Manchester and Barcelona in the context of post–2004 migration. It examined under-researched relations not only between these migrants and the majority communities but also with other migrants and ethnic minorities. Despite a rapidly growing and fascinating field of academic research from various disciplines on migration from Poland, little is known about the actual convivial experiences of Polish migrant women in multicultural cities. Hence, this book showed the importance of gendered encounters with difference in often gendered city spaces. The empirical examples also showed how whiteness and Otherness are produced through various encounters with white and non-white established population. In some situations, particularly in the context of Brexit, Polish migrants may become victims of racism and xenophobia; in other contexts, as privileged white Europeans (Rzepnikowska, 2019). There are also times when they facilitate connections between people across difference. This book contributes to the existing literature on conviviality by recognising the spatiality of convivial relations which seem to be closely linked with the dynamics of race, ethnicity, gender and class. The narratives in both cities have offered complex and multidimensional accounts of living in close proximity with difference.

In this Conclusion, I discuss further the main contributions of my research and draw on my key empirical findings by reflecting on different forms of conviviality, the importance of spatio-temporal characteristics and gendered, classed and raced dynamics. I also reflect on the question of difference which has been central to this book. I finish by considering future directions by referring to my participants' reflections about the future of living together in Manchester and Barcelona.

Different forms of conviviality

The concept of conviviality has opened a new understanding of living with difference which emerges from interaction between different groups and individuals in multicultural societies. The growing interest in the concept across various disciplines in recent years indicates that conviviality emerges in many societies and reflects the importance of studying this mode of living together. Nevertheless, the tendency to focus on problematic relations obscures current debates. By the same token, idealising urban encounters disguises hierarchies of power and inequalities. This book contributes to the field of studies on conviviality by adding more empirical depth to this concept, by exploring different factors, dynamics, discourses and contexts influencing it. The empirical findings illustrate various forms of conviviality situated at particular times and places, and examples of practices that underpin it, defining thus a set of convivial cultures.

In Chapter 3, the narratives about encounters with difference in both Manchester and Barcelona where people from different backgrounds live in close residential proximity showed examples of what I defined as *neighbourly conviviality* based on fleeting but habitual encounters between neighbours, including greetings and acknowledging each other, casual conversations and neighbourly help, as well as adaptation strategies by following existing practices. Neighbourly conviviality also involves more sociable forms, including socialising with the local residents during barbecues and home visits, where cultural differences are used as a resource in convivial interaction. The narratives of some research participants, especially in Barcelona, illustrate positive, fleeting but distant relations with the local residents with preference of intimacy when it comes to private relations. However, it does not mean that these fleeting encounters are unimportant. In fact, they seem to constitute an essential part of everyday interaction in both cities and they facilitate a certain level of familiarity with each other and recognition of difference. Furthermore, they are also important because they can have a real impact on how people feel about living in an area and whether they can settle and belong. Most interviewees, especially those with families, seemed satisfied with fleeting but distant relations with their neighbours manifested through everyday recognition, greetings and small talk, and they mostly did not feel the need to closely interact with their neighbours. On the other hand, several narratives in Manchester illustrated that neighbourly conviviality may generate more meaningful forms of engagement with neighbours in situations where contact goes beyond casual greetings and fleeting encounters, contrasting with the argument in the existing literature that conviviality is limited to superficial, fleeting and casual encounters in public spaces unlikely to generate meaningful engagement with difference (Amin, 2002; Heil, 2015; Valentine, 2008).

The narratives about encounters in both cities also revealed examples of *motherly conviviality* illustrating a significant connection between motherly activities, spaces for mothers and conviviality. Schools, nurseries, breastfeeding clubs and playgroups were discussed as important spaces of encounter and interaction between mothers from a range of backgrounds. This highlights the relationship between the use of some semi-public spaces and gender roles of mothers looking after their children. Furthermore, some research participants facilitated encounters between other mothers and children across difference, as observed in Judyta's and Emila's cases in Chapter 3. Judyta's narrative also showed that more meaningful engagement with other mothers happens with particular individuals with whom they identify or share experience of migration and/or common activities.

In Chapter 4, the narratives about relations at work have also revealed various forms of *workplace conviviality*. By closely examining the narratives, I discussed a *playful and light-hearted form of conviviality* highlighting the importance and the role of humour and language in shaping convivial interaction at work. Bogusia's and Krysia's narratives in Manchester showed that humour can be used as a strategy to overcome the language and communication barrier. Their accounts showed how humour and language differences may become integral parts of everyday interaction at work facilitating not only sociality but also a sense of inclusion and bonding. While there is a lot of pressure on migrants to learn English, the example of Bogusia's co-workers learning Polish phrases illustrates a rarely discussed practice of language-accommodating practices acknowledging a minority language.

Regular interaction at work may lead to more meaningful forms of contact at work with a potential to change racialised views over time. This means that certain views held upon arrival in multicultural environments may not only be shifted but also translated into acceptance and respect for different groups and individuals and their practices. These more meaningful forms of engagement are generated in situations when contact goes beyond casual greetings and fleeting encounters between people who become familiar through habits of everyday interaction and often move beyond the workplace. These forms of engagement at work raise the importance of *friendships* made at work, which are a more meaningful form of interaction based on deeper social bonds, care and respect for difference. In the discussions on workplace friendships and other meaningful forms of contact, the interviewees hardly paid any attention to ethnic, religious, cultural, gender and other differences which often become commonplace and, as Gilroy (2006a: 40) has argued, do not "add up to discontinuities of experience or insuperable problems of communication". Dorota's account highlighted the importance of friendship with other women. Socialising with female co-workers might possibly be a way to challenge social control (O'Connor, 1992) and patriarchal practices (Andrew and Montague, 1998). Gendered workplace relations may also be shaped by the gendered nature of certain employment sectors. The temporal characteristics (the length of time spent at a particular workplace), equal status, similar age and education level, and shared work tasks and interests are among significant factors shaping workplace relations. Another important characteristic of workplace friendships is 'voluntariness' since they develop by choice (Sias and Cahill, 1998). Therefore, the characteristic of voluntariness distinguishes workplace friendships from forced encounters marked by obligatory ties discussed in Bogusia's example with reference to strained relations with the black male supervisor, marked by both power asymmetries and racialised discourse.

This takes me to my next point showing that conviviality is not free from conflict and tensions between different groups and individuals characterised by hostility, prejudice and racialisation of Others. For instance, Bogusia's narrative showed that when conflicts at work arise, whiteness can be asserted, and differences become racialised. Nevertheless, migrants may use survival strategies in a form of everyday performances of forced encounters to get by at work. I defined this as *forced conviviality* characterised by involuntary and superficial interaction. This is particularly important in the case of workplaces where workers have little choice with whom they work and where they have to obey the rules and regulations with regard to diversity and equality. Bogusia's case illustrated how forced conviviality may thrive especially in cases of segregation between jobs along gender and ethnic lines.

Discriminatory practices in the labour markets and within the workplaces may lead to a limited contact between different groups and individuals. Several research participants in Barcelona highlighted that their paths hardly crossed with non-European and non-white migrants and ethnic minorities because they worked in occupations staffed largely by Spaniards and other white European nationals. In the British context, Lucyna's and Renia's accounts showed how negative perceptions of Polish migrants, partly shaped by a damaging media and political rhetoric, contribute to tensions between co-workers, long before and after the Brexit vote. These interviewees or their relatives experienced hostile and anti-migrant attitudes despite the workplace being regulated by diversity and equality regulations aiming to ensure that the workplace environment complies with the law. Strong principles of social justice are needed to protect the achievements of everyday conviviality (Amin, 2013).

Spatio-temporal, race, ethnicity, gender and class dynamics

In discussing engagement with difference, it is vital to highlight the role of shared spaces, including the streets, educational facilities, spaces for mothers, places of worship and workplaces in bringing diverse populations together. Multi-sitedness is a significant spatialised characteristic of conviviality which may transcend a single location and the extended interaction may take place in other locations which are often connected in some way, for example, after work through socialising in bars, restaurants, at homes and in other places.

The empirical chapters showed how spatio-temporal characteristics intersect with race, gender and class dynamics, socio-economic factors, political and public debates on immigration. Several narratives demonstrated that street encounters in the context of both cities were often gendered, classed and raced (see also Rzepnikowska, 2018a). I discussed how masculine domination is reproduced in particular spaces (Koskela, 1999) and how it contributes to the disparity in equal access to public space. Paulina's example in Chapter 3 demonstrated how the council estate where she lived become territorialised by anti-social youths and how it restricted her mobility in her local area. These encounters are situated in the context of new tensions and new forms of racism experienced by Polish migrants. They take place at the time of popular anxieties over jobs, housing and welfare, and socio-economic deprivation of the inner city areas where many migrants move and where they can be racialised and constructed as the unwanted Other. Paulina's narrative also showed how street encounters might be used by migrant women to understand difference within a racialised schema and reinforce stereotypical perceptions. The gendered spatial practices of the South Asian men discussed in Paulina's case were understood as racial practices reinforcing the construction of these men as dangerous and oppressive to women.

In contrast to these less convivial street encounters, Julia's example of street conviviality in Barcelona in Chapter 3, discussed in the interview and the focus group, illustrated a lively and convivial atmosphere on the streets and squares characterised by outdoor lifestyle and gathering of people. The image portraying people dancing to the music played by the street artists in Barceloneta discussed by the focus group participants portrayed the convivial and celebratory character of the city. Even though it is argued that public gatherings constituting part of Catalan *convivència* do not necessarily lead to extended interaction (Heil, 2014), some street interactions demonstrate the emergence of conviviality based on negotiation of difference, for instance through dance, music and enjoyment by crossing boundaries through touch, which might not be possible in other everyday encounters. These findings raise the importance of moments of sociality through fleeting interaction emerging from transitory street encounters.

The focus groups in both cities also raised the importance of educational facilities for adults allowing habitual contact and engagement in common activities with people from different backgrounds. This may facilitate the opportunity to get to know each other and shift stereotypical views, although this shift might be temporary. Contrary to the street encounters discussed in the context of Manchester, classroom or discussion space may promote social relations in a fairly safe manner.

Conviviality developed and enacted within private spaces of the home has been largely under-researched. The empirical examples in my study highlighted the importance of domestic space as a potential site of conviviality in the context of home visits and domestic work. Preparing and sharing food may not only constitute the making of home (Rabikowska and Burrell, 2009), but it may also serve as an important aspect of gathering together with neighbours, mingling and developing connections. Through domestic work, private household becomes a space of contact with individuals from social groups with which migrant women previously did not have any connection. Habitual contact in home spaces between private household owners and Krysia resulted in the emergence of closer and friendly relations and a sense of acceptance across difference. While this occupation is often associated with exploitation of migrant workers, Krysia's account showed the possibilities of conviviality characterised by the creation of emotional bonds, personal interaction, acceptance and care.

Temporality of experience manifested through frequent geographical mobility and changing life circumstances may result in lack of attachment to the place and mutual engagement with people. The interviewees in Barcelona were particularly mobile, changing accommodation quite frequently, influencing their relations with the local population. On the other hand, habitual contact over an extended period of time is likely to generate familiarity and lead to possibilities of convivial interaction across difference. The research participants also highlighted the importance of time required for relationships to develop. While visible racialised ethnic difference was a subject of surprise and fascination for many arrivals in both cities, as a result of habitual encounters over a period of time, particularly in the British context, this difference often became normalised and commonplace (Wessendorf, 2014b). The longitudinal perspective adopted in my research is particularly important in highlighting the importance of time and space which are central to conviviality. In the context of Brexit, Renia's narrative showed how "everything changes" and "constantly fluctuates". Even though racism and xenophobia were not new to Renia and her husband, they had not experienced hostility in such potency before the Brexit vote. In contrast, Krysia and Oliwia experienced strengthening of social relations with the local people over time, and they both observed that this was closely linked to the areas where they lived.

The question of difference

As I argued in this book and elsewhere (Rzepnikowska, 2016b, 2018b), the perceptions of difference are often affected by the media, political and public discourses in the sending and receiving countries which often sharpen differences between different groups. As Gilroy (2004: 157) suggested,

> we are informed not only that the mutually exclusive cultures of indigenes and incomers cannot be compatible but also mistaken attempts to mix or even dwell peacefully together can bring only destruction. From this perspective, exposure to otherness is always going to be risky.

Nevertheless, examples of conviviality illustrate that ethnic differences often become integral parts of everyday interaction. This is particularly the case of Bogusia's workmates learning and using Polish phrases, Paulina's example of hosting barbecue parties for her neighbours, during which she prepared Polish food and engaged in telling them about Polish culture, and Emila's birthday parties for children from various backgrounds in her local area. While the interviewees initially discussed the difficulty in establishing connections with Catalans in Barcelona, several narratives demonstrated the possibility of transcending the linguistic barriers and the discourse of Catalan closedness through relationships with Catalan partners, participating in community projects, as well as through empathy. As seen in the narratives of Krysia (Manchester) and Irena (Barcelona), ethno-religious difference becomes less important in the context of work relations based on respect for difference, deeper social bonds and care developed over time. Boundaries along ethno-religious lines become blurred through everyday interaction in the workplace. These examples showed that ethnic differences are not necessarily a hindrance to conviviality. In fact, they become an important resource for it, permitting the possibility to be different, contrary to the assumptions that to be convivial requires sameness or conformity (Amin, 2008).

The future of conviviality in Manchester and Barcelona

Lastly, I offer some reflections of my interviewees about the future of Manchester and Barcelona. When I asked how they see these cities in the next 10–20 years, the research participants mostly thought that both cities would become more multicultural and mixed with a rapidly increasing number of inter-ethnic relationships and mixed-race children. Many also thought that residents would become more used to various forms of difference. They noticed many new homes being built and restored in their neighbourhoods, with attractive areas for interaction offering optimistic prospects in both cities. This raises the importance of urban planning in facilitating conviviality and the creation of pedestrian-friendly and safe neighbourhoods (Wood et al., 2010) with accessible spaces welcoming people and encouraging convivial interaction (Fincher, 2003). However, material settings might not be sufficient to create spaces for conviviality (Nowicka and Vertovec, 2014), especially when encounters are marked by unequal power relations. Encouraging active participation of migrants in the social life of the neighbourhoods, for example, during *fiestas de barrios* (neighbourhood festivities) in Barcelona could help break the stereotypes and divisions between the established local population and migrants in Barcelona.

In several narratives about the future of both cities time was seen as a crucial characteristic shaping future social relations. Paulina's narrative highlights the importance of the temporal aspect influencing her perceptions of difference and relations with others:

> I think that I will not pay as much attention [to difference] in the future because I will adjust [*bedę już zaklimatyzowana*]. I think [Manchester] will still be multicultural ... now everything has been new to me, because they only opened the border in 2004.

While many believed that both cities would be more ethnically mixed, they stressed the importance of preserving their own culture. As a result of her fascination with mixed couples, Maryla pointed out she would like to have a multicultural household without a need to give up her own culture. Oliwia expressed her concerns about Polish children who "will lose their culture" as a result of their parents speaking English to them and, what she called, language "shortcuts" influenced by English language manifested through a common practice of combining Polish and English: 'Ponglish' (see also Nowicka, 2012). Nevertheless, she thought that living together in diverse environments and preserving own culture might and should be possible. She referred to the example of the Pakistani communities in Manchester. Similarly, Nina from Barcelona stressed the importance of preserving cultural difference and passing it on to the next generations and, at the same time, openness to difference and mixing:

> Everybody could learn something from others but not necessarily forgetting about where I come from. As in our example, I don't want my children to

forget they are from Poland, that they have their roots in Poland, but at the same time I want them to be open. If they have a partner from a different country it would be nice, but it would be also nice if they remembered that part of them is from somewhere else and they could pass this on, although in a mixed version, because there will be two cultures, not necessarily blurred but in a symbiosis.

These accounts raise the importance of negotiating difference which has been at the heart of my discussions about conviviality permitting the possibility to be different. They reflect Sennett's (1977: 255) argument that people "can act together without the compulsion to be the same".

The majority of the research participants in Barcelona expressed their uncertainty about the future of the city as a result of the economic crisis which some thought might result in a fear of anti-immigrant attitudes in the nearest future. A few feared the negative rhetoric observed in the British context. Another major concern with regard to the future of Barcelona was the question of Catalan independence. Like many other research participants, Ela feared that she would be less accepted if Catalonia became independent:

In twenty years Catalonia might be a separate country.... I'm afraid that then they would become more closed to people from the outside, the foreigners, and I am the one [laugh], who on top of everything does not speak Catalan, although I plan to learn it, but in any case, I will always feel more confident speaking Spanish, so from my point of view it would be better if Catalonia remained as part of Spain, because this would mean better acceptance of the people from the outside.

These concerns about the future raise the importance of structural socioeconomic and political factors influencing social relations. The idea of Catalan identity, often discussed in terms of Catalan independence, was viewed by most interviewees as synonymous with anti-immigration attitudes, although the research participants in Barcelona hardly witnessed these types of attitudes in contrast to the experiences of the interviewees in the British context. In fact, existing research shows that Catalan identity is related to lower levels of negative attitudes towards immigrants (Rodon and Franco-Guillén, 2014). Nevertheless, as Conversi and Jeram (2017: 63) warn,

one should be cautious about the possibility that, if the dialectic relationship between Spain and Catalonia were to be broken through secession, the successor Catalan state may reconsider the relationship between majority and minority cultures as has occurred in other historical instances of secessions.

In terms of Catalan language, migrants are expected to learn it or get excluded if they fail to do so (Pujolar, 2009). This poses questions with reference to multilingualism in Barcelona. Many research participants in Barcelona suggested that more encouraging and inclusive ways to learn Catalan would help transcend the communication difficulties. These complex sociolinguistic dynamics require further attention and could be addressed in future policy and research.

The research participants re-interviewed in 2017/18 in Manchester were particularly aware about anti-immigration and populist climate growing in the UK. As seen in Chapter 5, Renia highlighted the use of xenophobic and populist arguments by some politicians and tabloid press influencing people's views about migrants. Her narrative was marked by uncertainty about the future not only regarding her rights after Brexit, but also future relations with the local people. These concerns are particularly relevant in the times when "racism has become normalized in both elite political discourse and practice and everyday life, dramatically diminishing the spaces for Britain's racialized minorities to breathe and live life free from hate" (Virdee and McGeever, 2018: 1811). This climate of uncertainty, fear and resentment towards migrants, as well as a deeply-rooted nostalgia for the British Empire (Gilroy, 2004) pose a significant challenge to conviviality. EU migrants might experience further structural disadvantage and discrimination as their rights and entitlements are rewritten following Brexit (Benson and Lewis, 2019). However, it is not all bleak. Krysia's narrative shows a great example of a sustained neighbourly convivial culture resisting racism and xenophobia in post–Brexit-vote Britain. This convivial culture is characterised by peaceful interaction between neighbours, trust and acts of care and kindness. Furthermore, recent study findings show a positive shift in attitudes across the political and social spectrum since the Brexit vote (Ipsos MORI, 2017; Ford, 2018). They show that people have become more positive about immigration in the last few years, although the majority still want immigration reduced. It is important to consider the ageing British society and decreasing numbers of EU migrants (ONS, 2018), many of whom do the jobs which are unpopular among native workers. Therefore, after Brexit, the UK will still need migrant workers to fill in labour shortages.

There are more grounds for optimism in the context of an everyday multicultural reality. Several interviewees in Manchester and Barcelona mentioned the discourse of *peaceful coexistence* in the future of both cities. Aldona in Manchester hoped that the negative perceptions towards Polish migrants would change in favour of peaceful coexistence which carries a notion of 'common humanity' also present in several other narratives in both cities:

*Interviewer: You mentioned peaceful coexistence [*pokojowe współistnienie*],
what do you mean by that?*

Aldona: It means that, for example, when I tell somebody that I am Polish, he would not speak straight away with a very clear language [laugh], but would try to approach me as a human being, right? It is about not imposing stereotypes straight away, right? To try to get to know the person before making comments that he or she is like this or like that.

Weronika in Barcelona and Maryla in Manchester see peaceful coexistence as an outcome of learning about and getting to know the Other:

I think that peaceful coexistence requires respect towards another person and to look beyond his or her nationality or religion. Once there is respect and patience to get to know and to listen to this otherness [inność] then this will be a start and the beginning of a way to learn, because this is like when a dog sees a stranger it starts barking because it is terrified with a new situation and it prefers to warn you 'listen, this is my territory, stay away' and I think it is the same with people. When we don't know somebody, we start acting aggressively. But if we start getting to know each other we will realise that this is not so difficult. We will start getting used to the 'new'.

(Weronika)

Learning about different cultures and people enriches us and offers new experiences. You become more open. ... Just because someone eats with their hands doesn't mean they are inferior. It's about learning from and about others, about how they live, how they were brought up and about their customs and traditions. Because once you get to know it, it is no longer seen as a threat or something we can't deal with. ... It doesn't matter that I wear a headscarf. I am still the same person.

(Maryla)

These examples remind us that encounters with difference bring with it unavoidable exposure to the unknown and the stranger. Nevertheless, habitual encounters may help break some barriers, enable the learning process which then may enable individuals to rethink their perceptions of others, disrupt preconceived ideas, racial stereotypes and facilitate more positive ways of living together.

The examples of quotidian practices of social interaction I discussed in this book demonstrate the possibility of everyday-boundary crossings (not without tensions) which have the potential to break through classed, gendered and racialised discourses at an individual level. Furthermore, it is necessary not only for individuals, but for societies as a whole to address social inequalities and to facilitate new ways of thinking in the context of developing relations across difference.

Bibliography

Abrams, P. (1982) *Historical Sociology*. Shepton Mallet: Open Books.

Ahmed, S. (2004) 'Declarations of whiteness: The non-performativity of anti-racism', *Borderlands*, 3(2): 1–16. www.borderlands.net.au/vol3no2_2004/ahmed_declarations.htm.

Alarcón, A. and Garzón, L. (2013) 'Children of immigrants and social mobility in officially bilingual societies: The case of Catalonia', *Spanish in Context*, 10(1): 92–113.

Alén Garabato, C. (1999) 'Un país, una lengua, unos hablantes ... representaciones del catalán en los estudiantes de la Universidad de Santiago de Compostela', in M. T. García Sabell Tormo, M. Míguez Pan, E. Montero Cartelle, M. E. Vázquez Bujan, J. M. Viña Liste (eds.), *Homenaxe ó profesor Camilo Flores*. Santiago de Compostela: Servicio de Publicacións da Universidade de Santiago de Compostela, 3–16.

Alexander, C., Edwards, R. and Temple, B. (2007) 'Contesting cultural communities: Language, ethnicity and citizenship in Britain', *Journal of Ethnic and Migration Studies*, 33(5): 783–800.

Ali, S., Campbell, K., Branley, D. and James, R. (2004) 'Politics, identity and research', in C. Seale (ed.), *Researching Society and Culture*. 2nd edn. London: Sage, 21–32.

Amin, A. (2002) 'Ethnicity and the multicultural city: Living with diversity', *Environment and Planning A*, 34(6): 959–980.

Amin, A. (2008) 'Collective culture and urban public space', *City*, 12(1): 5–24.

Amin, A. (2010) *Cities and the Ethic of Care for the Stranger*. Joint Joseph Rowntree Foundation, University of York Annual Lecture, 1–15. www.jrf.org.uk/report/cities-and-ethic-care-stranger.

Amin, A. (2012) *Land of Strangers*. Cambridge: Polity Press.

Amin, A. (2013) 'Land of strangers', *Identities: Global Studies in Culture and Power*, 20 (1): 1–8.

Amrith, M. and Sahraoui, N. (2018) *Gender, Work and Migration*. London: Routledge.

Anderson, B., Ruhs, M., Rogaly, B. and Spencer, S. (2006) *Fair Enough? Central and East European Migrants in Low-Wage Employment in the UK*. York: Joseph Rowntree Foundation/COMPAS.

Andrew, A. and Montague, J. (1998) 'Women's friendship at work', *Women's Studies International Forum*, 21(4): 355–361.

Anthias, F. and Yuval-Davis, N. (1983) 'Contextualising feminism: Gender, ethnic & class divisions', *Feminist Review*, 15: 62–75.

Anthias, F. and Yuval-Davis, N. (1992) *Racialized Boundaries: Race, Nation, Gender, Colour and Class and Anti-racist Struggle*. London and New York: Routledge.

Arnal Sarasa, M. D. (1998) *Inmigrantes polacos en España. El camino como concepto teórico para el estudio de la adaptación*. PhD. Universidad Complutense de Madrid.

Ashe, S. and Nazroo, J. (2017) *Equality, Diversity and Racism in the Workplace: A Qualitative Analysis of the 2015 Race at Work Survey*. http://hummedia.manchester.ac.uk/institutes/code/research/raceatwork/ Equality-Diversity-and-Racism-in-the-Workplace-Full-Report.pdf.

Back, L. (2015) 'Losing culture or finding superdiversity?', *Discover Society*, 20. http://discoversociety.org/2015/05/05/losing-culture-or-finding-superdiversity-2/.

Back, L. and Sinha, S. (2016) 'Multicultural conviviality in the midst of racism's ruins', *Journal of Intercultural Studies*, 37(5): 517–532.

Balibrea, M. P. (2001) 'Urbanism, culture and the post-industrial city: Challenging the "Barcelona model"', *Journal of Spanish Cultural Studies*, 2(2): 187–210.

Barbería, J. L. (2008) 'Los niños que Hitler robó. Huérfanos de la barbarie nazi', in *Polonesos a Barcelona. Un munt d'histories*. Barcelona: Ajuntament de Barcelona, 24–31.

Barcelona City Council (2010) *Pla Barcelona Interculturalitat* [Barcelona Interculturality Plan]. www.bcn.cat/novaciutadania/pdf/es/PlaBCNInterculturalitatCast130510_es.pdf.

Barcelona City Council (2012a) *Població estrangera a Barcelona. Informació Sociodemografica, Gener 2012*. www.bcn.cat/novaciutadania/pdf/ca/estudis/pob_estrangera_2012.pdf.

Barcelona City Council (2012b) *Padró Municipal d'Habitants. Gener 2012*. Departament d'Estadística. www.btv.cat/btvnoticies/wp-content/ftp_btvnoticies/2012/agost/poblacio_estrangera/.

Barcelona City Council (2015a) *La població estrangera a Barcelona. Gener 2015*. www.bcn.cat/estadistica/catala/dades/inf/pobest/pobest15/pobest15.pdf.

Barcelona City Council (2015b) *Lectura del Padrón Municipal de Habitantes. Evolución de la población extranjera de Barcelona 2006–2015*. Departament d'Estadística. www.bcn.cat/estadistica/castella/dades/inf/pobest/pobest15/part1/t13.htm.

Barrett, G. A. and McEvoy, D. (2006) 'The evolution of Manchester's "Curry Mile": From Suburban shopping street to ethnic destination', in D. Kaplan and W. Li (eds.), *Landscapes of the Ethnic Economy*. Lanham, MD: Rowman and Littlefield, 193–207.

Barrett, J. R. and Roediger, D. (1997) 'Inbetween peoples: Race, nationality and the "new immigrant" working class', *Journal of American Ethnic History*, 16(3): 3–44.

Bell, D. and Valentine, G. (1997) *Consuming Geographies: We Are Where We Eat*. New York: Routledge.

Benson, M. and Lewis, C. (2019) 'Brexit, British People of Colour in the EU-27 and everyday racism in Britain and Europe', *Ethnic and Racial Studies*, doi:10.1080/01419870.2019.1599134.

Botterill, K. and Burrell, K. (2018) '(In)visibility, privilege and the performance of whiteness in Brexit Britain: Polish migrants in Britain's shifting migration regime', *Environment and Planning C: Politics and Space*, 37(1): 23–28.

Botterill, K., Hopkins, P., Isakjee, A., Lorne, C., Nagel, C. Finlay, R. and Nayak, A. (2019) 'Brexit, race and migration', *Environment and Planning C: Politics and Space*, 37(1): 3–40.

Bottero, W. (2009) 'Class in the 21st century', in K. P. Sveinsson (ed.), *Who Cares About the White Working Class*. London: Runnymede Trust.

Bowman, C. G. (1993) 'Street harassment and the informal ghettoization of women', *Harvard Law Review*, 106(3): 517–580.

Boyd, R. (2006) 'The value of civility?', *Urban Studies*, 43: 863–878.

Bridge, G. (2002) 'The neighbourhood and social networks', *CNR Paper*, 4. www.urbancenter.utoronto.ca/pdfs/curp/CNR_Neighbourhoods-Social-N.pdf.

British Council (2013) *Culture at Work: The Value of Intercultural Skills in the Workplace.* www.britishcouncil.org/sites/britishcouncil.uk2/files/culture-at-work-report-v2.pdf.

Buchowski, M. (2006) 'The specter of orientalism in Europe: From exotic other to stigmatized brother', *Anthropological Quarterly*, 79(3): 463–482.

Burnett, J. (2017) 'Racial violence and the Brexit state', *Race and Class*, 58(4): 85–97.

Burrell, K. (2009) *Polish Migration to the UK in the 'New' European Union: After 2004.* Farnham: Ashgate.

Byrne, B. (2003) 'Reciting the self: Narrative representations of the self in qualitative interviews', *Feminist Theory*, 4(1): 29–49.

Byrne, B. (2006) *White Lives: The Interplay of 'Race', Class and Gender in Everyday Life.* London: Routledge.

Byrne, B. (2017) 'Testing times: The place of the citizenship test in the UK immigration regime and new citizens' responses to it', *Sociology*, 51(2): 323–338.

Byrne, B. and De Tona, C. (2013) 'Multicultural desires? Parental negotiation of multiculture and difference in choosing secondary schools for their children', *Sociological Review*, 62(3): 475–493.

Çağlar, A. and Glick Schiller, N. (2018) *Migrants & City-Making: Dispossession, Displacement, and Urban Regeneration.* Durham and London: Duke University Press.

Cantle, T. (2001) *Report of the Independent Community Cohesion Review Team.* London: Home Office. http://resources.cohesioninstitute.org.uk/Publications/Documents/Document/DownloadDocumentsFile.aspx?recordId=96&file=PDFversion.

Carling, J., Erdal, M. B. and Ezzati, R. (2014) 'Beyond the insider–outsider divide immigration research', *Migration Studies*, 2(1): 36–54.

Castro, A. (1948) *España en su historia: cristianos, moros y judíos.* Buenos Aires: Editorial Losada S.A.

Castro, A. (1971) *The Spaniards: An Introduction to their History* (trans. by W. F. King and S. Margaretten). Los Angeles and London: University of California Press.

CBOS (Centrum Badania Opinii Społecznej) [Centre for Public Opinion Research in Poland] (2007) *Społeczna percepcja przemocy werbalnej i mowy nienawiści.* www.mowanienawisci.info/wp-content/uploads/2014/04/K_074_07.pdf.

Cesari, J. and DeWan, P. (2006) *Securitization and Religious Divides in Europe: Islamophobia in Western Europe.* Project Report. Unset.

Climent-Ferrando, V. (2012) *Immigration in Catalonia. In Search of a Public Philosophy.* Barcelona: Interdisciplinary Research Group on Immigration. www.eurac.edu/en/research/autonomies/minrig/Documents/ALIAS/immigration_Catalonia_climent.pdf.

Clua i Fainé, M. (2012) 'Multiculturalism, identities and national uncertainties in Southwest Europe: The rise of xenophobia and populism in Catalonia (Spain)', *EASA Workshop, Working Papers, 3.* https://scholarworks.umass.edu/chess_easa/3.

CoDE (2013) *Geographies of Diversity in Manchester. Local Dynamics of Diversity: Evidence from the 2011 Census.* The University of Manchester: Centre on Dynamics of Ethnicity. www.ethnicity.ac.uk/census/local/CoDE-Manchester-Geographies-Of-Diversity-Census-Briefing.pdf.

Cohen, P. (1988) 'The perversions of inheritance: Studies in the making of multi-racist Britain', in P. Cohen and H. S. Bains (eds.), *Multi-Racist Britain.* London: Macmillan Education, 9–118.

Colectivo Ioé (1998) *Inmigración y trabajo: trabajadores inmigrantes en el sector de la construcción: polacos y marroquíes en Madrid y Barcelona.* www.colectivoioe.org/uploads/bb572a2da1ba0023a2283ee7287e8a796f4d1afb.pdf.

Collier, J. and Collier, M. (1967) *Visual Anthropology: Photography as a Research Tool*. Albuquerque: University of New Mexico Press.

Conversi, D. and Jeram, S. (2017) 'Despite the crisis: The resilience of intercultural nationalism in Catalonia', *International Migration*, 55(2): 53–67.

Cook, J., Dwyer, P. and Waite, L. (2011a) 'The experiences of accession 8 migrants in England: Motivations, work and agency', *International Migration*, 49(2): 54–79.

Cook, J., Dwyer, P. and Waite, L. (2011b) '"Good relations" among neighbours and workmates? The everyday encounters of accession 8 migrants and established communities in urban England', *Population, Place and Space*, 17(6): 727–741.

Council of Europe (2011) *Barcelona: Results of the Intercultural Cities Index*. Intercultural Cities: Joint Action of the Council of Europe and of the European Commission, 9 August, 1–12. www.coe.int/t/dg4/cultureheritage/culture/Cities/Index/Barcelona_en.pdf.

Council of Europe (2017) *Results of the Intercultural City Index: Barcelona*. https://rm.coe.int/16802ff6f2.

Crenshaw, K. (1994) 'Mapping the margins: Intersectionality, identity politics and violence against women of color', in M. A. Fineman and R. Mykitiuk (eds.), *The Public Nature of Private Violence*. London: Routledge, 93–118.

D'Angelo, A. and Ryan, L. (2011) 'Sites of socialisation: Polish parents and children in London schools', *Przegląd Polonijny*, 37(1): 237–258.

Darlington, Y. and Scott, D. (2002) *Qualitative Research in Practice: Stories from the Field*. Buckingham: Open University Press.

Datta, A. (2009) 'Places of everyday cosmopolitanism: East-European construction workers in London', *Environment and Planning A*, 41(2): 350–370.

Day, K. (1999) 'Embassies and sanctuaries: Women's experiences of race and fear in public space', *Environment and Planning D*, 17: 307–328.

Degen, M. M. (2008) *Sensing Cities: Regenerating Public Life in Barcelona and Manchester*. London and New York: Routledge.

Denis, M. and Matas Pla, M. (2002) *Entrecruzar culturas: Competencia intercultural y estrategias didácticas*. Brussels: De Boeck & Lacier.

DiAngelo, R. (2011) 'White fragility', *The International Journal of Critical Pedagogy*, 3(3): 54–70.

Douglas, M. (1984) *Food in the Social Order: Studies of Food and Festivities in Three American Communities*. New York: Russell Sage Foundation.

Drinkwater, S., Eade, J. and Garapich, M. (2006) 'Poles apart? EU enlargement and the labour market outcomes of immigrants in the UK', *Discussion Papers in Economics*. www.surrey.ac.uk/economics/files/apaperspdf/2006_DP17-06.pdf.

Duda-Mikulin, E. A. (2018a) *"I Love the UK But it Broke My Heart and I Will Leave": Speculating About Brexodus*. https://genderplaceandculture.wordpress.com/2018/03/05/post-4-of-gpc25-i-love-the-uk-but-it-broke-my-heart-and-i-will-leave-speculating-about-brexodus-by-eva-duda-mikulin/.

Duda-Mikulin, E. A. (2018b) *EU Migrant Workers, Brexit and Precarity: Polish Women's Perspectives From Inside the UK*. Bristol: Policy Press.

Dustmann, C. and Frattini, T. (2014) 'The fiscal effects of immigration to the UK', *The Economic Journal*, 124(580): 593–643.

Duvell, F. (2004) 'Polish undocumented immigrants, regular high-skilled workers and entrepreneurs in the UK', *Institute for Social Studies Working Paper*, 54: 1–28.

Dyer, R. (1997) *White: Essays on Race and Culture*. London: Routledge.

Dziekan, M. (2011) 'History and culture of Polish Tatars', in K. Górak-Sosnowska (ed.), *Muslims in Poland and Eastern Europe Widening the European Discourse on Islam.* Warsaw: University of Warsaw, 27–39.

Eade, J., Drinkwater, S. and Garapich, M. P. (2006) *Class and Ethnicity – Polish Migrants in London.* University of Surrey. www.surrey.ac.uk/cronem/files/POLISH_FINAL_RE SEARCH_REPORT_WEB.pdf.

ECRI [European Commission against Racism and Intolerance] (2015) *Raport ECRI Dotyczący Polski.* www.coe.int/t/dghl/monitoring/ecri/Country-bycountry/Poland/POL-CbC-V-2015-20-POL.pdf/.

ECRI (2016) *ECRI Report on the United Kingdom.* www.coe.int/t/dghl/monitoring/ecri/Countryby-country/United_Kingdom/GBR-CbC-V-2016-038-ENG.pdf/.

England, K. V. L. (1994) 'Getting personal: Reflexivity, positionality, and feminist research', *The Professional Geographer*, 46(1): 80–89.

Erel, U. (2009) *Migrant Women Transforming Citizenship: Life-Stories From Britain and Germany.* Aldershot: Ashgate.

Erickson, B. (2011) 'Utopian virtues: Muslim neighbors, ritual sociality, and the politics of convivència', *American Ethnologist*, 38(1): 114–131.

Escandell, X. and Ceobanu, A. M. (2009) 'When contact with immigrants matters: Threat, interethnic attitudes and foreigner exclusionism in Spain's Comunidades Autónomas', *Ethnic and Racial Studies*, 32(1): 44–69.

Estlund, C. L. (2003) *Working Together: How Workplace Bonds Strengthen a Diverse Democracy.* New York: Oxford University Press.

Falzon, M. (2009) 'Introduction: Multi-sited ethnography: Theory, praxis and locality in contemporary research', in M. Fazon (ed.), *Multi-Sited Ethnography: Theory, Praxis and Locality in Contemporary Research.* Ashgate: Farnham, 1–24.

Favell, A. (2008) 'The new face of east-west migration in Europe', *Journal of Ethnic and Migration Studies*, 34(5): 701–716.

Favell, A. and Nebe, T. M. (2009) 'Internal and external movers: East-West migration and the impact of EU enlargement', in E. Recchi and A. Favell (eds.), *Pioneers of European Integration: Citizenship and Mobility in the EU.* Cheltenham: Edward Elgar, 205–223.

Fenster, T. (2005) 'The right to the gendered city: Different forms of belonging in everyday life', *Journal of Gendered Studies*, 14(3): 217–231.

Fincher, R. (2003) 'Planning for cities of diversity, difference and encounter', *Australian Planner*, 40(1): 55–58.

Fomina, J. and Kucharczyk, J. (2016) 'Populism and protest in Poland', *Journal of Democracy*, 27(4): 58–68.

Fong, E. and Isajiw, W. (2000) 'Determinants of friendship choices in multiethnic society', *Sociological Forum*, 15(2): 249–271.

Ford, R. (2018) *How Have Attitudes to Immigration Changed Since Brexit?* http://ukandeu.ac.uk/how-have-attitudes-to-immigration-changed-since-brexit/.

Ford, R. and Goodwin, M. (2018) 'Britain after Brexit: A nation divided', *Journal of Democracy*, 28(1): 17–30.

Fortier, A. (2008) *Multicultural Horizons: Diversity and the Limits of the Civil Nation.* London: Routledge.

Fox, J. E. (2013) 'The uses of racism: Whitewashing new Europeans in the UK', *Ethnic and Racial Studies*, 36(11): 1871–1889.

Fox, J. E., Moroşanu, L. and Szilassy, E. (2012) 'The racialization of the new European migration to the UK', *Sociology*, 46(4): 680–695.

Fox, J. E., Moroşanu, L. and Szilassy, E. (2015) 'Denying discrimination: Status, "race", and the whitening of Britain's new Europeans', *Journal of Ethnic and Migration Studies*, 41(5): 729–748.

Frankenberg, F. (1993) *White Women Race Matters: The Social Construction of Whiteness*. Minneapolis: University of Minnesota Press.

Gampel, B. (1992) 'Jews, Christians, and Muslims in medieval Iberia: "Convivencia" through the eyes of sephardic Jews', in V. B. Mann, T. F. Glick and J. D. Dodds (eds.), *Convivencia: Jews, Muslims, and Christians in Medieval Spain*. New York: George Braziller, 11–37.

Ganga, D. and Scott, S. (2006) 'Cultural "insiders" and the issue of positionality in qualitative migration research: Moving "across" and moving "along" researcher-participant divides', *Forum: Qualitative Social Research*, 7(3).

Garapich, M. (2008) 'Odyssean refugees, migrants and power: Construction of the "other" within the Polish community in the United Kingdom', in D. Reed-Danahay and C. Brettell (eds.), *Citizenship, Political Engagement and Belonging: Immigrants in Europe and the United States*. New Brunswick and London: Rutgers University Press, 124–144.

Garner, S. (2009) 'Home truths: The white working class and the racialization of social housing', in K. P. Sveinsson (ed.), *Who Cares about the White Working Class*. London: Runnymede Trust, 45–50.

Gawlewicz, A. (2014) 'Language and translation strategies in researching migrant experience of difference from the position of migrant researcher', *Qualitative Research*, 11: 1–16.

Gawlewicz, A. (2016) 'Beyond openness and prejudice: The consequences of migrant encounters with difference', *Environment and Planning A*, 48(2): 256–272.

Gazeta.pl Forum (2018) *Biali Murzyni*. http://dyskusje24.pl/szukaj/forum/biali+murzyni.

Generalitat de Catalunya (2009) *El Govern promou la campanya institucional de sensibilització 'Som Catalunya. País de Convivència'*. https://govern.cat/salapremsa/notes-premsa/1837/govern-promou-campanya-institucional-sensibilitzacio-catalunya-pais-convivencia.

Gilroy, P. (1987) *There Aint No Black in the Union Jack*. London: Hutchinson.

Gilroy, P. (2004) *After Empire: Melancholia or Convivial Culture?* London: Routledge.

Gilroy, P. (2006a) 'Multiculture in times of war: An inaugural lecture given at the London School of Economics', *Critical Quarterly*, 48(4): 27–45.

Gilroy, P. (2006b) 'Colonial crimes and convivial cultures', *Rethinking Nordic Colonialism Exhibition*. Keynote Speech. www.rethinking-nordic-colonialism.org/files/pdf/ACT2/ESSAYS/Gilroy.pdf.

Gilroy, P. (2008) 'Melancholia or conviviality: The politics of Belonging in Britain', in S. Davison and J. Rutherford (eds.), *Race, Identity and Belonging: A Soundings Collection*. London: Lawrence and Wishart, 48–59.

Giménez Romero, C. and Lorés Sánchez, N. (2007) 'Convivencia. Conceptualización y sugerencias para la praxis', *Inmigración y gobierno local: experiencias y retos*, 77–100 www.cidob.org/content/download/6416/64398/version/2/file/08_gimenez_cast.pdf.

Glick Schiller, N. and Çağlar, A. (2011) *Locating Migration: Rescaling Cities and Migrants*. New York: Cornell University Press.

Glick Schiller, N. and Çağlar, A. (2016) 'Displacement, emplacement and migrant newcomers: Rethinking urban sociabilities within multiscalar power', *Identities*, 23(1): 17–34.

Glick Schiller, N., Çağlar, A. and Guldbrandsen, T. C. (2006) 'Beyond the ethnic lens: Locality, globality, and born-again incorporation', *American Ethnologist*, 33(4): 612–633.

Glick Schiller, N., Darieva, T., Gruner-Domic, S. (2011) 'Defining cosmopolitan sociability in a transnational age. An introduction', *Ethnic and Racial Studies*, 34(3): 399–418.

Glick Schiller, N. and Schmidt, G. (2016) 'Envisioning place: Urban socialities within time, space and multiscalar power', *Identities: Global Studies in Culture and Power*, 23(1): 1–16.

Glick, T. F. (1992) 'Convivencia: An Introductory Note', in V. B. Mann, T. F. Glick, and J. D. Dodds (eds.), *Convivencia: Jews, Muslims, and Christians in Medieval Spain*. New York: George Braziller, 1–10.

González Leandri, R. (2003) 'Wizerunek polskiej imigracji w Hiszpanii', in E. González Martínez and M. Nalewajko (eds.), *Hiszpania-Polska spotkania*. Warszawa: Wydawnictwo Neriton, 169–177.

González Yanci, M. P. and Aguilera Arilla, M. J. (1996) 'Los polacos en los nuevos flujos inmigratorios en España: una aceptación social diferente', *Espacio, Tiempo y Forma*, Serie VI, *Geografía*, 9: 73–91.

Górak-Sosnowska, K. (2011) 'Muslims in Europe: Different communities, one discourse? Adding the Central and Eastern European perspective', in K. Górak-Sosnowska (ed.), *Muslims in Poland and Eastern Europe: Widening the European Discourse on Islam*. Warsaw: University of Warsaw, 12–26.

Grabowska-Lusińska, I. and Okólski, M. (2008) 'Migracja z Polski po 1 maja 2004 r.: jej intensywność i kierunki geograficzne oraz alokacja migrantów na rynkach pracy krajów Unii Europejskiej', *Centre of Migration Research Working Paper*, 33(91): 1–139.

Grabowska-Lusińska, I. and Okólski, M. (2009) *Emigracja ostatnia?* Warsaw: Scholar.

Graham, E. E. (1995) 'The involvement of sense of humor in the development of social relationships', *Communication Reports*, 8(2): 158–169.

Graham, E. E., Papa, M. J. and Brooks, G. P. (1992) 'Functions of humor in conversation: Conceptualization and measurement', *Western Journal of Communication*, 56(2): 161–183.

Grasseni, C. (2009) *Developing Skill, Developing Vision*. New York and Oxford: Berghahn.

Gray, B. (2008) 'Putting emotion and reflexivity to work in researching migration', *Sociology*, 42(5): 935–952.

Griffin, A. and May, V. (2012) 'Narrative analysis and interpretative phenomenological analysis' in C. Seale (ed.), *Researching Society and Culture*. London: Sage, 441–458.

Grzymała-Kazłowska, A. (2007) *Konstruowanie innego. Wizerunki imigrantow w Polsce*. Warszawa: Wydawnictwo Uniwersytetu Warszawskiego.

Grzymała-Kazłowska, A. and Okólski, M. (2003) 'Influx and integration of migrants in Poland in the early XXI century', *Prace Migracyjne*, 50: 1–51.

Guma, T. and Dafydd Jones, R. (2019) '"Where are we going to go now?" European Union migrants' experiences of hostility, anxiety, and (non-) belonging during Brexit, *Population, Space and Place*, 25(2): 1–10.

Gutiérrez Rodríguez, E. (2010) *Migration, Domestic Work and Affect: A Decolonial Approach on Value and the Feminization of Labor*. London and New York: Routledge.

Hage, G. (2014) 'Continuity and change in Australian racism', *Journal of Intercultural Studies*, 35(3): 232–237.

Haque, Z. (2017) *Racism and Inequality: The Truth about Brexit*. www.runnymedetrust.org/blog/immigration-racism-and-inequality.

Haraway, D. J. (1988) 'Situated knowledges: The science question in feminism and the privilege of partial perspective', *Feminist Studies*, 14(3): 575–599.

Harding, S. (1987) 'Introduction', in S. Harding (ed.), *Feminism and Methodology*. Bloomington: Indiana University Press, 1–14.

Harries, B. (2014) 'We need to talk about race', *Sociology*, 48(6): 1107–1122.

Harries, B., Byrne, B., Rhodes, J. and Wallace, S. (2018) 'Diversity in place: Narrations of diversity in an ethnically mixed, urban area', *Journal of Ethnic and Migration Studies*, doi:10.1080/1369183X.2018.1480998.

Harris, C., Jackson, L., Piekut, A. and Valentine, G. (2017) 'Attitudes towards the "stranger": Negotiating encounters with difference in the UK and Poland', *Social & Cultural Geography*, 18(1): 16–33.

Harris, C. and Valentine, G. (2016) 'Encountering difference in the workplace: Superficial contact, underlying tensions and group rights', *Tijdschrift voor economische en sociale geografie*, 107(5): 582–595.

Heil, T. (2014) 'Are neighbours alike? Practices of conviviality in Catalonia and Casamance', *European Journal of Cultural Studies*, 17(4): 452–470.

Heil, T. (2015) 'Conviviality: (Re)negotiating minimal consensus', in S. Vertovec (ed.), *Routledge International Handbook of Diversity Studies*. Oxon and New York: Routledge, 317–324.

Hellermann, C. and Stanek, M. (2006) 'Estudios sobre la inmigración de Europa Central y Oriental en España y Portugal', *Papeles del Este*, 11: 1–20. www.geps.es/uploads/tx_geps/041_PAPE0606120008A.pdf.

Hellgren, Z. (2016) *Immigrants' Perceptions on Integration in Two Institutional Frameworks: Sweden and Spain*. Final Project Report. www.upf.edu/documents/3329791/0/Hellgren+Integration+project+report/43ca249d-03e6-40ae-babd-67737d91f6fc.

HESA [Higher Education Statistics Agency] (2015) *Top Ten Other European Union Countries of Domicile in 2013/14 for HE Student Enrolments by Location of HE*. www.hesa.ac.uk/free-statistics.

Holmes, J. (2006) 'Sharing a laugh: Pragmatic aspects of humour and gender in the workplace', *Journal of Pragmatics*, 38(1): 26–50.

Holmes, J. and Marra, M. (2002) 'Humour as a discursive boundary marker in social interaction', in A. Duszak (ed.), *Us and Others: Social Identities Across Languages, Discourses and Cultures*. Amsterdam and Philadelphia: John Benjamins, 377–400.

Hopkins, P. E. (2009) 'Responding to the "crisis of masculinity": The perspectives of young Muslim men from Glasgow and Edinburgh, Scotland', *Gender, Place & Culture: A Journal of Feminist Geography*, 16(3): 299–312.

Ignatiev, N. (1995) *How the Irish Became White*. New York and London: Routledge.

Ilahi, N. (2009) 'Gendered contestations: An analysis of street harassment in Cairo and its implications for womens access to public spaces surfacing', *An Interdisciplinary Journal for Gender in the Global South*, 2(1): 83–89.

Imre, A. (2005) 'Whiteness in post-socialist Eastern Europe: The time of the Gypsies, the end of race', in A. J. López (ed.), *Postcolonial Whiteness: A Critical Reader on Race and Empire*. Albany: State University of New York Press, 79–100.

Ipsos MORI (2016) *Immigration Is Now the Top Issue for Voters in the EU Referendum*. www.ipsos.com/ipsos-mori/en-uk/immigration-now-top-issue-voters-eu-referendum.

Ipsos MORI (2017) *Shifting Ground: 8 Key Findings From a Longitudinal Study on Attitudes Towards Immigration and Brexit*. www.ipsos.com/sites/default/files/ct/news/documents/2017-10/Shifting%20Ground_Unbound.pdf.

Jamieson, M. (2000) 'Compassion, Anger and Broken Hearts: Ontology and the role of language in the Miskity lament', in J. Overing and A. Passes (eds.), *The Anthropology of Love and Anger: The Aesthetics of Conviviality in Native South America*. London: Routledge, 82–98.

Jayaweera, H. and Anderson, B. (2008) *Migrant Workers and Vulnerable Employment: A Review of Existing Data*. Report for TUC Commission on Vulnerable Employment, COMPAS. www.vulnerableworkers.org.uk/wp-content/uploads/2008/08/analysis-of-migrant-worker-data-final.pdf.

Johnson, L. C. (1994) 'What future for feminist geography?', *Gender, Place & Culture*, 1(1): 103–113.

Kalra, V. (2014) 'Writing British Asian Manchester: Vernacular cosmopolitanism on the "Cury Mile"', in S. McLoughlin, W. Gould, A. J. Kabir, E. Tomalin (eds.), *Writing the City in British Asian Diasporas*. Oxon and New York: Routledge, 70–88.

Kamen, H. A. (2014) *The Spanish Inquisition: A Historical Revision*. New Haven and London: Yale University Press.

Karner, C. and Parker, D. (2011) 'Conviviality and conflict: Pluralism, resilience and hope in inner-city Birmingham', *Journal of Ethnic and Migration Studies*, 37(3): 355–372.

Karpieszuk, W. (2009) 'Czy "Murzynek Bambo" obraża Afrykanów?', *Wyborcza*, 28 November. http://warszawa.wyborcza.pl/warszawa/1,34889,7306439,Czy__Murzynek_ Bambo__obraza_Afrykanow_.html.

Keith, M. (2005) *After the Cosmopolitan*. London: Routledge.

Kempny, M., Kapciak, A. and Łodzinski, S. (1997) *U progu wielokulturowosci. Nowe oblicza społeczeństwa polskiego*. Warszawa: Oficyna Naukowa.

Kershen, A. (2015) *London the Promised Land Revisited*. London: Routledge.

Khan, O. and Shaheen, F. (2017) *Minority Report: Race & Class in Post-Brexit Britain*. Runnymede Trust. www.runnymedetrust.org/uploads/publications/pdfs/Race%20and% 20Class%20Post-Brexit%20Perspectives%20report%20v5.pdf.

Kim Y. J. (2012) 'Ethnographer location and the politics of translation: Researching one's own group in a host country', *Qualitative Research*, 12(2): 131–146.

Kindler, M. and Napierała, J. (2010) 'Wstęp', in M. Kindler, and J. Napierała (eds.), *Migracje kobiet: przypadek Polski*. Warsaw: Scholar.

Kinney, P. (2017) 'Walking interviews', *Social Research Update*, 67: 1–4.

Kłosowska, A. (1994) 'Nation, race and ethnicity in Poland', in P. Ratcliffe (ed.), *Race, Ethnicity and Nation: International Perspectives on Social Conflict*. London: Routledge, 199–220.

Koch, R. and Latham, A. (2011) 'Rethinking urban public space: Accounts from a junction in west London', *Transactions of the Institute of British Geographers*, 37(4): 515–529.

Komaromi, P. and Singh, K. (2016) *Post-Referendum Racism and Xenophobia: The Role of Social Media Activism in Challenging the Normalisation of Xeno-Racist Narratives*. www.irr.org.uk/app/uploads/2016/07/PRRX-Report-Final.pdf.

Komter, A. E. (2005) *Social Solidarity and the Gift*. Cambridge: Cambridge University Press.

Kornak, M., Tatar, A. and Pankowski, R. (2016) *Katalog Wypadków – Brunatna Ksiega. 2014–2016*. www.nigdywiecej.org/pdf/pl/pismo/22/katalog_wypadkow-brunatna_ ksiega.pdf.

Koskela, H. (1999) '"Gendered exclusions": Women's fear of violence and changing relations to space', *Human Geography*, 81(2): 111–124.

Krotofil, J. (2011) '"If I am to be a Muslim, I have to be a good one", Polish migrant women Embracing Islam and reconstructing identity in dialogue with self and others', in K. Górak-Sosnowska (ed.), *Muslims in Poland and Eastern Europe: Widening the European Discourse on Islam*. Warsaw: University of Warsaw, 154–168.

Kruszelnicki, J. (2008) 'Los estudiantes polacos en España: IV ola de migraciones después del 1 de mayo de 2006', in *El cambio de imagen mutua de Polonia y España desde la transición*. Warsaw: Instituto Cervantes de Varsovia. Instytut Historii PAN, 215–235.

Kymlicka, W. (2012) *Multiculturalism: Success, Failure, and the Future*. Washington, DC: Migration Policy Institute, 1–32.

L'Hospitalet City Council [Ajuntament de L'Hospitalet] (2013) *Anuari Estadístic de la ciutat de L'Hospitalet: Demografia*. www.l-h.cat/utils/obreFitxer.aspx?Fw9EVw48 XS7hfkw3bv2c3msaDJoVRwXfpqazCiYuUkBpBgqazB.

Lancee, B. and Dronkers, J. (2011) 'Ethnic, religious and economic diversity in Dutch neighbourhoods: Explaining quality of contact with neighbours, trust in the neighbourhood and interethnic trust', *Journal of Ethnic and Migration Studies*, 37(4): 597–618.

Laurier, E. and Philo, C. (2006) 'Cold shoulders and napkins handed: Gestures of responsibility', *Transactions of the Institute of British Geographers*, 31: 193–207.

Leadbeater, C. (2014) *The London Recipe: How Systems and Empathy Make the City*. London: Centre for London. https://publicpurpose.com.au/wp-content/uploads/2017/01/CFL_THE-LONDON-RECIPE.pdf.

Leitner, H. (2012) 'Spaces of encounters: Immigration, race, class, and the politics of belonging in small-town America', *Annals of the Association of American Geographers*, 102(4): 828–846.

Leyden, K. (2003) 'Social capital and the built environment: The importance of walkable neighbourhoods', *American Journal of Public Health*, 93(9): 1546–1551.

Lofland, L. H. (1973) *A World of Strangers: Order and Action in Urban Public Space*. New York: Waveland Press.

Lofland, L. H. (1989) 'Social life in the public realm. A review', *Journal of Contemporary Ethnography*, 17: 453–482.

Lopez Rodriguez, M. (2010) 'Migration and a quest for "normalcy": Polish migrant mothers and the capitalization of meritocratic opportunities in the UK', *Social Identities: Journal for the Study of Race, Nation and Culture*, 16(3): 339–358.

Lorde, A. (1984) *Sister Outsider: Essays and Speeches*. Trumansburg, NY: The Crossing Press.

Lund, H. (2002) 'Pedestrian environments and sense of community', *Journal of Planning Education and Research*, 21: 301–312.

Mahler, S. and Pessar, P. (2006) 'Gender matters: Ethnographers bring gender from the periphery toward the core of migration studies', *International Migration Review*, 40(1): 27–63.

Main, I. (2013) 'High mobility of Polish women: The ethnographic inquiry of Barcelona', *International Migration*, 52(1): 130–145.

Manchester City Council (2007) *Moss Side and Rusholme District Centre Local Plan*. www.manchester.gov.uk/download/downloads/id/10184/moss_side_and_rusholme_local_plan.pdf.

Manchester City Council (2010) *Community Cohesion in Manchester: Manchester City Council Report for Information*. www.manchester.gov.uk/download/meetings/id/8847/5_community_cohesion.

Manchester City Council (2012) *2011 Census – Ethnic Group of Residents by Ward*. www.manchester.gov.uk/downloads/download/4220/.

Manchester City Council (2014a) *Equality Framework for Local Government: Manchester City Council Report for Resolution*. 27 August, 7: 24–84. www.manchester.gov.uk/download/meetings/id/17366/7_equality_framework_for_local_government.

Manchester City Council (2014b) *Baguley Ward Electoral Registration Summary: Information to Assist the Introduction of Individual Electoral Registration (IER)*. www.man chester.gov.uk/downloads/download/5983/baguley_ward_plan.

Manchester City Council (2015) *Manchester Migration: A Profile of Manchester's Migration Patterns*. www.manchester.gov.uk/download/downloads/id/22894/a05_profile_of_ migration_in_manchester_2015.pdf.

Marra, M. and Holmes, J. (2007) 'Humour across cultures: Joking in the multicultural workplace', in H. Kotthoff and H. Spencer-Oatey (eds.), *Handbook of Intercultural Communication*. Berlin and New York: Mouton de Gruyter, 153–172.

Martiniello, M. (2013) 'Comparisons in migration studies', *Journal of Comparative Migration Studies*, 1(1): 7–22.

Massey, D. (2005) *For Space*. London: Sage.

Matejskova, T. and Leitner, H. (2011) 'Urban encounters with difference: The contact hypothesis and immigrant integration projects in eastern Berlin', *Social and Cultural Geography*, 12(7): 717–741.

Maynard, M. (1994) '"Race", gender and the concept of "difference" in feminist thought', in H. Afshar and M. Maynard (eds.), *The Dynamics of 'Race' and Gender: Some Feminist Interventions*. London: Taylor & Francis, 9–26.

McDowell, L. (2007) 'Constructions of whiteness: Latvian women workers in post-war Britain', *Journal of Baltic Studies*, 31(1): 85–107.

McDowell, L. (2009) 'Old and new European economic migrants: Whiteness and managed migration polices', *Journal of Ethnic and Migration Studies*, 35(1): 19–36.

McDowell, L., Batnitsky, A. and Dyer, S. (2007) 'Division, segmentation and interpellation: The embodied labours of migrant workers in a Greater London Hotel', *Economic Geography*, 83(1): 1–25.

McGregor-Smith Review (2017) *Race in the Workplace*. www.gov.uk/government/uploads/ sy stem/uploads/attachment_data/file/594336/race-in-workplace-mcgregor-smith-review. pdf.

Miles, R. (1982) *Racism and Migrant Labour*. London: Routledge.

Ministerio de Empleo y Seguridad Social (2012) *Evolución de extranjeros con certificado de registro o tarjeta de residencia en vigor a 31 de diciembre según sexo, nacionalidad y régimen de residencia. 2002–2011*. http://extranjeros.empleo.gob.es/es/Estadisticas/ operaciones/con-certificado/index.html.

Ministerio de Empleo y Seguridad Social (2014) *Extranjeros residentes en España a 31 de diciembre de 2014. Principales resultados: Anexo de Tablas*. http://extranjeros. empleo.gob.es/es/Estadisticas/operaciones/con-certificado/201412/Residentes_Tablas_ PR_31122014.pdf.

Ministerio de Trabajo e Inmigración (2014) *Plan Esratégico de Ciudadanía e Integración 2011–2014*. http://extranjeros.empleo.gob.es/es/Programas_Integracion/Plan_estrate gico2011/pdf/PECI-2011-2014.pdf.

Modood, T. (2005) 'A defence of multiculturalism', in S. Davison and J. Rutherford (eds.), *Race, Identity and Belonging. A Soundings Collection*. London: Lawrence and Wishart, 82–91. www.lwbooks.co.uk/ebooks/raceident.pdf.

Modood, T. (2015) 'What is multiculturalism and what can it learn from interculturalism?', *Ethnicities*, 16(3): 11–20.

Mohammad, R. (2001) '"Insiders" and/or "outsiders": Positionality, theory and praxis', in M. Limb and C. Dwyer (eds.), *Qualitative Methodologies for Geographers: Issues and Debates*. London: Arnold, 101–120.

Mohanty, C. T. (1988) 'Under western eyes: Feminist scholarship and colonial discourses', *Feminist Review*, 30: 61–88.

Moore, M. and Ramsay, G. (2017) *UK Media Coverage of the EU Referendum Campaign*. London: Kings College Centre for the Study of Media Communication and Power. www.kcl.ac.uk/sspp/policy-institute/CMCP/UK-media-coverage-of-the-2016-EU-Referendum-campaign.pdf.

Morawska, E. (2014) 'Composite meaning, flexible ranges, and multi-level conditions of conviviality: Exploring the polymorph', *European Journal of Cultural Studies*, 17(4): 357–374.

Mullings, B. (1999) 'Insider or outsider, both or neither: Some dilemmas of interviewing in a crosscultural setting', *Geoforum*, 30(4): 337–350.

Multilingual Manchester (2013) *Multilingual Manchester: A Fact Sheet*. http://mlm. humanities.manchester.ac.uk/pdf/MLMFactsheet.pdf.

Nalborczyk, A. S. (2006) 'Islam in Poland: The past and the present', *Islamochristiana*, 32: 225–238.

Nalewajko, M. (2012) *Nieznani a bliscy. Historyczne i społeczne uwarunkowania recepcji polskiej imigracji przełomu XX i XXI tieku w Hiszpanii*. Warszawa: Instytut Historii PAN.

Narkowicz, K. and Pedziwiatr, K. (2017) 'Why are Polish people so wrong about Muslims in their country?' *Open Democracy*. www.opendemocracy.net/can-europe-make-it/kasia-narkowicz-konrad-pedziwiatr/why-are-polish-people-so-wrong-about-muslims-in.

Nava, M. (2002) 'Cosmopolitan modernity: Everyday imaginaries and the register of difference', *Theory, Culture & Society*, 19(1–2): 81–99.

Nayak, A. (2007) 'Critical whiteness studies', *Sociology Compass*, 1(2): 737–755.

Nayak, A. (2009) 'Beyond the pale: Chavs, youth and social class', in K. P. Sveinsson (ed.), *Who Cares About the White Working Class*. London: Runnymede Trust, 28–35.

Neal, S., Bennett, K., Cochrane, A. and Mohan, G. (2013) 'Living multiculture: Understanding the new spatial and social relations of ethnicity and multiculture in England', *Environment and Planning C*, 31: 308–323.

Neal, S., Bennett, K., Cochrane, A. and Mohan, G. (2018) *The Lived Experiences of Multiculture: The New Spatial and Social Relations of Diversity*. Oxon and New York: Routledge.

Neal, S., Iqbal, H. and Vincent, C. (2016) 'Extended encounters in primary school worlds: Hared social resources, connective spaces and sustained conviviality in socially and ethnically complex urban geographies', *Journal of Intercultural Studies*, 37(5): 464–480.

Niessen, J., Huddleston, T. and Citron, L. (2007) *Migrant Integration Policy Index*. Brussels: British Council and Migration Policy Index. www.integrationindex.eu/multiver sions/2712/FileName/MIPEX-2006-2007-final.pdf.

Noble, G. (2009) 'Everyday cosmopolitanism and the labour of intercultural community', in A. Wise and S. Velayutham (eds.), *Everyday Multiculturalism*. Basingstoke: Palgrave Macmillan, 46–65.

Nogué, J. and Vincente, J. (2004) 'Landscape and nationality identity in Catalonia', *Political Geography*, 23: 113–132.

Nowicka, M. (2012) 'Transcultural encounters of diversity. The case of Polish presence in the UK', in A. Dziewulska and A. M. Ostrowska (eds.), *New Neighbours: On the Diversity of Migrants' Political Involvement*. Warsaw: Centre for Europe, University of Warsaw, 111–124.

Nowicka, M. (2018) 'Cultural precarity: Migrants' positionalities in the light of current anti-immigrant populism in Europe', *Journal of Intercultural Studies*, 39(5): 527–542.

Nowicka, M. and Cieślik, A. (2014) 'Beyond methodological nationalism in insider research with migrants', *Migration Studies*, 2(1): 1–15.

Nowicka, M. and Krzyżowski, Ł. (2017) 'The social distance of poles to other minorities: A study of four cities in Germany and Britain', *Journal of Ethnic and Migration Studies*, 43(3): 359–378.

Nowicka, M. and Vertovec, S. (2014) 'Introduction. Comparing convivialities: Dreams and realities of living-with-difference', *European Journal of Cultural Studies*, 17(4): 341–356.

O'Connor, P. (1992) *Friendships Between Women*. London: Harvester Wheatsheaf.

Oakley, A. (1981) 'Interviewing women: A contradiction in terms?', in H. Roberts (ed.), *Doing Feminist Research*. London: Routledge and Kegan Paul, 30–61.

ONS [Office for National Statistics] (2011a) *Polish People in the UK – Half a Million Polish Residents*. www.ons.gov.uk/ons/rel/migration1/migration-statistics-quarterly-report/august-2011/polish-people-in-the-uk.html.

ONS (2011b) *Language in England and Wales*. www.ons.gov.uk/ons/rel/census/2011-census-analysis/language-in-england-and-wales-2011/rpt–language-in-england-and-wales–2011.html.

ONS (2012) *International Migrants in England and Wales 2011*. www.ons.gov.uk/ons/dcp171776_290335.pdf.

ONS (2015) *Births by Parents' Country of Birth, England and Wales: 2014*. www.ons.gov.uk/peoplepopulationandcommunity/birthsdeathsandmarriages/livebirths/bulletins/parentscountryofbirthenglandandwales/2015-08-27/pdf.

ONS (2016) *Population by Country of Birth and Nationality, 2015*. London: Office for National Statistics.

ONS (2018) *UK and Non-UK People in the Labour Market: November 2018. Estimates of Labour Market Activity by Nationality and Country of Birth*. www.ons.gov.uk/employmentandlabourmarket/peopleinwork/employmentandemployeetypes/articles/ukandnonukpeopleinthelabourmarket/november2018.

Overing, J. and Passes, A. (eds.) (2000) *The Anthropology of Love and Anger: The Aesthetics of Conviviality in Native South America*. London: Routledge.

Owczarzak, J. (2009) 'Introduction: Postcolonial studies and postsocialism in Eastern Europe', *Focaal*, 53: 3–19.

Padilla, B., Azevedo, J. and Olmos-Alcaraz, A. (2015) 'Superdiversity and conviviality: Exploring frameworks for doing ethnography in Southern European intercultural cities', *Ethnic and Racial Studies*, 38(4): 621–635.

Pain, R. (1991) 'Space, sexual violence and social control: Integrating geographical and feminist analyses of women's hear of crime', *Progress in Human Geography*, 15: 415–431.

Parutis, V. (2011) 'White, European, and hardworking: East European migrants' relationships with other communities in London', *Journal of Baltic Studies*, 42(2): 263–288.

Peattie, L. (1998) 'Convivial cities', in M. Douglass and J. Friedmann (eds.), *Cities for Citizens: Planning and the Rise of Civil Society in a Global Age*. Chichester: Wiley, 247–253.

Pérez-Rincón, S. Vives, A. García, A. and Expósito, C. (2012) 'Reproducción de la Otredad Inmigrante en Barcelona y Recepción Popular del Espacio Urbano Representado como "Gueto"', *Revista de Ciencias Sociales*, 29: 160–182.

Perry, J. (2011) *UK Migration: The Leadership Role of Housing Providers*. Joseph Rowntree Foundation. www.jrf.org.uk/sites/default/files/jrf/migrated/files/migration-housing-policy-summary_0.pdf.

Peters, K. (2011) *Living Together in Multi-Ethnic Neighbourhoods: The Meaning of Public Spaces for Issues of Social Integration*. Wageningen: Wageningen Academic Publishers.

Phizacklea, A. (1983) *One Way Ticket: Migration and Female Labour*. London: Routledge.

Phizacklea, A. (2003) 'Transnationalism, gender and global workers', in U. Erel, M. Morokvasic-Muller and K. Shinozaki (eds.), *Crossing Borders and Shifting Boundaries: Gender on the move*. Opladen: Leske and Budrich, 79–100.

Pietka, E. (2011) 'Encountering forms of co-ethnic relations: Polish community in Glasgow', *Studia Migracyjne – Przegląd Polonijny*, 1: 129–151.

Pink, S. (2012) *Situating Everyday Life: Practices and Place*. London: Sage.

Piróg, P. (2010) '"Murzynek Bambo w Afryce mieszka", czyli jak polska kultura stworzyła swojego "Murzyna"', *Opposite* 1. http://opposite.uni.wroc.pl/2010/pirog.htm.

Podemski, K. (2012) 'Doświadczanie świata. Kontakty międzykulturowe Polaków', in K. Frysztacki and P. Sztompka (eds.), *Polska początku XXI wieku: przemiany kulturowe i cywilizacyjne*. Warszawa: Wydawnictwo PAN, 197–221.

Pujolar, J. (2006) 'African women in Catalan language courses: Struggles over class, gender and ethnicity in advanced liberalism', in B. McElhinny (ed.), *Words, Worlds and Material Girls: Language, Gender, Global Economies*. Berlin: Mouton de Gruyter, 305–346.

Pujolar, J. (2009) 'Immigration in Catalonia: Marking territory through language', in M. Baynham, S. Slembrouck and J. Collins (eds.), *Globalization and Language Contact: Spatiotemporal Scales, Migration Flows, and Communicative Practices*. London: Continuum.

Pujolar, J. (2010) 'Immigration and language education in Catalonia: Between national and social agendas', *Linguistics and Education*, 21(3): 229–243.

Pujolar, J. and Gonzalez, I. (2013) 'Linguistic "mudes" and the de-ethnicization of language choice in Catalonia', *International Journal of Bilingual Education and Bilingualism*, 16(2): 138–152.

Rabikowska, M. and Burrell, K. (2009) 'The material worlds of recent Polish migrants: Transnationalism, food, shops and home', in K. Burrell (ed.), *Polish Migration to the UK in the 'New' European Union. After 2004*. Aldershot: Ashgate, 211–232.

Ramírez Goicoechea, E. R. (2003) 'La comunidad polaca en España. Un colectivo particular', *Reis*, 102(3): 63–92.

Rawlins, W. K. (1992) *Friendship Matters: Communication, Dialectics, and the Life Course*. New York: Aldine de Gruyter.

Ray, J. (2005) 'Beyond tolerance and persecution: Reassessing our approach to medieval Convivencia', *Jewish Social Studies*, 11(2): 1–18.

Razack, S. (2004) 'Imperilled Muslim women, dangerous Muslim men and civilised Europeans: Legal and social responses to forced marriages', *Feminist Legal Studies*, 12(2): 129–174.

Reay, D., Hollingworth, S., Williams, K., Crozier, G., Jamieson, F., James, D. and Beedell, P. (2007) '"A darker shade of pale?" Whiteness, the middle classes and multi-ethnic inner city schooling', *Sociology*, 4(6): 1041–1060.

Rienzo, C. and Vargas-Silva, C. (2014) *Migrants in the UK: An Overview*. Oxford: University of Oxford, The Migration Observatory. www.migrationobservatory.ox.ac.uk/sites/files/migobs/Migrants%20in%20the%20UK-Overview_0.pdf.

Riessman, C. K. (1993) *Narrative Analysis*. London: Sage.

Riessman, C. K. (2002) 'Narrative analysis', in A. M. Huberman and M. Miles (eds.), *The Qualitative Research Companion*. London: Sage, 217–270.

Riessman, C. K. (2008) *Narrative Methods for Human Sciences*. London: Sage.

Rishbeth, C. and Rogaly, B. (2017) 'Sitting outside: Conviviality, self-care and the design of benches in urban public space', *Transactions of the Institute of British Geographers*, 43(2): 284–298.

Rodman, M. C. (1992) 'Empowering place: Multilocality and multivocality', *American Anthropologist*, 94(3): 640–656.

Rodon, T. and Franco-Guillén, N. (2014) 'Contact with immigrants in times of crisis: An exploration of the Catalan case', *Ethnicities*, 14(5): 650–675.

Roediger, D. (1994) *Towards the Abolition of Whiteness*. New York: Verso.

Román, M., et al. (2011) 'Tratamiento informativo de la mujer inmigrante en la prensa española', *Cuadernos de Información*, 29: 173–186.

Rosenbaum, M. (2017) *Local Voting Figures Shed New Light on EU Referendum*. www.bbc.co.uk/news/uk-politics-38762034.

Ryan, L. (2001) 'Irish female emigration in the 1930s: Transgressing space and culture', *Gender, Place and Culture*, 8(3): 271–282.

Ryan, L. (2007) 'Who do you think you are? Irish nurses encountering ethnicity and constructing identity in Britain', *Ethnic and Racial Studies*, 30(3): 416–438.

Ryan, L. (2010) 'Becoming Polish in London: Negotiating ethnicity through migration', *Journal for the Study of Race, Nation and Culture*, 16(3): 359–376.

Ryan, L. (2015a) 'Friendship-making: Exploring network formations through the narratives of Irish highly qualified migrants in Britain', *Journal of Ethnic and Migration*, 41(10): 1664–1683.

Ryan, L. (2015b) '"Inside" and "outside" of what or where? Researching migration through multi-positionalities', *Forum: Qualitative Social Research*, 16(2).

Ryan, L. (2015c) *'Another Year and Another Year': Polish Migrants in London Extending the Stay Over Time*. Middlesex University: Social Policy Research Centre. http://sprc.info/wp-content/uploads/2012/07/Polish-Migrants-in-London-extending-the-stay.pdf.

Ryan, L., Rodriguez, M. L. and Trevena, P. (2016) 'Opportunities and challenges of unplanned follow-up interviews: Experiences with Polish migrants in London', *Forum Qualitative Sozialforschung*, 17: 1–20.

Ryan, L., Sales, M., Tilki, M. and Siara, B. (2009) 'Family strategies and transnational migration: Recent Polish migrants in London', *Journal of Ethnic and Migration Studies*, 35(1): 61–77.

Ryan, L. and Webster, W. (2008) *Gendering Migration Masculinity, Femininity and Ethnicity in Post-War Britain*. Aldershot: Ashgate.

Rzepnikowska, A. (2016a) 'Convivial cultures in Manchester and Barcelona: Exploring the narratives of Polish migrant women', *Migration Studies – Polish Diaspora Review*, 42(2): 119–134.

Rzepnikowska, A. (2016b) 'Imagining and encountering the other in Manchester and Barcelona: The narratives of Polish migrant women', *Journal of the Institute of Ethnology and Anthropology* (Special Issue: Postsocialist Mobilities), 15: 55–108.

Rzepnikowska, A. (2017) 'Conviviality in the workplace: The case of Polish migrant women in Manchester and Barcelona', *Central and Eastern European Migration Review*, 6(2): 51–68.

Rzepnikowska, A. (2018a) 'Polish migrant women's narratives about language, raced and gendered difference in Barcelona', *Gender, Place and Culture* (Special issue: Gendered, Spatial and Temporal Approaches to Polish intra-EU Migration), 25(6): 850–865.

Rzepnikowska, A. (2018b) 'Racism and xenophobia experienced by Polish migrants in the UK before and after Brexit vote', *Journal of Ethnic and Migration Studies*, 45(1): 61–77.

Rzepnikowska, A. (2019) 'Shifting racialised positioning of Polish migrant women in Manchester and Barcelona', in P. Essed. K. Farkuharson, K. Pillay and E. White (eds.), *Relating World of Racism: Dehumanisation, Belonging and the Normativity of European Whiteness*. London: Palgrave, 191–219.

Said, E. W. (1995) *Orientalism*. London and New York: Penguin Books.

Salicrú, R. (2008) 'Crossing boundaries in late Medieval Mediterranean Iberia: Historical glimpses of Christian–Islamic intercultural dialogue', *International Journal of Euro-Mediterranean Studies*, 1(1): 33–51.

Salmon, P. and Riessman, C. K. (2008) 'Looking back on narrative research: an exchange', in M. Andrews, C. Squire and Tamboukou, M. (eds.), *Doing Narrative Research*. London: Sage, 197–204.

Salt, J. and Okólski, M. (2014) 'Polish emigration to the UK after 2004: Why did so many come?', *Central and Eastern European Migration Review*, 2: 11–37.

Sánchez-Albornoz, C. (1962) *España, un enigma histórico*. Buenos Aires: Editorial Sudamericana.

Sennett, R. (1977) *The Fall of Public Man*. Cambridge: Cambridge University Press.

Sias, P. M. and Cahill, D. J. (1998) 'From coworkers to friends: The development of peer friendships in the workplace', *Western Journal of Communication*, 62(3): 273–299.

Sias, P. M. and Gallagher, E. (2009) 'Developing and maintaining workplace relationships', in R. Morrison and S. Wright (eds.), *Friends and Enemies in Organisations: A Work Psychology Perspective*. Hampshire: Palgrave Macmillian, 78–100.

Sigona, N. (2018) 'Theresa May's dog-whistle rhetoric on EU citizens jumping the queue – and its effect on my four-year-old', *The Conversation*. https://theconversa tion.com/theresa-mays-dog-whistle-rhetoric-on-eu-citizens-jumping-the-queue-and-its-effect-on-my-four-year-old-107303.

Simon, S. (1996) *Gender in Translation: Cultural Identity and the Politics of Transmission*. Routledge: London and New York.

Simonsen, K. (2008) 'Practice, narrative and the 'multicultural city': A Copenhagen case', *European Urban and Regional Studies*, 15(2): 145–158.

Simpson, P. (2011) 'Street performance and the city: Public space, sociality, and intervening in the everyday' *Space and Culture*, 14(4): 412–430.

Sivanandan, A. (2009) 'Foreword', in L. Fekete (ed.), *A Suitable Enemy: Racism, Migration and Islamophobia in Europe*. London: Pluto, viii–x.

Sivanandan, A. (2016) 'Foreword', in J. Burnett (ed.), *Racial Violence and the Brexit State*. London: Institute of Race Relations.

Skeggs, B. (1997) *Formations and Class and Gender: Becoming Respectable*. London: Sage.

Skeggs, B. (2009) 'Haunted by the spectre of judgement: Respectability, value and affect in class relations', in K. P. Sveinsson (ed.), *Who Cares about the White Working Class*. London: Runnymede Trust.

Smith, J. (2010) *Where Next for Ethnic Diversity Policymaking at the Local Level? Lessons From a Comparative Study of Manchester and Copenhagen*. Manchester: Centre for Local Economic Strategies (CLES). www.cles.org.uk/wp-content/uploads/2011/01/Diversity.pdf.

Soifer, M. (2009) 'Beyond convivencia: Critical reflections on the historiography of interfaith relations in Christian Spain', *Journal of Medieval Iberian Studies*, 1(1): 19–35.

Solé, C. and Parella, S. (2003) 'The labour market and racial discrimination in Spain', *Journal of Ethnic and Migration Studies*, 29(10): 121–140.

Średziński, P. (2010) *Public Opinion Research with Regards to the Integration of the Citizens of African Countries in Poland*. Warsaw: Fundacja Afryka Inaczej. https://ec.europa.eu/migrant-integration/.

Stanek, M. (2007) 'Hiszpańskie Badania nad Migracjami z Europy Środkowo-Wschodniej', in J. Zamojski (ed.), *Migracje i społeczeństwa współczesne*. Warszawa: Instytut Historii Polskiej Akademii Nauk, 107–125.

Stanfield II, J. H. (1993) 'Epistemological considerations', in J. H. Stanfield II and R. M. Dennis (eds.), *Race and Ethnicity in Research Methods*. Newbury Park, London and New Delhi: Sage, 16–36.

Stanley, L. and Wise, S. (1993) *Breaking Out Again: Feminist Ontology and Epistemology*. Routledge: London.

Suárez-Navaz, N. (2004) *Rebordering the Mediterranean: Boundaries and Citizenship in Southern Europe*. New York and Oxford: Berghahn Books.

Sveinsson, K. P. (ed.) (2009) *Who Cares about the White Working Class*. London: Runnymede Trust.

Tarantino, F. (2014) *La Estrategia BCN Antirumores y la Red BCN Antirumores*. Informe de Investigación de la Academia Europea para la Integración de los Inmigrantes. www.eu-mia.eu/media/library/19-09-2014-16-58-12/at_download/AttachmentFile.

Temple, B. (2011) 'Polish migrants' narratives of "us", "them", language and integration', in A. Stenning and A. Słowik (eds.), *Post-Accession Migration in Europe – A Polish Case Study*. Kraków: Impuls, 39–54.

Tremblay, D. and Battaglia, A. (2012) 'El Raval and mile end: A comparative study of two cultural quarters between urban regeneration and creative clusters', *Journal of Geography and Geology*, 4(1): 56–74.

Trevena, P. (2018) *Brexit and Attracting and Retaining Migrants in Scotland*. https://spice-spotlight.scot/2018/10/08/guest-blog-brexit-and-attracting-and-retaining-migrants-in-scotland/.

Trzebiatowska, M. (2010) 'The advent of the "EasyJet Priest": Dilemmas of Polish Catholic integration in the UK', *Sociology*, 44: 1055–1072.

Urry, J. (1995) *Consuming Places*. London: Routledge.

Valentine, G. (1989) 'The geography of women's fear', *Area*, 21(4): 385–390.

Valentine, G. (2002) 'People like us: Negotiating sameness and difference in the research process', in P. Moss (ed.), *Feminist Geography in Practice: Research and Methods*. Oxford: Blackwell, 116–126.

Valentine, G. (2008) 'Living with difference: Reflections on geographies of encounter', *Progress in Human Geography*, 32(3): 323–337.

Valentine, G. and Harris, C. (2016) 'Encounters and (in)tolerance: Perceptions of legality and the regulation of space', *Social and Cultural Geography*, 17(7): 913–932.

Valentine, G. and Sadgrove, J. (2012) 'Lived difference: A narrative account of spatio-temporal processes of social differentiation', *Environment and Planning A*, 44(9): 2049–2063.

Valluvan, S. (2016) 'Conviviality and multiculture a post-integration sociology of multi-ethnic interaction', *Young*, 24(3): 204–221.

van Dijk, T. A. (2002) 'Discourse and racism', in D. Goldberg and J. Solomos (eds.), *The Blackwell Companion to Racial and Ethnic Studies*. Oxford: Blackwell, 145–159.

van Riemsdijk, M. (2010) 'Variegated privileges of whiteness: Lived experiences of Polish nurses in Norway', *Social & Cultural Geography*, 11(2): 117–137.

Vertovec, S. (2007a) 'Super-diversity and its implications', *Ethnic and Racial Studies*, 29(6): 1024–1054.

Vertovec, S. (2007b) *New Complexities of Cohesion in Britain: Super-Diversity, Transnationalism and Civil-Integration, Commission on Integration & Cohesion*. COMPAS. www.compas.ox.ac.uk/fileadmin/files/Publications/.

Vertovec, S. (2014) 'Reading super-diversity', in B. Anderson and M. Keith (eds.), *Migration: The COMPAS Anthology*. Oxford: COMPAS.

Virdee, S. and McGeever, B. (2018) 'Racism, crisis, Brexit', *Ethnic and Racial Studies*, 41(10): 1802–1819.

Watson, S. (2006) *City Publics: The (Dis) Enchantments of Urban Encounters*. London: Routledge.

Wawryk, J. (2012) *Klechdy sezamowe i Przygody Sindbada Żeglarza jako prolegomena do twórczości poetyckiej Bolesława Leśmiana*. PhD. Uniwersytet Śląski.

Werbner, P. (1999) 'Global pathways. Working-class cosmopolitans and the creation of transnational ethnic worlds', *Social Anthropology*, 7(1): 17–35.

Wessendorf, S. (2014a) '"Being open, but sometimes closed". Conviviality in a super-diverse London neighbourhood', *European Journal of Cultural Studies*, 17(4): 392–405.

Wessendorf, S. (2014b) *Commonplace Diversity: Social Relations in a Super-Diverse Context*. Basingstoke: Palgrave Macmillan.

White, A. (2010) 'Young people and migration from contemporary Poland', *Journal of Youth Studies*, 13(5): 565–580.

White, A. (2011a) *Polish Families and Migration Since EU Accession*. Bristol: Policy Press.

White, A. (2011b) 'Polish migration in the UK – Local experiences and effects', *AHRC Connected Communities Symposium: Understanding Local Experiences of New Migration*. Sheffield, 26 September 2011, 1–20.

Wilk, P. (2010) 'Images of poles and Poland in the Guardian, 2003–2005', in B. Korte, E. U. Pirker and S. Helff (eds.), *Facing the East in the West: Images of Eastern Europe in British Literature, Film and Culture*. Amsterdam and New York: Rodopi, 335–348.

Wilson, H. F. (2011) 'Passing propinquities in the multicultural city: The everyday encounters of bus passengering', *Environment and Planning A: Economy and Space*, 43(3): 634–649.

Wilson, H. F. (2013a) 'Collective life: Parents, playground encounters and the multicultural city', *Social & Cultural Geography*, 14: 625–648.

Wilson, H. F. (2013b) 'Learning to think differently: Diversity training and the "good encounter"', *Geoforum*, 45: 73–82.

Wilson, H. F. (2017) 'On geography and encounter', *Progress in Human Geography*, 41: 451–471.

Wimmer, A. (1997) 'Explaining xenophobia and racism: A critical review of current research approaches', *Ethnic and Racial Studies*, 20(1): 17–41.

Wimmer, A. and Glick Schiller, N. (2002) 'Methodological nationalism and beyond: Nation-state building, migration and the social sciences', *Global Networks, A Journal of Transnational Relations*, 2(4): 301–334.

Wise, A. (2009) 'Everyday multiculturalism: Transversal crossings and working class cosmopolitans', in A. Wise and S. Velayutham (eds.), *Everyday Multiculturalism*. London: Palgrave, 21–45.

Wise, A. (2016) 'Convivial labour and the "Joking Relationship": Humour and everyday multiculturalism at work', *Journal of Intercultural Studies*, 37(5): 481–500.

Wise, A. and Noble, G. (2016) 'Convivialities: An orientation', *Journal of Intercultural Studies*, 37(5): 423–431.

Wise, A. and Velayutham, S. (2014) 'Conviviality in everyday multiculturalism: Some brief comparisons between Singapore and Sydney', *European Journal of Cultural Studies*, 17(4): 406–430.

Władyka, D. and Morén-Alegret, R. (2013) 'Polish immigration in Barcelona: The Sagrada familia neighbourhood as an arena for interaction', *International Migration*, 52(1): 146–164.

Wolff, L. (1994) *Inventing Eastern Europe: The Map of Civilisation on the Mind of the Enlightenment*. Stanford, CA: Stanford University Press.

Wood, L, Frank, L. and Giles-Corti, B. (2010) 'Sense of community and its relationship with walking and neighborhood design', *Social Science and Medicine*, 70: 1381–1390.

Wood, N. and Waite, L. (2011) 'Editorial: Scales of belonging', *Emotion, Space and Society*, 4: 201–202.

Woolard, K. A. (2003) '"We don't speak Catalan because we are marginalized": Ethnic and Class meanings of language in Barcelona', in R. Blot (ed.), *Language and Social Identity*. Westport: Praeger Publishers, 85–104.

Yuval-Davis, N. (1997) *Gender and Nation*. London and New Delhi: Thousand Oaks.

Ząbek, M. (2007) *Biali i Czarni. Postawy Polaków wobec Afryki i Afrykanów*. Warszawa: Instytut Etnologii i Antropologii Kulturowej UW & Wydawnictwo DiG.

Ząbek, M. (2009) 'Afrykanie w Polsce. O stosunkach rasowych we współczesnym społeczeństwie polskim', in A. Jasińska-Kania and S. Łodziński (eds.), *Obszary i formy wykluczenia etnicznego w Polsce*. Warszawa: Wydawnictwo Naukowe Scholar, 169–180.

Zapata-Barrero, R. (2014) 'The limits to shaping diversity as public culture: Permanent festivities in Barcelona', *Cities*, 37: 66–72.

Index